Kipling and Afghanistan

Kipling and Afghanistan

*A Study of the Young Author as
Journalist Writing on the
Afghan Border Crisis of 1884–1885*

NEIL K. MORAN

McFarland & Company, Inc., Publishers
Jefferson, North Carolina, and London

LIBRARY OF CONGRESS CATALOGUING-IN-PUBLICATION DATA

Moran, Neil K.
　　Kipling and Afghanistan : a study of the young author as journalist writing on the Afghan Border Crisis of 1884–1885 / Neil K. Moran.
　　　　p.　　cm.
　　Includes bibliographical references and index.

　　ISBN-13: 978-0-7864-2282-1
　　(softcover : 50# alkaline paper) ∞

　　1. Kipling, Rudyard, 1865–1936 — Knowledge — Afghanistan.
　　2. Afghanistan — History — 19th century — Historiography.
　　3. Afghanistan — Press coverage — History — 19th century.
　　4. Kipling, Rudyard, 1865–1936 — Travel — Afghanistan.
　　5. Journalism — Afghanistan — History — 19th century.
　　6. British — Afghanistan — History — 19th century.
　　7. Authors, English — 19th century — Biography.
　　8. Journalists — Great Britain — Biography.　I. Title.
PR4856.M66　　2005
828'.809 — dc22　　　　　　　　　　　　　　　　　　　　　　　　2005021000

British Library cataloguing data are available

©2005 Neil K. Moran. All rights reserved

No part of this book may be reproduced or transmitted in any form or by any means, electronic or mechanical, including photocopying or recording, or by any information storage and retrieval system, without permission in writing from the publisher.

On the cover: Rudyard Kipling (*New York Times*); background ©2005 fStop Images

Manufactured in the United States of America

McFarland & Company, Inc., Publishers
　Box 611, Jefferson, North Carolina 28640
　　www.mcfarlandpub.com

Acknowledgments

In view of the relatively recent date of the Afghan Boundary Commission, it seemed advisable to first contact the families of the original members. It therefore was a pleasure to be informed on my first foray through the pages of *Who's Who* that Peter Digby Lumsden of Toronto had in his possession the papers of his great-uncle Sir Peter Lumsden, head of the commission. This initial success encouraged me to send dozens of letters overseas in the hope of eliciting more information.

In particular I appreciated the long letters over a period of 15 years from the daughter of the Honorable George Milo Talbot, a surveyor with the ABC. The Honorable Rose Talbot had moved to Australia, after the family home, Malahide Castle, had been sold to the Irish government. The history of the Talbot family in Ireland encompasses 800 years, back to the time of Henry II. Rose Talbot had documents about the commission from her father and what she called some "Bochara" rugs. Her letters were always a source of delight. She sent me photographs of her Turkoman carpets and directed me to documents at Oxford. Responding to a description of what her father went through as a surveyor, she wrote (May 31, 2002), "They all had a rough time and my father certainly had much to put up with from Holdich's idleness. He would have been 30 to 31 at that period."

An Internet search in 2000 led to the discovery that the National Army Museum in London had acquired the letters and diaries of Dr. Charles Owen, the ethnologist with the ABC, in 1998. Owen's diary covered the entire period of the ABC campaign from September 1884 to October 31, 1886, and the collection included more than 100 long letters to his wife. In addition, he contributed more than 40 newsletters to the *Civil and Military Gazette* in Lahore as its ABC correspondent.

The *Civil and Military Gazette* provided the link to Rudyard Kipling, for this was the newspaper for which he worked as an assistant editor from 1882 to 1887. Charles Owen knew both Rudyard Kipling and his father. In fulfilling his daily newsprint quota with translations, scraps and cut-and-paste items on Central Asia and Afghanistan, Rudyard Kipling developed a more intimate knowledge of the Afghan/Russian border conflict than almost anyone else in the Raj. In March 1885 he attended the Rawal Pindi conference between the amir of Afghanistan and the viceroy of India as a correspondent for the CMG. I wish to thank the Kipling librarian at Dalhousie University, Karen Eliz May Smith, for making the microfilms of the *Civil and Military Gazette* from 1884 to 1886 available to me. Joy Eldridge, Kipling specialist at the University of Sussex library, provided me with information on Kipling's scrapbooks and on his Turkoman carpets.

Another important contact was Peter Harrington of Brown University. Peter Harrington was preparing a study of William Simpson, the artist with the ABC. Harrington had contacted the great-grandson of Simpson in Australia, who possessed Simpson's diary of the Second Afghan War. Harrington was able to persuade a colleague of his, Fred Sharf, to purchase this manuscript for the Brown University Library. Sharf acquired Simpson's Abyssinian diary and a number of letters written by Owen. Since I had been searching for material on Owen for several years without success, this was welcome news. Sharf not only kindly offered to make transcriptions of the letters available but also generously arranged for the National Army Museum to provide me with transcripts of Owen's correspondence and diaries.

I am furthermore indebted to Jennifer Wearden and Marjorie Trusted for information on carpets and silver ornaments in the Victoria and Albert Museum. Even though the answers were generally negative, I appreciated the responses from various museums, libraries, ministries and institutes in the United Kingdom, Ireland as well as in Europe, the United States, Pakistan and India.

Lady Durand, wife of the fourth baronet, informed me that nearly all of the possessions of another ABC participant, Edward Durand, were unfortunately lost in the Blitz. She said they had been put for safekeeping in a depository which later suffered a direct hit, whereas the house in Sloane Square remained unharmed.

Another fortuitous event was the organization of an exhibition of the paintings of William Simpson by the Fine Art Society in 1987. Peter Harrington of the Brown University Library put me in contact with Simon Peers, who was organizing the exhibition. In 1984 Peers reported that he was not aware of any original works from 1884 and 1885, but three years later he informed me that he had located Simpson's grandson, who had "a very comprehensive scrap/sketch book of all the goings on of the Afghan Boundary Commission." Simpson related in his autobiography that he had personally shown his album together with some Turkoman jewelry to Queen Victoria at Balmoral after his return to England in 1885. The silver ornaments were later donated in 1900 by his wife to the Victoria and Albert Museum.

Through a circuitous route involving Harrington, I learned that Simpson's grandson had sold the album at Christie's London. Christie's would of course not divulge the name of the owner but kindly passed on my letter to him, together with a supporting letter from Jon Thompson. I thus learned that the album was in the possession of the Right Honorable Lord Viscount Cranborne. Lord Cranborne immediately gave me permission to inspect the album.

Steven Tomlinson of the Bodleian Library in Oxford promptly provided me with further information about the papers of Lord Talbot. Jennifer Wearden responded to a simple question about the spelling of a name within hours. An Internet search came up with the name of Peter Hoffenberg in Hawaii, who was working on a biography of John Lockwood Kipling. By the next day, he had sent me some valuable leads on the father of Rudyard Kipling.

It was a pleasure to receive a positive response from David Page, editor of the *Kipling Journal*, to my article "Dr. Charles Owen and the Kiplings." He and John Slater informed me that the sketch of the office of the *Civil and Military Gazette* from 1885 had originally been printed in their journal in mirror image. I wish to thank Page for providing me with the corrected reproduction. My chapter on Lahore was enriched by material sent to me by Omar Khan, author of *From Kashmir to Kabul*. He kindly offered to help me to track down certain photos of the officers of the ABC by John Burke. Robin Harcourt Williams at Hatfield House was able to provide me with color transparencies of William Simpson's ABC album from the Marquess of Salisbury's library.

For the preparation of the photographs from the *Illustrated London News* I wish to thank Brian Musselwhite of the Royal Ontario Museum.

During the many years of research I received assistance from many institutions and organizations, and I wish to thank them for their cooperation: The Royal Photographic Society (Bath, U.K.), Fitzwilliam Museum (Cambridge, U.K.), University Museum of Archaeology and Anthropology (Cambridge, U.K.), Royal Engineers Corps Library (Chatham, U.K.), Oriental Museum (Durham, U.K.), Bankfield Museum (Halifax, U.K.), Military Heritage Museum (Lewes, U.K.), British Library (London), British Museum (London), Cavalry & Guards Club (London), Horniman Museum (London), Imperial War Museum (London), London Illustrated News Library (London), Museum of Mankind (London), National Army Museum (London), Pharmaceutical Society of Great Britain (London), Royal Anthropological Society (London), Royal Commission on Historical

Manuscripts (London), Royal Geographical Society (London), Royal Society for Asian Affairs (London), Victoria and Albert Museum (London), Windsor Castle Royal Library (London), Whitworth Art Gallery (Manchester, U.K.), Gordon Reece Gallery (North Yorkshire, U.K.), Ashmolean Museum (Oxford, U.K.), Bodleian Library (Oxford, U.K.), Pitt Rivers Museum (Oxford, U.K.), St. Anthony's College Middle East Centre (Oxford, U.K.), Royal Botanic Gardens (Richmond, U.K.), Galerie Azadi (Hamburg, Germany), Linden-Museum (Stuttgart, Germany), Geological Survey of India (Calcutta), Indian Museum (Calcutta), Survey of India (Dehra Dun), Government Central Museum (Jaipur, India), Maharaja Sawai Man Singh II Museum (Jaipur, India), State Museum (Lucknow, Uttar Pradesh, India), India International Photographic Council (New Delhi), National Archives of India (New Delhi), Malahide Castle (Dublin, Ireland), Lahore Museum (Lahore, Pakistan), House of Lumsden Association (Fife, Scotland), National Galleries of Scotland (Edinburgh), National Library of Scotland (Edinburgh), Royal Botanic Garden (Edinburgh, Scotland), Royal Scottish Museum (Edinburgh), Glasgow Museums and Art Galleries (Glasgow, Scotland), Mitchell Library (Glasgow, Scotland), Museum of Photography (Rochester, N.Y.), National Museum of Natural History (Washington, D.C.), Embassy of Pakistan (Washington, D.C., USA), Textile Museum (Washington, D.C.).

Finally I wish to thank the following individuals for their advice and encouragement: Peter Andrews (Cologne, Germany), S. Asplin (Fife, Scotland), Siawosch Azadi (Hamburg, Germany), Miss Campbell of Kilberry (Tarbert Lochfyne, Scotland), Lady Durand (Yonghal, Ireland), Joy Eldridge (Brighton, U.K.), Ekaterina Ermakova (Moscow), Brigadier Javed Hassan (Washington, D.C.), Farideh Giahi (Toronto), Katharine Green (Toronto), Peter Harrington (Providence, R.I.), Peter Hoffenberg (Honolulu, Hawaii), Jerzy Jatczak (Toronto), Pauline Johnstone (Lewes, U.K.), Ned and Joan Long (Akron, Ohio), Peter Digby Lumsden (Toronto), the Most Honorable the Marquess of Salisbury (Winborne, U.K.), Brian Musselwhite (Toronto), Natalia Nekrassova (Toronto), Frances Olsen (Ottawa), Shir and Parviz Khosrow Parwand of Herat Carpets (Toronto), Simon Peers (Antananarivo, Madagascar), Robert Pinner (London), Thomas Pinney (California), Robert Pittenger (New York), Abdul Rasouli (Toronto), Fred Sharf (Chestnut Hill, Mass.), John Slater (of the Kipling Society, U.K.), Karen Smith (Halifax, N.S.), Mrs. Peter Sparks (Cheltenham, U.K.), the Honorable Rose Talbot de Malahide (Tasmania, Australia), Jon Thompson (London), Steven Tomlinson (Oxford, England), Elena Tzareva (St. Petersburg), Jennifer Wearden (London), Robin Harcourt Williams (Hatfield House, U.K.) and Georges Yeremian (Toronto).

Table of Contents

Acknowledgements	v
Preface	1
1: Prologue	3
2: The Journey to Sarakhs	14
3: The ABC Reaches Its Destination	29
4: Her Majesty's Troops Retreat	48
5: England and Russia Face to Face in Asia	69
6: Forging the Boundary	86
7: The ABC in Lahore	96
Introduction to the Appendices	107
Appendix I: Articles by Rudyard Kipling	110
Appendix II: Articles on Central Asia and Afghanistan Attributed to Kipling or Wheeler	189
Appendix III: Translations by Rudyard Kipling	190
Appendix IV: Afghan Boundary Commission Reports from Correspondents	204
Appendix V: Members of the Afghan Boundary Commission	206
Notes	213
Selected Bibliography	221
Index	225

When you're wounded and left on Afghanistan's plains,
And the women come out to cut up what remains,
Jest roll to your rifle and blow out your brains
   An' go to your Gawd like a soldier.
    Go, go, go like a soldier,
    Go, go, go like a soldier,
    Go, go, go like a soldier,
      So-oldier of the Queen!

      Last stanza of *The Young British Soldier* (1892)
                      by Rudyard Kipling

Preface

The acquisition of the papers of Dr. Charles Owen by the National Army Museum (London) in 1998 opened a new perspective on Rudyard Kipling as assistant editor of the *Civil and Military Gazette* in Lahore, British India. Owen belonged to the same social circle as John Lockwood and Alice Kipling and became a fellow employee of their 19-year-old son after being hired as a correspondent for the *Civil and Military Gazette* in 1884. In that year the British set up the Afghan Boundary Commission in response to Russian incursions into Afghanistan. For two years Owen participated in this mission as medical officer and ethnologist. Between November 1884 and October 1886 he sent more than 40 newsletters to his newspaper in Lahore, most of which went through Rudyard Kipling's hands before appearing in print.

Even before formation of the commission, Rudyard Kipling had become knowledgeable about Russian aspirations in Central Asia, because his duties involved translating reports on the advance contained in Russian newspapers for the *Civil and Military Gazette*. In March and April 1885 Kipling attended a conference between the amir of Afghanistan and the viceroy of India as a correspondent of the *Civil and Military* Gazette. John Lockwood Kipling called the assignment his son's "first big thing."

The efforts of the British to demarcate the Russian–Afghan border ended in a disaster after the Russians overwhelmed the Afghans at Penjdeh on 30 March 1885 when the amir arrived in India. For the editor of the Lahore paper, Owen's description of the attack and the humiliating British retreat was "the best letter he has read since he has been in India."

After a summer of saber rattling, a group of Russian and British officers began demarcating the border on 12 November 1885. Owen continued with his newsletters until the Afghan Boundary Commission returned to India on 31 October 1886. These newsletters, together with the letters and diary at the National Army Museum, reveal the public and private aspects of the commission.

Rudyard Kipling played a major part in the welcoming ceremonies for the mission in Lahore, presided over by the viceroy of India and the Duke of Connaught, favorite son of Queen Victoria. A piece in the *Civil and Military Gazette* describes the dinner for the returning officers attended by Kiplings and his father.

Later in life, Rudyard Kipling and his wife attempted to destroy all early manuscript material and letters. After John Lockwood Kipling died, Rudyard Kipling made a huge bonfire of his father's papers. A search of the Kipling archives at Sussex University could not turn up a single reference to Dr. Charles Owen. Kipling's office diary for 1885 did survive the purge, however, and it is one of the treasures of Harvard University

Kipling's newsletters from the conference between the viceroy and the amir give an intriguing insight into his development as an artist. A few pieces, such as the picture of Peshawar titled "The City of Evil Countenances," absolutely sparkle with brilliance. His lifelong mistrust of Russians dates from these years, and his experiences with the amir and his troops found expression in his writings.

1

Prologue

During the latter half of the nineteenth century Russia gradually strengthened its grip on Central Asia. In 1866 there was war with Bokhara and in 1868 Samarkand was taken. In 1873 the Russians added Khiva to their acquisitions, and after a long siege the Tekke Turkmens were defeated in January 1881 at the bloody battle of Geok Tepe in Krasnovodsk. The Trans-Caspian Railway began creeping its way across Central Asia. Merv fell in February 1884.[1]

With their stake in India and Afghanistan the British could not view these events without a certain amount of trepidation. By this date the British had fought two vicious wars with Afghanistan, suffering in January 1842 the most terrible retreat in the history of British arms, when of 17,000 soldiers and camp followers proceeding through the Khyber Pass only one single survivor reached Jalalabad.

After Sir Louis Cavagnari, the resident in Kabul, was murdered on September 3, 1879, Major-General Frederick Roberts was dispatched from India on a mission of vengeance to the Afghan capital. Roberts had hardly finished devastating Kabul and setting a rival amir, Abdur Rahman, on the throne on July 22, 1880, when he received word that the British under General Burrows had been defeated by Afghan troops at Maiwand on July 27. Roberts then marched to Kandahar and by September 1 he had overwhelmed the enemy. The British withdrew under the condition that they would retain the right to handle Afghanistan's foreign relations. Since Abdur Rahman had spent his years of exile in Samarkand and Russian Turkestan, the British could never, however, be sure of his true sentiments.

The hero of the Second Afghan War, General Frederick Roberts, described the capture of Merv as "by far the most important step ever made by Russia on her march toward India."[2] The specter of the Russians taking advantage of the unsettled state of Afghanistan by extending their field of influence right up to the border of India threw the Anglo-Indian military establishment centered at Simla into a quandary. Not only was the military hampered in its operations by a weak liberal-minded viceroy, Lord Ripon, but the parliament at home seemed to have little interest in Indian affairs. The fall of Merv served as the catalyst. It finally brought home to Lord Ripon and the British public that the jewel of the British crown might be at risk. If Afghanistan fell, how could a common border with Russia be defended?

An insight into the diplomatic manipulations in response to the Russian advance is provided by the secret diary kept by Arthur F. Barrow, the private secretary and aide-de-camp of General Lumsden. According to Barrow's unpublished manuscript, titled "Precis respecting Afghan Frontier from January 1884 to April 9th, 1885," the viceroy of India telegraphed the India Office on Feb. 24, 1884, emphasizing the necessity of coming to a clear understanding with Russia as to the Northern and North-Western frontier of Afghanistan. The viceroy urged the government to appoint a joint commission with representation from the British, Afghan, Russian and possibly Persian governments.[3]

Realizing that Russian momentum for a further thrust to the south was rapidly building, Prime Minister William Gladstone for once was not long in formulating a plan of action. The Foreign Office dug out maps of Central Asia, and diplomatic enquiries were made at St. Petersburg. The news of the Russian annexation of Sarakhs on the frontier of the Persian province of Khorassan only served to heighten the sense of urgency. The *Illustrated London News* of May 31, 1884, carried a brief notice with two maps highlighting the area in dispute. The Central Asian authority Charles Marvin was quoted as urging "the necessity of ordering an immediate delimitation of the Afghan frontier in proximity to Sarakhs, to be conducted by British officers."[4]

These news releases emanating from London, Simla and St. Petersburg naturally aroused a great deal of interest in India, but nowhere were these developments more closely followed than in the offices of the *Civil and Military Gazette* in Lahore. This provincial newspaper had forged a market niche by combining a competent distilling of international news with a strong dose of local gossip. It was close enough to the headquarters of the British military in Simla to be among the first to learn about developments, yet it was far enough away to maintain an independent point of view. As an antidote to the official papers from the presidency cities of Calcutta, Bombay and Madras, the *Civil and Military Gazette* had been able to build up a loyal following among the British officer corps on the North West frontier. The owners were the wealthy entrepreneur James Walker of Simla and William Rattigen, a lawyer from Lahore.

Learning that the newspaper was looking for an assistant editor, John

1. Prologue

Lockwood Kipling approached the owners about considering his son Rudyard for the position. As curator of the Lahore museum and principal of the New Mayo School of Art, Kipling was regarded as one of the more illustrious citizens of the city. His son was in his final year at Westward Ho! in Devon. A university education for Rudyard was beyond his family's means, so the best alternative seemed to be giving him a start in life as a journalist.

To further this plan, John Lockwood Kipling and his wife, Alice, decided to take up residency in Simla in the summer of 1882. Simla was not only the headquarters of India's military, but the civilian government moved from Calcutta to Simla during the hot months as well. Every civil servant worth his salt deemed a presence in Simla as essential for networking. Kipling's reputation as an ethnologist had gained him entry to the social circle around James Walker, and the Kiplings must have applied all their guiles to obtaining a post at the *Gazette* for their son. The tactics worked, and the editor of the newspaper, Stephen Wheeler, was more or less forced to accept a 16-year-old as his assistant. As a sop, James Walker sent Wheeler to England to interview the candidate. In October Rudyard joined a staff of three Europeans overseeing some 70 workers.[5] Walker seems to have taken a special interest in the boy as he was invited to stay with the Walkers at Kelvin Grove in July 1883.

The *Civil and Military Gazette* Building in 1885 from *The Kipling Journal*, no. 16 (December 1930), p. 112–113. John Slater of the Kipling Society says the sketch was originally printed in mirror image. Rudyard Kipling is leaning against the right side of a pillar. (Photograph courtesy of David Page, Kipling Society.)

By the fall of 1884 Kipling had almost two years experience with the newspaper, proving his worth with a routine of translations, proof-reading, correspondence and "cut-and-paste" layouts. Wheeler gradually allowed Kipling to publish a few of his poems in the newspaper. Moreover, Wheeler's frequent illnesses meant that all the editorial work often fell on Kipling's shoulders.[6] Already in November 1882 Kipling was complaining: "I am responsible for every scrap of the paper except the first two pages. That is to say, I bear the blame of correspondents' blunders–it is my duty to correct them — misprints and bad lettering — it is my business to find them out — vulgarities, bad grammar and indecency — we get *that* sometimes?— have to be looked to carefully and I have a large correspondence all over India with men of all sorts."

Since Kipling knew French, editor Stephen Wheeler gave him the task of translating reports in French on the Russian advance into Central Asia reported in *Novoie Vremya* and *Journal de St. Petersbourg*. He was to pay particular attention to events in Afghanistan and Central Asia. With the fall of Merv, this aspect of his apprenticeship acquired an added dimension. On February 27, 1884, the *Civil and Military Gazette* published a number of telegrams and letters dealing with the threat the Russian advance posed for Balkh and Herat. On February 29 the newspaper featured an article on "The Trade Routes of Central Asia" based on extracts from the *St. Petersburg Gazette* with a map of the region. On March 21 the *Gazette* offered its readers a translation from the *Allgemeine Zeitung* on "The Russians in Merve." During the following months the political maneuverings were followed very closely.

"Major-General Sir Peter Stark Lumsden, K.C.B., C.S.I." Lithograph based on a photograph in the Afghan Boundary Commission album of William Simpson, The Marquess of Salisbury Library. *Illustrated London News*, September 13, 1884, p. 245.

As head of what came to be called the Afghan Boundary Commission, Gladstone and Lord Granville at the Foreign Office selected Major-General Sir Peter Stark

1. Prologue

Lumsden, K.C.B., C.S.I. Lumsden came from a distinguished Anglo-Indian military family, and his brother was Sir Harry Burnett Lumsden, who formed the famous Corps of Guides in 1847 and was credited with introducing the khaki uniform into the Indian army. In 1857 Peter Lumsden had accompanied his older brother on a mission to Kandahar, where they were held in virtual house arrest during the Indian Mutiny. This was followed by a series of military appointments in India and London, culminating in 1871 with his designation as aide-de-camp to the Queen.

Lumsden took as his own ADC Captain Arthur F. Barrow, who was said to be "peculiarly fitted for such a duty; as he is a first-class Russian scholar."[7] For the Persian side of his political department Lumsden chose Nawab Mirza Hassan Ali Khan. His first assistant commissioner was A. Condie Stephen, E.B., of the British embassy at Teheran. As his second assistant commissioner, Lumsden called upon a fellow veteran from the Indian Mutiny, Col. Charles E. Stewart. A gifted linguist, he had traveled through Persia in disguise and written about the devastation caused by Turkoman raids. Prior commitments delayed his departure from London, and he planned to join the party in Afghanistan.

The last member of the Commission was William Simpson, the distinguished foreign correspondent and artist with the *Illustrated London News*. Simpson's publication of a two-volume illustrated history of the Crimean War in 1855 had made him a celebrity.[8] He was sent as a correspondent by the *Illustrated London News* to the Abyssinian War in 1867–1868, the German-French War of 1870 and the war in Afghanistan in 1878. In 1875–1876 he accompanied the Prince of Wales on his official visit to India. The participation in the Afghan Boundary Commission was the last major assignment of his career.[9] His principal duty as special artist was to furnish the government with a series of sketches of the countries and people through which the mission would have to travel.

The instructions to Lumsden, dated August 25, 1884, were explicit. The definition of the duties of the commission included not only ascertaining the exact limits of Afghan territory by conducting surveys of the region but also compiling information on the Saryk Turkoman tribe at Penjdeh. The question of whether Penjdeh was in Afghanistan was to be given special attention. The investigation of this question determined to a large extent the composition of the Commission in India.

In Simla it was assumed that General Roberts would be called upon to head the Indian section, but the Foreign Office made it clear that a more neutral candidate would be preferred. The British would after all have to depend on the good faith of Amir Abdur Rahman for passage through the country. Their selection fell on Lieutenant-Colonel Joseph West Ridgeway, who had accompanied Roberts on the march from Kabul to Kandahar. At the time of his appointment, Ridgeway was junior under-secretary of the government of India, in the Foreign Department. The selection of the officers accompanying him lay largely in his hands.

The Indian Section of the commission initially consisted of 30 Europeans, an escort of 465 and 900 camp-followers.[10] The Foreign Office assigned the participating officers to three branches—political, survey and intelligence—to which was appended a group of scientific experts. The 11th Bengal Lancers and the 20th Panjab Infantry formed the escort. The *Illustrated London News* for September 13th named the individual members as follows:

> The actual surveying operations will be conducted by three officers of the Royal engineers, Major Hill, Captain Gore, and Lieutenant Talbot. Dr. Aitchison will study the natural history and botany, and Mr. Griesbach the geology, of the region to be traversed, which is likely to yield some interesting contributions to scientific knowledge. Oriental archaeology, history, and ethnology may also be expected to gain valuable additions to the existing stores of learning.

"Lieutenant-Colonel B. K. Ridgeway, V.C." Lithograph based on a photograph in the Afghan Boundary Commission Album of W. Simpson, The Marquess of Salisbury Library. *Illustrated London News*, May 25, 1885, p. 534.

The Major Hill mentioned in the *Illustrated London News* was invalided, so Major Thomas Holdich replaced him at the last moment. Captain Edward Durand and Captain Charles E. Yate were sent as Political Officers. Captain Pelham J. Maitland, first intelligence officer of the Bombay Staff Corps, headed the Intelligence Branch. Danish linguist Albert De Laessoe acted as official interpreter. Captains Durand and De Laessoe were responsible for collecting archaeological specimen and the medical attaché, Dr. Charles Owen, was to prepare an ethnological report.[11] Thomas Weir with his "photographic apparatus" participated as the representative of the *Times of India*.

On August 25, 1884, Lord Granville sent word to St. Petersburg that Lumsden had been appointed British Commissioner.[12] The initial suggestion that the Russian Commission would be led by Major Alikhanoff brought a storm of protest in London and Simla. Alikhanoff had come to fame by writing a report on the Turkomans and Merv with minute details about the land and its people. He was also the first Russian officer to make his way in disguise into the Turcoman stronghold of Merv. The *Civil and Military Gazette* wrote:

> The dashing Mohamedan soldier, Ali Khan, has doubtless been thoroughly Russianised in nature as well as in name, but it may be questioned whether he is a sufficiently important personage to satisfy the purely ceremonial requirements of the occasion. It cannot be supposed that the Russian Government are ignorant of the meaning which our native subjects in India may naturally attach to such an appointment; and perhaps, it would not be going too far, even yet, to suggest to Russia the necessity of appointing a Commissioner who is at least a Russian by birth.[13]

It was said that his appointment would only serve to throw ridicule on the commission and he could hardly be placed at a negotiating table opposite Lumsden. In response to these protests, the Foreign Office of St. Petersburg found a more senior officer, General Zelenoy, to head its Commission.

Among Kipling's translations were the memoirs of Major Alikhanoff, whose activities contributed in a major way to the fall of Merv.[14] In his autobiography *Something of Myself*, Kipling described this task with particular distaste:

> One cut-and-come-again affliction was an accursed Moscovite paper, the *Novoie Vremya*, written in French, which, for weeks and weeks, published the war diaries of Alikhanoff, a Russian General then harrying the Central Russian Khanates. He gave the name of every camp he halted at, and regularly reported that his troops warmed themselves at fires of *sax-aul*, which I suppose is perhaps sage-brush. A week after I had translated the last of the series every remembrance of it passed from my normal memory.

But even if most of the mundane tasks of publishing the newspaper landed on his desk, Kipling soon realized that his translations from the Russian press gave him a particular edge in understanding the Central Asia conflict and thus the discussions about the establishment of a boundary mission suddenly put him in a very favorable position.[15] Paraphrasing the discussion on the subject in St. Petersburg papers, Kipling wrote in the Oct. 21, 1884, issue of the *Gazette*, that with respect to material interests "the situation of England in Asia was a far better one than [Russia's] ... nevertheless the success of Russia in Central Asia disguieted her." (See Appendix III.1.) Kipling continued, the English "looked then for a barrier against this advance beyond her own frontiers, and found it in Afghanistan, a country which in the year 1857, had entered into a treaty of alliance with the Viceroys of India."

The English had at first thought of setting up a "neutral zone," but, the translator continued, "this was abandoned in the face of the many difficulties which would attend on its establishment," so it was resolved "to lay down a line of demarcation which should be respected not only by the two Powers, but also by the Khans which came within the range of their respective influences." Kipling went on to say, "particular importance had been attached to the eastern portion of the line of demarcation — that is to say, the line running from Soree-Kul lake in the Panier [sic] district to the Afghan outpost of Khodga Salekh, on the left bank of the Oxus, as it served as a boundary between the possessions of the Khan of Bokhara and those of the Amir of Afghanistan." However, with the Russian conquest of the Tekke Turkomans, the necessity for "a fresh demarcation of the line of limitation" between the Oxus and Persia arose.

As the negotiators in London soon learned, the conflict had boiled down to being essentially a question about the ethnicity of certain Turkoman tribes. In his discussions with the Russians, Gladstone's Foreign Secretary, Lord Granville, had been presented with the argument that the Salor Turkomans used Badghiz and the region around Penjdeh as pastureland and therefore the Salors, *ergo* Russia, had an ethnographical claim to the territory. In the same region, however, were also the Saryk Turkomans, who had never submitted to the Russians and they were asking for protection from the Amir of Afghanistan. For this reason the Foreign Office laid particular weight upon ascertaining the allegiance of the native populations inhabiting this region. St. Petersburg claimed that the Saryks had sent representatives to Merv. Kipling knew what he was talking about when he translated the line: "Russia sealed her right to Turcomania by the blood spilt under the walls of Geok Tepe" (See Appendix III.5).

Kipling's involvement with the ABC during the first months of 1885 can be followed almost day by day through his work diary for 1885. At the beginning of his diary he recorded that he had supplied 230 columns matter for the newspaper in 1884.[16] For the period beginning in January 1885, he set his quota at two and a half columns per issue.[17]

A shrewd businessman, James Walker viewed the formation of the Afghan Boundary Commission as a perfect opportunity to increase his readership, so he augmented the reportage by hiring two participants of

1. Prologue

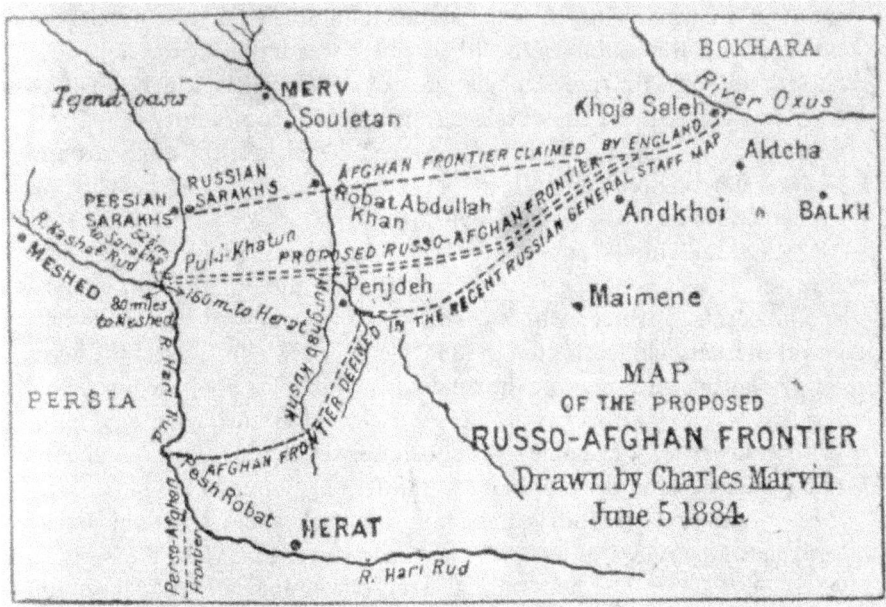

Map of the proposed Russo-Afghan frontier, drawn by Charles Marvin. *Illustrated London News,* June 14, 1884, p. 574.

the mission as correspondents for the *Civil and Military Gazette*. Political officer Edward Durand was an obvious first choice. The Central Asian authority Charles Marvin described him as "a son of the hero Sir Henry Durand, and for several years had been acting as political agent attached to the ex–Ameer Yakoob Khan, the ruler who connived at Cavagnari's murder at Cabul."[18] His brother Henry Mortimer Durand was one of the most influential members of the Indian Foreign Office and, in fact, he was named head of the political department before the year was out. Their father's memoirs of the First Afghan War were published by Henry Mortimer Durand in 1879. Few officers in Simla had closer links to the Foreign Office than Edward Durand, who in addition was a brilliant linguist.

As his second correspondent Walker obtained the services of an old Simla colleague, Dr. Charles Owen, the medical officer and ethnologist with the ABC. Owen had served on the personal staff of Sir Frederick Roberts during the Second Afghan War and after Roberts defeated Ayub Khan's Afghan army near Kandahar, Owen could count himself "in." In 1880 Owen acceded to the plum posting of Civil Surgeon in Simla.

Owen's appointment gained him access into the close-knit and secretive Simla society. That he numbered himself among the cousins of an influential figure in Indian politics, the Honorable Courtenay Ilbert, did not hinder Owen's ambitions either. Ilbert was father of the notorious "Ilbert Bill" allowing Indian magistrates to try Europeans, which provoked such an outcry in the conservative Anglo-Indian community. The Ilbert connection and his medical work brought Owen into the circle around Walker. When Owen volunteered for service in Egypt in 1882, his wife was invited to reside in the Walker mansion.

After returning from Egypt, Owen found a post in Jaipur as resident surgeon. His duties appear to have been more diplomatic than medical and he became involved with an exhibition of Jaipur artifacts for the Calcutta International Exhibition in 1883. He not only helped select the items for display but he also wrote the catalogue, which was published in 1883.[19] For this task he fell back on the expertise of John Lockwood Kipling in Lahore. Owen was thus able to establish himself in a small way as an ethnologist, at least in the eyes of a few influential people in Simla.

Owen's career in India can be followed in great detail with his letters and diaries from 1878 to 1900, which were acquired in 1998 by the National Army Museum.[20] The material has been chronologically organized and includes three letters Owen sent to his fiancée, Miss Barry, from 1878, Owen's diary and 15 letters to his wife from the Egyptian Expedition (1882), diary notes and six letters from Jaipur (1882–1884) and diaries and more than 100 letters to his wife from the Afghan mission (1884–1886).

Writing from Egypt, Owen mentions John Lockwood Kipling and his wife, whom he had met in Simla at the time they were pressuring Walker to accept their son as an assistant editor at the *Gazette*: "You seem to like the Kiplings. I quite agree with you about their intelligence but I think they are both horrid cads" (letter to his wife dated August 30, 1882).[21] In a commentary on this material at the museum, the compiler of the register notes that Owen, as civil surgeon of Simla, had access to a wide social circle and adds that "Walker, together with a lawyer from Lahore called William Rattigen, founded the *Civil & Military Gazette* in Lahore on which Rudyard Kipling had his first post — see page 50 — and was a close friend of the elder Kiplings, John Lockwood and Alice. Indeed during June 1883, Rudyard stayed with the Walkers in Simla for his month's holiday from the heat of Lahore, and it is quite possible for Mrs. Owen to have met him there if she was in Simla at the time."

According to a report in the Allahabad based newspaper *Pioneer* on August 29, 1884, Owen was in charge of submitting to the government a report on the ethnography, arts, manufacture, trades and agriculture of the peoples and tribes through whose territory the Commission passed.[22] The same statement appeared again on November 28, 1884: "Dr Owen will prepare and submit to Government a report on the ethnography ... of the people and tribes through whose territory we pass, illustrating it with photographs and sketches representing the dress and types of the inhabitants."[23] A young native draughtsman from the Jaipur School of Art was to illustrate the report with sketches.[24] Owen described his assignment in a letter to his wife dated April 24, 1885:[25]

> But I don't ever take any trouble about them and sometimes keep them a month without a line, anyhow it is bread and butter to me in a small way, and it does one good to have a Press connection no matter how insignificant it may be.

The itinerary as it was formulated was that Sir Peter Lumsden would leave London on September 4, and meet the Russian Commissioner, General Zelenoy, at Sarakhs near the Persian-Afghan border in the first week of November. The members of the commission would travel via Vienna and the Black Sea to Tiflis, where they hoped to meet briefly on September 16 with Zelenoy. From Baku the party would sail by steamer over the Caspian Sea to the Persian port city of Resht. The commission planned to arrive in Teheran at the end of September. After consultation with the Persian government, Lumsden would travel to Meshed, near the eastern border of Khorassan, and reach Sararks about November 7.[26]

Quetta on the border of Afghanistan was chosen as the assembling point for the Indian military escort under command of Major Ridgeway. From Quetta the convoy had to make its way "across 400 miles of untraversed wilderness, commencing with the arid flats of Baluchistan lying south of the Helmund (much of which is absolute desert), concluding with the wide rolling scrub-covered 'dashts,' which stretch all the way from the Helmund river to Herat along the Perso-Afghan border."[27] The *Illustrated London News* gave further particulars about the route and mission:

> It is expected in India that a mixed English and Russian commission will proceed in the autumn to the northern border of Afghanistan to mark out the frontier. An agreement has, it is understood, been arrived at between the British and Russian Governments, providing in general terms that the frontier shall follow the course of the Oxus as far as Khoja Saleh, whence it will proceed south and west, taking a circular course along the margin of cultivation of Pul-i-Khatun, on the Hari Rud river.[28]

This report was accompanied by a map drawn by Charles Marvin showing the area in dispute.

2

The Journey to Sarakhs

For a provincial newspaper dependent on maintaining good lines of communication to the military establishment in Simla, the position of the *Civil and Military Gazette* with regard to the formation of the Afghan Boundary Commission appears at first glance to be strangely negative. Its reaction in the August 4 issue to the announcement that Lieutenant Colonel Ridgeway had been appointed head of the Indian section was that it seemed "almost incredible," when much more experienced officers such as General Roberts, Sir Auckland Colvin and Sir Charles McGregor had been overlooked. The author of the article admitted that "it is no fault of Colonel Ridgeway that he is a comparatively young man," as young men such as Lord Metcalfe, Mr. Elphinstone and Sir John Malcolm had achieved remarkable exploits, "but before they were placed in positions of responsibility and power, they had proved their merits to masters who were as well qualified to judge of the ability of officers as any of their generation." "But," the *Gazette* asked, "can the same be said of Colonel Ridgeway, whose claims to reputation may be said to lie in the fact that he accompanied General Roberts on the march from Cabul to Kandahar, and that he has been Under-Secretary in the Foreign Department of the Government of India for some three years?" Recent decisions of the Foreign Department had moreover already inspired political observers with such a profound distrust of its operations that "the appointment of this officer to the Commission is so far from being one which commands general confidence, that it is one in which no general confidence is felt."

A "newswriter from Simla" is suggested as the author of this piece but the criticism is so acute that it could not have been published without the sanction of James Walker. The article speaks of those who maintain that the constitution of a Boundary Commission was imperatively called for, but "there are other, ourselves included, who believe that the result of such a proceeding cannot be otherwise than unsatisfactory." The actual formulation of the attack can probably be attributed to editor Stephen Wheeler.

James Walker did not hesitate to use his newspaper to promote the policies of his colleagues General Roberts and Sir Charles MacGregor, author of *The Gazetteer of Central Asia, Part II*. In his book MacGregor advocated an active "Forward Policy" in response to the Russian incursions. The ostensible grounds for the Second Afghan War in 1878 were that Amir Shere Ali Khan had accepted an embassy in Kabul from the Russians, whereas a similar request on the part of the British was refused. A revealing photograph taken in Kabul by John Burke in February 1880 shows General Roberts and Charles MacGregor to either side of a round table at the center of which MacGregor's book is prominently featured.[1]

Gladstone's appointment of the Marquess of Ripon as Viceroy in 1880, however, put a serious dent in the influence of the Simla military establishment on the Foreign Office. The formation of the ABC was viewed by the military as another example of Gladstone doing too little, too late.

The *Gazette* article commented that the way the political winds were blowing had been indicated when "an unfortunate telegram from home announced the selection of Sir Peter Lumsden." Regrettably the selection of the other officers of the ABC would now be largely in Ridgeway's hands. Since "no officers senior to him in rank or position can be nominated to serve under him, even if it were possible that they should consent to do so ... the field of selection is therefore almost inevitably narrowed to a class of officer of whom the public knows nothing, and in whom consequently it can feel no confidence."

This cut at the commission was followed on August 18 by a letter to the editor from an anonymous "X.Y.Z." criticizing the latest antics of the "Gladstone-Ripon *regime*." The author said "in two ways only can we profit by this picnic, reserved, as is inevitable, for some of the Simla clique, not — as is their right — for men who live on the frontier." What was needed to impress the Russians was "a few members of the Quarter-Master General's department, and a very picked and showy-looking escort, [rather] than any amount of diplomatic talent." The Foreign Office should have sent "a smart and carefully chosen sample" keyed to "impress the imagination of all spectators.... Instead of this, interest or talent for office work seems alone to have guided the powers that be ... and the members, clever though they *may* be, are one and all more at home at a desk than in the saddle." The writer continued, "along side the picked lot of smart soldiers, who will undoubtedly represent the Czar, they will cut a very sorry appearance indeed." In short, this ABC staff consisted of "would be" officers, reveling in double rations, pay and the newest uniforms, accompanied by "a guard of men hurried off in kit they may happen to have at the time, without probably the smallest grant of batta or warm clothing, and the usual flour and ghee Hindoo rations doled out, *minus* either firewood or comforts."

Since most of the officers for the ABC had been selected by this date, the writer's criticism must have been a bitter pill to swallow. In particular the reference to the "picnic" rankled and was often referred to by ABC officers later while they were crossing the deserts of Afghanistan or freezing in their yurts on the border of Turkestan.

The *Gazette* position found almost immediately a sharp rebuttal in a letter to the editor of the rival newspaper *Pioneer*, published in Allahabad. An "EX-POLITICAL" wrote that the remarks in the Lahore paper were the reflection of a "small provincial clique ... practically left out in the cold in connection with a matter in which they deem themselves peculiarly fitted to shine." Rather than being inexperienced as implied in the *Gazette*, Colonel Ridgeway had "24 years' service, of which 15 have been in political employ." Before the march to Kandahar, Ridgeway had served many months in Kabul and he had been highly recommended by General Roberts. He had three years service in the Foreign Office and "an intimate knowledge of the views of the Government of India on the whole question."

Like any good editor, Stephen Wheeler was never happier than when being the recipient of rabid letters to the editor, so he dutifully reprinted the Allahabad letter in his own newspaper. Two further long letters to the editor from a "CONSERVATIVE" and a "FRONTIER" on the subject appeared on August 25 and 30.

Having ruffled enough feathers in Simla, Wheeler and Walker began to direct their attention to the Amir. Here they were more condescending allowing that the money spent on maintaining the good will of Abdur Rahman was well spent, for, as the anonymous "FRONTIER" mentioned in his letter to the editor, "the real strength of Afghanistan is and always will be its stubborn and hardy people."[2] Yet the British had to make it clear that if Russia crossed any border set down by the Afghan Boundary Commission then it would be a *casus belli*. The English people at home had to finally realize that a powerful European nation was setting up frontier posts along a border for all practical purposes conterminous with their own in India.

Since the fall of Merv Wheeler and assistant editor Kipling had been assembling and setting aside for future publication a series of "cut-and-paste" items on preparations for the campaign and on Central Asia from various English, Russian and Indian newspapers. They were also aware that the *Gazette* would have to adopt a more balanced view of the boundary commission if they were to not completely antagonize their two ABC correspondents Edward Durand and Dr. Charles Owen. Their quibble focused after all on the Foreign Office, not on the military.

Nevertheless, the newspaper could not leave the subject without printing a report from a Simla correspondent commenting on the indecorous "hustle" at the Foreign Office, "for what do men go to the Highlands of India save to recruit their health, adorn official festivities with their presence, chaperon grass-widows and draw their pay?" The writer began his piece with the words, "The curtain is up: the Farce has begun!"[3]

On September 9 the *Gazette* came up with an editorial recapitulating a Central Asian policy "marked by a series of disasters and reverses." In light of this long record of failures, the aims and actions of the Delimitation Commission had to be very carefully considered. But instead of this the government was sending "a fourth-rate man to do work which requires exceptional ability," in fact, "General Sir Peter Lumsden was about the worst man who could have been found for the important duty assigned to him." As for Colonel Stewart, he might be able to write an interesting narrative about his experiences as an Armenian horse-dealer in Persia, yet he lacked "the wide experience, the tact, and the readiness of resource, which should be required from all leading members of the Boundary Commission." The *Gazette* concluded, "we can only hope that Colonel Ridgeway will falsify the opinion of his abilities expressed in these columns."

Colonel Ridgeway accompanied by Captain Yate arrived in Quetta on the second of September and gradually troops and participants filtered in.[4] On September 3, 244 rifles of the 20th Panjab under Lieutenant Meikeljohn and five native officers checked in as well as Captain Gore of the survey. The mission required 1,600 camels, of which 1,100 were then there with 200 more on the way, whence another 300 extra camels had to be procured. On September 5, 64 sabres of the 11th Bengal Lancers under Lieutenant Wright arrived, with another 100 under Colonel Prinsep expected the next day. The logistical staff calculated that the mission would comprise of not less than 1,600 people and 600 horses and mules. By September 14, there were 300 sabres of the 11th Bengal Lancers and 240 bayonets of the 20th Panjab Infantry in the camp.[5]

On September 12 Edward Durand sent his first ABC newsletter from Quetta.[6] The arrangement with the *Gazette* seems to have been that Durand would cover the first part of the campaign from Quetta to Herat, but on reaching the border to Turkestan, Owen would take over the duties as *Gazette* correspondent. Owen expected to be fully occupied with his duties as a medical officer on the long march through the deserts of Baluchistan, but once the troops had reached the area in dispute he would turn his attention to ethnographical matters.

Durand began his first letter by referring to the "picnic" they were enjoying in the intense heat — the thermometer stood at about 120 degrees in the shade. Several roads were being considered by Colonel Ridgeway for getting "his party over the waste with as little loss of life as possible, either in men or animals." The water supply posed the greatest difficulty.

The other *Gazette* correspondent, Dr. Owen, had left Jaipur, or Jeypore as it was then spelled, on August 27 at 9:40 A.M. With him on the train, but of course not in the first class section, were his kit, dog, photographic equipment, the artist from the Jaipur School of Art and his servants.[7] At Delhi he changed into the Lahore mail (on the Sind, Punjab and Delhi Railway mentioned on the first page of *Kim*). The train left Delhi at 9 P.M., arriving the next day at Lahore at 5 P.M. While shifting his baggage to the Mooltan side of the station, Owen ran into Dr. Aitchison, the naturalist with the ABC. Owen had only time for a quick soup and tea before the train to Mooltan started. At Mooltan on August 29, everybody changed to the Indus-Valley-State-Railway train en route to Sukkar. The heat, Owen says, was considerable. At one station his dog jumped out and the train had to be stopped so he could retrieve it.

At 7 A.M. on August 30, they reached Rohri Bunder and had a pleasant trip across the Indus on a steamer. At Sukker the luggage was shifted onto the Kandahar and Sind Railway train, which left at 9:15 A.M. At Jacobabad he was joined by ABC members Lt. Arthur Yate and Lt. (the Hon.) M.G. Talbot of the Royal Engineers. Rindli, the terminus, was reached about 10:15 P.M., where some soldiers of the 11th Bengal Lancers helped transport his baggage to the Dak Bungalow.

August 31 was spent sorting out stores, tents, etc., in the intense heat in preparation for the trip by land to Quetta. Despite the name, the Kandahar State Railway ran in 1884 only as far as Rindli, and in fact never did make it to Kandahar.

Col. Ridgeway arrived in Rindli on September 1 and he immediately set off for Quetta. From September 2 to 9, Owen was fully occupied with arranging his photographic kit and the dispensary for the long march to Quetta. Everyone suffered considerably from the heat and flies.

On September 9, they marched from Rindli to Kirta, some 18 miles, on September 10 from Kirta to Bibuiani (12½ miles). Passing through Mach (September 11) and Dogan (September 13), the convoy reached the large ABC camp at Siriab at 7 A.M. on September 14. Siriab was about six miles from Quetta.

On September 18, the political officers from Simla arrived, setting the whole camp in an uproar by announcing the devastating news that the Foreign Office had ordered the force be reduced to 900 men, taking only 200 cavalry and 200 infantry as escort. The field and civil hospitals were to be amalgamated. Owen wrote in his diary, "I doubt the wisdom of this alteration as it seems to me that the medico-political work is all important in a business of this kind," but he decided to keep his peace until the orders were sent to him from headquarters.

On September 21, orders were given for the force to leave the camp in two relays the next day. Owen with half the hospital ended up in the first group. His *Gazette* colleague Edward Durand would be traveling with him. Durand had sent his second report on the ABC from Camp Quetta, i.e. Sairiab, on September 18, deploring the heat, dust, reduction of forces and the difficulty in obtaining camels (See Appendix IV.2). Yet "the troops are in good health and spirits, and all keen to be moving."

As Holdich of the royal engineers later commented: "the outfit of the Commission was on a scale of liberality which left nothing to be desired. Tents such as had never before been seen in Turkistan, mess equipment and mess attendants, stores of wine and delicacies such as might serve the purpose of a series of royal banquets in the Turkistan wilderness, were all provided."[8] Lt. Arthur Yate noted that "all the English members of the Mission have been fitted out with Kashmir tents 240 lb. in weight; while for the use of the British Commissioner and the mess on the frontier, large hill and double poled tents and *shamianahs* have been procured.[9] Even two collapsible boats arrived from Bombay, the purpose of which was debated, although it was agreed that they would be good for duck-shooting on the Oxus or Murghab. A special problem was posed by the flag staff. About 45 feet high, it was carried in three sections, each 16 feet long. Also included was a bulldog to keep watch at the foot of the British flag staff.

It was estimated that during the winter of 1884–85 there must have been between 2,000 and 3,000 members of the British commission in Turkestan. "It was evidently intended that the English Commission should carry with it the prestige of India's wealth and luxury."[10] William Simpson mentions the large amount of luggage being brought from London as well, "the greater part of it being presents for the chiefs who may be met along the route.[11]

Durand's third report appeared in the October 8 issue of the *Gazette*. Wheeler and Kipling must have been very pleased with it. It filled up a full two and half columns, which meant all the less work for them. Essentially the report described how the force was divided into sections, so as to not deplete the water supply on the march. For a 60-mile stretch between Nushki and the Helmund River, water had to be conveyed in skins as this wasteland was without usable wells. The report "from our own Correspondent" dated September 20 began:

> The Afghan Mission is now at Camp Nushki, having descended a good thousand feet or more, probably, since leaving Quetta, and are hard at work making the last preparations for crossing the desert. The march down from Quetta has been very trying, by reason of the intense heat by day and the biting cold by night. The ground all the way, when not composed of stones with slight intervals between them, has been sand, and this becomes cold at once, when the sun goes down. The camping grounds have been all on such dust, for it is more like the dust of an Indian bullock-cart road than sand, and the result of its being blown over clothes and saddlery, is that everything is grimed and gritty. Even the bullock trunks cannot quite keep it out, the "scentless and delicate dust" finding its way to packed kit, as well as to the nostrils and eye-lids of everything mortal.

Durand managed, however, to expand on this meager material with considerable wit. Details about the activities of the scientific experts were augmented with praise for the logistical accomplishments of Colonel Ridgeway. The naturalist discovered a new species of tadpole allied to one only found in the Swiss lakes, the surveyors calculated the distances, two or three pigeons were shot — "not much bigger than doves but still pigeons — diminutive blue rocks with slight bars on the wing." Durand ended with a sketch of Azad Kan, Sirdar of Kharsan: "He sits his horse as upright as ever, and though over 97 gives a grip that would make a Bengali Baboo sink to the ground with agony."

Pleased with having a correspondent with a literary bent, Durand's employers encouraged him to give free rein to his talents. His next report on October 20 therefore almost doubled in size to four columns and a bit. He laced his description of the terrain ("The march was a very pleasant one of some 15 or 16 miles, over "*put*," or hard white sandy loam, this time unbroken by sand hills. "You might have gone this march on roller skates; a plain after the first few miles as smooth as a race course") with his worries about his favorite horse and observations on a poisonous plant, which caused the death of nine camels:

> My own pet horse, that no money would buy, went last night in this way. He carried me gamely all the march through. I knew that he was wrong before I had been 5 minutes on him. On arrival in camp he showed that

2. The Journey to Sarakhs

he was thoroughly wrong. If anything happened to him, I shall agree with Fitz James: "O Woe worth this chase, woe worth this day, That cost thy life my gallant grey." I hope he may pull through, I sat up with him, put a huge mustard poultice over his loins and a large bag of heated sand over that; gave him opium and calomel.

In his next report on October 27 he was able to fill up almost three columns, but grown weary of counting wells, camels and miles, Durand seems to have gone overboard with his literary chatter. He began with a comparison of the frapping of his *pal* in the night to a cyclone "off the Cape":

> I heard the flapping of the canvas, the cracking of the timbers, the rush back of the broken chains of the steering gear, saw the white foam lying sheeted, level with the bulwarks, felt again the great ship stagger and sway in the crush of the mighty waves, felt the awful darkness enshrouding us, heard the topsail crack like a whip and watched it disappear into the night like a sea bird.

The letter ended with a reference to Homer and the sound of the men drinking their whiskey to the tune of:

> *Carpe diem quam minimum credula postero* — or as Lord Derby has it — "E'en while we speak time's slipping fast away. Trust not the morrow, grasp the fleeting day"— Who shall blame us? For us, no sweet strains of music at Benmore — no *grata puellae visus ab angulo* — but *nunc pulsanda tellus* to a different tune, stumbling along in the dark, our hope a bonfire and our dream a spring.

All of Durand's classical education was put on view as the mission approached the marsh lands of Seistan, birthplace of the legendary Persian hero Rustam and one of Alexander's stations on his march to India (*Gazette*, November 18, 1884). Kipling, whose duties included proofreading the newsletters, would have delighted in all the obscure references. Kipling and Durand both spoke the *patois* of Anglo-Indian children raised by servants until they were of an age to be sent off to an English boarding school.

> I mention these things, to shew how classic is the dead ground we have been treading. I have no doubt, but that Semiramis, the great Queen, more fierce in her wars than the Macedonian founder of Empires, more terrible in her loves than the Macedonio-Egyptian cosmopolites, who followed, at some distance, her unbridled lead, had a pleasure-place on the shores of the lake, then beautiful with buildings, where Assyrian music

lulled her willing victims to sleep. The lake, whose only music now is the whisper of the rushes, the whirr of the wild-fowl, or the desolate sough of the wind along the wave-swept shore, we have history at our back for the surmise. Did not her great empire stretch far towards India? Did she not found, and name Cophes, the modern Abistada?

That hairy-limbed, cynical, amusing old sinner, Montaigne, if my reference memory does not fail me, lets one into strange secrets, culled, as usual with him, from hidden classic sources, anent the loves of Semiramis and their deadly nature. She was delicate in her choice of lovers—men "burnt red with Indian suns"—but once her pick was made, they never lived again to the world. Translated to some high rock, or fairy palace, for the amusement of an idle hour, they found their rest for ever. At any rate, none ever returned to boast that the Great Queen had loved him. I had, amongst other curios, half of a beautifully cut seal of undoubted Assyrian workmanship, picked from the ruins for Saro Tar. A standing Assyrian female figure, intact on the right; in front of her, high up, a king's head crowned, and below that again the ends of the wings and quarters of a lion.

Between Camp Nushki and Camp Kuhsan near Herat, Durand supplied his newspaper with 11 lengthy reports.[12] Most of the reports are accompanied by very detailed maps highlighting the line of march. These were probably prepared by the *Gazette* draftsman Corp. Wilson. He appears alongside Rudyard Kipling in a sketch of the *Gazette* building from 1885 (see illustration in Chapter 1) and is said to have taken Kipling on occasion to the sergeants' mess.[13]

Additional material on the march is to be found in Owen's extensive diary notes.[14] When not dealing with his patients and the difficult native doctor assigned to him (who halfway to Herat applied to return to India), Owen devoted his spare moments to collecting ethnographical material as well as specimens of pottery, coins and seals. His draftsman was instructed to prepare drawing of Biluch vessels and native costumes.

Owen was particularly intrigued by the varying carpet weavings of the districts they passed through and began purchasing examples. On October 20, near Rudbar, he found some well constructed carpets with all the colors fast except for the green, but he regretted that the camp was moving at such a fast pace, that it was impossible to collect either information or specimens or verify the truth of the information given." On October 26, he purchased a "good specimen of Kurzin or carpet camel bag" and on November 13, he bought a fairly coarse carpet for 30 rupees. He said it added much to the appearance and comfort of his tent.

Of his charitable dispensary, he wrote that it was a first-rate move and "should counteract the bad effect the Amir's agent tries to produce by

2. The Journey to Sarakhs

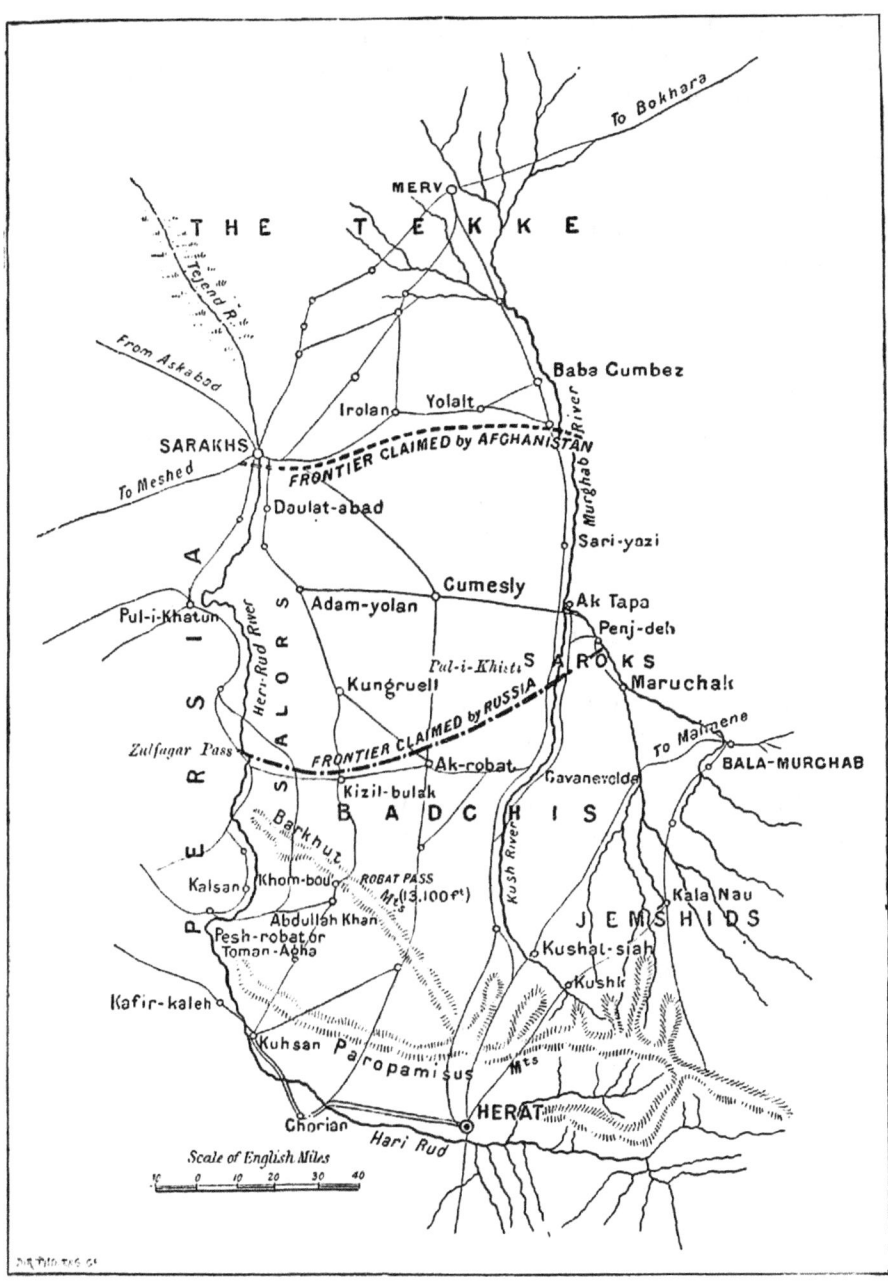

Map showing the disputed frontier between Turkestan and Afghanistan. *Illustrated London News*, March 7, 1885, p. 48.

taking supplies from the country and not paying for them and then saying it is the English who do not pay." There were so many patients that it was impossible to attend to them.[15] After he performed one successful cataract operation, he "was immediately seized by the shoulders, leg and feet by a crowd of other blind people who begged to have their sight restored."

The *Pioneer* reported that "Dr. Owen, who is also a photographer, has his hands so full of medical work that ... men, women and children throw themselves at his feet."[16] Arthur Yate commented that "Dr. Owen ... has his hands so full of medical work that he is obliged to devote such leisure moments as he can snatch from philanthropy to archaeological pursuits and inquiries into local arts and manufactures.... No sooner do we reach a camping-ground than Dr. Owen is surrounded by a crowd of patients."[17]

A fortnight after Ridgeway left Quetta, the *Gazette* offered its readers a "cut-and-paste" item on Alikhanoff from the *Times* published on September 15 in response to the suggestion that Major Alikhanoff would be appointed as chief commission opposite Major General Sir Peter Lumsden. By October 13 this was "old news" but since Ridgeway's troops were approaching the boundary region, Wheeler and Kipling must have thought it deserved to be rehashed. Alikhanoff, in his capacity of Governor of Merv, was now awaiting the British north of Herat.

The *Times* had commented that this "subaltern in the Army of the Caucasus" was hardly an officer of sufficient standing to negotiate with Sir Peter Lumsden, ADC to the Queen. Alikhanoff, formerly Ali Khan from Dagestan, had suddenly gained fame after he made his way "in disguise into the Turcoman stronghold of Merv."[18] He then wrote a detailed description of the geography and ethnography of Turkestan in which every road, oasis, settlement, river, tribe, manufacture and industry was examined from a military point of view.

All this was familiar to Kipling as he had translated Alikhanoff's reports for the *Gazette* earlier in the year. Even though Kipling maintained in his memoirs that he forgot these "scraps" as soon as they left his pen, the details of his weeks of translations gave back vividly to him years later in a nightmare he experienced in New York.

> Ten or twelve years later, I fell sick in New York and passed through a long delirium which, by ill-chance, I remembered when I returned to life. At one stage of it I led an enormous force of cavalry mounted on red horses with brand-new leather saddles, under the glare of a green moon, across steppes so vast that they revealed the very curve of earth. We would halt at one of the camps named by Alikhanoff in his diary (I would see the name of it heaving up over the edge of the planet), where we

warmed ourselves at fires of *sax-aul*, and there, scorched on one side and frozen on the other, I sat till my infernal squadrons went on again to the next fore-known halt; and so through the list.[19]

After arriving in Kuhsan on November 17, the men were allowed a week's rest while the forces were regrouped in preparation for the next stage of the march. On the day before he passed over command of his forces to Major General Sir Peter Lumsden, Col. Ridgeway read his farewell order to his troops, which Durand forwarded on to the *Gazette*. Ridgeway noted that the march had been brought to a successful close "without a single serious contretemps." The first stage of their "Long Road" between Quetta and Nushki, where the camp assembled on September 28, was followed by the desert stage from Nushki to Khawaja Ali, which was reached on October 16. Lash Juwain marked the end of the third stage, which was reached on November 1. The last stage, the Herat march, ended on November 17.

Excluding halts the average rate of marching had been 18 miles a day, a remarkable record considering the great vicissitudes of heat and cold. In addition not a single adverse representation had been made to the amir's officials about the conduct of the troops during the long march and not a single unfriendly shot had been fired. The survey department had run a traverse from Quetta to Kuhsan, a distance of 767 miles, and mapped an area of 15,000 square miles.

In his concluding remarks, Ridgeway said he could not "close this brief summary, without thanking Dr. Owen for his earnest labours in the Civil Department, which must have alleviated much misery on the road traversed by the Force. 1681 patients have been attended and 307 operations performed of which 103 were major."

While Ridgeway and his troops were crossing the deserts in western Afghanistan, Lumsden was approaching Sarakhs from the other direction. The first sketches Simpson sent back from Persian to his editors recaptured for his English readers glimpses of the lives of her majesty's officials in Persia and of the ceremonial reception provided by the shah for the members of the commission. They appeared in the *Illustrated London News* on November 1, i.e. one month after the commission's arrival in Teheran.[20] The editors in London drew attention to the reputation of "Our Special Artist" by elaborating on the favors bestowed on Simpson by the shah.

The journey from Teheran to Meshed took some 29 days. The party left Teheran on October 2 and passed through Lasgird, Shahrud, Miandasht (October 19), Sabzewar and Nishapore. They arrived at Meshed, the Holy City of the Imam Reza, on October 31. Once the party had embarked on their mission and drew away from civilization, Simpson's reports and sketches became more and more involved with the Turkoman tribesmen and the havoc their raids had inflicted upon their neighbors. Hardly 100 miles from the Persian capital they came upon Lasgird, a city of refuge, which bore all the marks of the recent Turkoman intrusions. The impression this first encounter with the marauders of the Great Salt Desert left, is recorded in a half dozen published sketches and a large two-page illustration titled "Tower of Refuge — a Turkoman Raid" in the issue of April 25, 1885.[21] The engraving illustrated the system of refuge towers, which had been established as a means of escape from the Turkomans:[22]

> Our large Engraving is from a Sketch designed by him to illustrate, with complete accuracy in the details of scenery and costume, one of those fierce attacks by the wild horsemen of the Kara-Kum Desert, baffled here, apparently, by the "Tower of Refuge," which were of yearly occurrence, at one point or another, over the entire region. The last of the terrified fugitives, running for their lives from the fields where they have been laboring, or from their village homes beyond, are speeding to the still open door of the fortress: while in the tower outside a few brave men, directed by the chief, who waves his hand and shouts from the roof, begin to fire upon the Turkomans as they gallop up the hill, so as to gain a few minutes for their friends seeking refuge in the main citadel. There is another tower on the rock in the background, the elevated position of which must have commanded a distant view of the coming enemy. The stone cisterns or wells, for use when the stream dries up in summer, the small gardens inclosed with low fences and two or three small structures looking like tombs or Moslem shrines, are such as may be found about a collection of native dwellings.

The account which Simpson later wrote for *Harper's* after his return to England reveals a better understanding of the Turkomans but it was obviously written under the influence of literature on the conquest of the Turkomans by the Russians. The Russians, who had only just freed their own serfs in 1861, were not tardy in finding in the Central Asian slave trade a sanctified justification for their conquest.

> These predatory excursions were known as "chapows" by the Persians, and as "alamans" by the Turkomans. The number of men engaged in one of them depended much on the character of the leader: if he had a previous reputation for success in such expeditions, large numbers would flock to him when a new raid was projected: at times as many as five or six thousand men would engage in one of these expeditions. Horses were put under a peculiar diet and training to fit them for the necessary endurance, for it must be understood the Turkoman's horse formed the

2. The Journey to Sarakhs

"Tower of Refuge." Drawing by William Simpson from the Afghan Boundary Commission album. The Marquess of Salisbury Library, fol. 17 recto. By permission of the Most Honorable The Marquess of Salisbury. The drawing appeared as a lithograph in the *Illustrated London News* on April 25, 1885, pp. 446-7.

essential part of the raider, where long rides and sudden surprises were the main tactics of the game. As the Thugs of India converted their system of murder into a kind of worship, so the Ishans, or Mohammedan mollahs, gave a religious sanction to the foray by blessing it before starting. At first the "alaman" would move slowly across the desert; but as soon as the Persian frontier was passed, it made long and stealthy marches by unfrequented routes, avoiding all large towns, till the selected district was reached. Small parties were then detached: these in the dusk of the early dawn crept under of hollows or rising ground toward villages, on which they came down with a lightning sweep, so as to catch the men or women at work in the fields, or by the surprise to seize the cattle before they could be driven in. Men, women, and children, as well as horses, cattle, and sheep, were all fish to the Turkomans' net, and whatever was taken they carried off to the main body of the alaman, who guarded the plunder while the detachments carried on the work. If a village could be taken, then every living thing in it became spoil: whatever the robber's horse could carry, or whatever could be forced to move on its own legs, was borne away. Young girls—if they were pretty—and children were looked upon as the most valuable prizes, as they could be sold to the highest advantage in the bazars of Khiva or Bokhara; it was also considered a luck stroke when any one of wealth or rank was caught, a heavy ransom being expected for his release. We were told of one raid in which 130,000 sheep, goats, and other animals had been swept away: this large number has much the appearance of an exaggeration, but supposing we subtract a large discount from the figures—say twenty-five or even fifty per cent— the sum will yet present a calamitous loss to the people who were despoiled. When the operations on the ground selected were completed, the alaman began its retreat, generally taking another route from that by which it came. If not too much overburdened with spoil, the plundering would go on during the return march. When a successful expedition had been made, and each returned rich from robbery and crime, there was great rejoicing in the auls, or collections of kibitkas, which form the village of Turkestan; the Ishans again came forth and uttered prayers of thanks to Allah for all the good things which had come to them.[23]

3

The ABC Reaches Its Destination

Sir Peter Lumsden reached Sarakhs, the designated site for the initial negotiations, on November 8. Russian Commissioner General Zelenoy, however, was nowhere in sight, even though the Russians had clearly taken possession of the town.[1] General Lumsden managed to give the impression to his troops that this was unexpected, but Barrow's "Precis" reveals that Sir Peter Lumsden had received a telegram at "Shukrood" on October 18 stating that the Russian Commissioner would probably not arrive in Turkestan before January.

Realizing that waiting in Sarakhs for a Russian response would be fruitless, Lumsden made plans to join forces with Ridgeway, then at a camp east of Herat. After negotiations with the Afghan authorities in Herat, the town of Kuhsan was selected as the collection point. Despite the failure of the meeting at Sarakhs, it remained for Lumsden to attend to the geographical survey and the study of the native populations in the disputed area. The British knew as well that they had to get on with setting up their winter quarters at a location south of the disputed oasis of Penjdeh, where they would await the arrival of General Zelenoy.

The route from Sarakhs to Kuhsan is described in great detail in the reports because it was realized that the area might be of strategic importance should a conflict arise between England and Russia over the demarcation of the border.[2] Starting out on November 11, Sir Peter Lumsden proceeded up the Heri-Rud valley to Pul-i-Khatun and on to Goolar, opposite the Zulfagar Pass. Passing through Tut-i-Kurkht and Tomaun-Agha, he finally met the troops under Colonel Ridgeway at Kuhsan on November 19. The Indian force had reached Kuhsan on November 17 with "about 500 fighting men, 700 followers, and 1,800 camels."[3] The diary notes of Owen set the scene for the meeting:

> The thermometer registered 11½ [degrees] of frost and we were all frozen when daylight put in its appearance. However we had to get up as at 11 A.M. we expected General Lumsden to arrive. About 10 A.M. Col. Ridgeway and the political staff rode out some miles from camp to meet the British contingent and surely enough a few minutes before 11 A.M. notice was given that the General was coming and sure enough before we could almost reach the Mess tent where we were to meet him, Sir Peter Lumsden arrived. He was received by a Guard of Honour of the 20th B.N.I., 100 men, fine stalwart fellows, looking like thorough solders which they have proved themselves to be on many occasions. All I can say is that I shall be surprised if the Russians can turn out such men.[4]

After an impressive welcoming "durbar" in the presence of the governor of the province of Herat, the British informed the Afghans of their course of action. Lumsden and a small part of the camp was to move on November 24 into the Kushk valley and descend in a northeasterly direction to Ak Tapa, going to the winter quarters at Bala Murghab by way of Penjdeh. The main body of the camp under Ridgeway was to travel to Bala Murghab by way of the upper valley of the Murghab river.

The route to Penjdeh was covered by William Simpson in a long report of December 19 in the *Illustrated London News*.[5] The lay-out of the country through which they traveled found illustration as well in *Harper's Magazine*, accompanied by a very accurate topographical map. Col. Ridgeway described the southern route for British readers in the *Times*.

Kuhsan marked the point where Owen took over from Durand as correspondent for the *Gazette*. In his final report written on November 19, Durand wrote, "In view of our immediate march from here, I fear that correspondence must cease, as gentle Editors are sometimes constrained to say, but arrangements have been made to carry on the game, and another pen than mine will, I hope, keep you informed of the fortunes of the Mission." Owen was designated in the newspaper first as "another Correspondent" and later as "our own Correspondent." In Kuhsan however he appears to have been overwhelmed with tending patients in neighboring villages. Owen does not mention writing for the *Gazette* in his diary until an entry on November 26: "I wrote to Meb [his wife] and sent off a letter to C&M up to this date. No news from Durand." The entries in this first newsletter are dated November 19, 20, 21 and 22. What Owen essentially did was to go back to his diary for these days and embellish his notes for

3. The ABC Reaches Its Destination

the *Gazette*. The newsletter published on November 29 is taken almost verbatim from the diary. Similarly he mentions the quaint trappings of the Persian mules (diary, November 21), the facial crow's feet due to the cold and the serviceable Russian boots and cots (diary, November 21): "I have also seen a Russian camp bedstead with iron framework, very comfortable and strong, which packs into an exceeding small compass." His letter to his wife from November 26 might have explained the arrangements with the *Gazette*, but it does not survive. It was not until Ridgeway's march got under way that Owen began to find the time to compose completely new reports for the newspaper.

On November 24, Owen was awakened by the "noisy jingle of the bells worn by the Persian mules" as the expeditionary force under Lumsden left Kuhsan direction Penjdeh. "Talk about a bugle for reveille," he wrote, "these bells are ten times more efficient."[6] Lumsden's group was made up of Captain Barrow, A.D.C., Assistant Commissioner A. Condie Stephen, Nawab Mirza Hassan Ali Khan, Major Holdich of the Survey Department, Captains Durand and De Lassoe and a Native Attache, Mohammed Aslam Khan. Surgeon Charles went as the medical officer in charge. William Simpson from the *Illustrated London News* and Thomas Weir of the *Times of India* with his "photographic apparatus" represented the press. The escort was provided by 50 men of the 11th Bengal Lancers under Captain Heath and an Afghan contingency provided by the Amir of Afghanistan Abdur Rahman Khan.

As their guide the British had some unreliable maps, which marked little more than the paths the Turkomans followed on their raids. Watering places were difficult to find because the Turkomans customarily filled in the sources after they had dug them up. The group had to rely in the main on Turkoman scouts.

At Kara Tapa they came upon a clear stream, the Kushk-Rud, and a fertile area which had once been under cultivation but which now had long lain fallow. Simpson remarked: "The Turkomans have laid waste all this region, as they did that of the country bordering on the Heri-Rud: from this cause towns and villages have ceased to exist, and mounds only remain to mark the sites. About a century ago there was a large population in the valley."[7] On the march to Chaman-i-Bed near the Chapgal Pass they encountered "ploughs at work, and men digging out the old filled-up water-courses for irrigation. These men were Sarouks from Penjdeh, and they were bringing this part of the ground into cultivation for the first time since the former population had left it."

On December 2 Lumsden finally came to the bridge at Pul-i-Khisti, a locality which was to play an important role in the months ahead. At Ak

Tapa on the junction of the Kushk and Murghab rivers they were greeted by the Afghan garrison under Ghous-ud-din Khan. Lumsden moved to Penjdeh on the fourth and halted there on the fifth and sixth.

> We stopped a day at Ak Tapa, and then moved on to Penjdeh. About six miles to the south nearly the whole distance is covered with Sarok villages, formed of kibitkas. The Sarok Turkomans have come south from the Merv district, and have become Afghan subjects. The Murghab, as well as the Kushk valley, was without inhabitants, and its fields were lying waste. Some years ago the Saroks arrived, and they have restored the place to life again. Some of their chiefs came along the Kuskh valley, and met Sir Peter Lumsden on the third march from Ak Tapa; crowds of the Saroks turned out to see our arrival, and the outskirts of the camp were generally fringed with them, eager to look at the Feringees, and watch what they [were] doing. There was a good deal of trade going on in the purchase of carpets, and other articles, by our people. A considerable quantity of Indian rupees and Persian crans was left among them, so we may suppose that they will retain a pleasant recollection of us. At Penjdeh we remained two days; one of these days was principally occupied by a visit from the Governor of Herat, who had followed us up; and Sir Peter Lumsden paid a visit to Yalintoosh Khan, the chief of the Jamsheedies.[8]

On December 25 the *Gazette* provided its readers with a description of the settlement as well. Since Owen had been left behind in Kuhsan, the report presumably came from Edward Durand.

> We halted on the 3rd, and visited the Kibitkas of Panjdeh, buying the carpets that closed the tent doors. These are hand made and the colours quiet and agreeable. The old and young ladies came out to see us, and the men bargained — but neither gold nor rupees were of any use. They wanted Krans — a good door Carpet was worth from 50 to 70 tomans or say £2–10 — though, of course, they could not give such prices themselves.... The Kibitkas are like a parrots cage made large, of wood instead of wire, and over this frame-work felts are roped, with a movable one on the top to let light in, and smoke out. Some of them have matting up the outside for 6 feet or so, and inside they are nicely felted or carpeted. Some of the little girls wear a rounded or conical silver helmet ornamented, (when they can afford it I suppose), and the little boys all a "Babari" cap, which is as big as Papa's, and which they can just peep out from underneath. This is almost met by the boots they look out from. I was smoking and all the boys asked for a pull from my pipe! The women wear head-dresses of sorts; the more well to do — a yellow silk cap of the shape of a Persian domed felt, with a handkerchief round it. They were none of them pretty, and the hard work they do soon ages them. The men have a peculiar three cornered look about the eye which is remarkable. All are

3. The ABC Reaches Its Destination

"Kibitkas, Camp of the Afghan Frontier Commission, Bala Murghab, 5. Jan. 1885." Drawing by William Simpson from the Afghan Boundary Commission album, The Marquess of Salisbury Library, fol. 53 recto. By permission of the Most Honorable The Marquess of Salisbury. The drawing appeared as a lithograph in the *Illustrated London News* on April 11, 1885, p. 366.

good tempered and friendly. I have seen no really good horses amongst them as yet—though the horses are all necklaced with silver bands.[9]

While in Penjdeh Durand purchased a girl's cap and earrings for his wife and daughter, as well as a number of weavings. He included two sketches of the Saryk Turkoman girls in letters he sent to his wife and daughter in November 1884.[10] In a letter to "My Dear Little Marion" he asked his daughter, "Would you like to wear a silver cap like a little Turkoman girl like this? Perhaps if Neddy can find one at Panjdeh he will buy it for you." At the bottom of the page appears a picture of two Turkoman girls in front of a yurt. In another letter of his daughter he says he "had bought you a little Sarok girl's cap all made of funny little bits of silver and with a red tuft on the top, like this. Isn't she a funny little girl?" And Papa has got a big pair of earrings for Mummy, such funny long things—like this."[11]

The Bombay correspondent Thomas Weir took photographs, and

Simpson ran through the settlement making his sketches. Facing annihilation from Russian troops gathering at Merv, the Saryks afforded Lumsden all due honors. With their gifts, bright-colored uniforms and liberal purchases of carpets, the troops must have made a favorable impression.

Thomas Holdich included a picturesque description of his attempt to acquire one of the prized door rugs in an excursus on the Saryk weavings and silverwork:

> We went to Panjdeh, and we made friends amongst the weather-beaten Turkmans of the Sarik fraternity, who gave us good welcome, and were not above taking our rupees in exchange for their inimitable carpets and saddle-bags and silver-mounted harness. I have seen many carpets since, but I still think that those of the Sariks of Panjdeh are unmatched. They have backs like boards; stitches infinite in number and minuteness; they are soft, but firm in pile, and harmonious (though a trifle monotonous) in colour. Some of the best of these Sarik rugs were to found hanging across the doors of the "kibitkas"—those round felt tents which are called "akoi" by the Kirghiz, but which are exactly the same in construction whether you find them on the sands of Merve or the grass plateaux of the Pamirs. Between wood-smoke and the tanning effects of wind and weather many of the door-rugs acquire a tone, which is not to be matched by any other artificial process; and we took them eagerly whenever we could persuade the fierce, wrinkled old Turkman women to part with them. First advances were usually made through the rosy-cheeked, cheery little Turkman children. A present of a few beads would produce ecstacies of pleasure; but it wasn't always that the children were allowed to retain the beads by their parents. I remember one little damsel of six or eight whose delight was expressed in every line of her sweet little form when she first took a string of blue beads from my hand. Then she showed the beads to her grandmother, a wizened old hag who was watching proceedings with fierce but bleary eyes from the darkness of a kibitka interior. I don't know what passed between those two, but the young lady returned with an expression of infantile dignity that stiffened her little limbs, and curled her lips into the funniest affection of disdain that ever was seen. She flung the beads down at my feet with a scorn that would have done justice to an actress. So far it was exceedingly well done, but she waited just a little too long. A childish look of longing stole into her eye; and it stayed there, and disturbed the theatrical pose of her head, and then a large, unbidden tear appeared. I did not wait to see any more, and I do not know what became of the beads.[12]

Another amusing description about the acquisition of Turkoman artifacts was printed in the *Daily News*, which a member of the ABC, probably Simpson, had sent to the newspaper from the frontier. It is dated "Penjdeh, Dec. 7, 1884" and appeared in February of the following year.

3. The ABC Reaches Its Destination

> Everyone here has been busy, and I regret to have to report that the officers, without an exception, have by their conduct during the last day or so, rendered themselves liable to called "carpet knaves." The Turkoman young ladies have a deft way of working a peculiarly fine kind of carpet and some of the finest of these serve as doors of the kibitkas; they are hung up like a curtain. There has been quite a run on these carpets or "doors" here. Prices have gone up to fabulous sums. Our winter quarters are to be kibitkas, and everyone wants a carpet or two, and a "door" as well. Judging by some purchases, it looks as if some of our party are going to have very large kibitkas, a kibitka say, with half-a-dozen doors at least. The largest and finest kibitkas I have yet seen in Penjdeh had only one door. This was a very handsome residence; It was hung round with fringes and tassels, and the door was covered with a very beautiful carpet. It had a bloom on it like a peach. Some suggested that it would be the Lord Mayor's residence, and it was at once christened "The Mansion House." At first new carpets were brought for sale but someone brought an old one, beautifully toned down from the time it had hung on a door. This was bought up at a high figure; and as soon as the value of old doors was discovered there was a rush on the kibitkas, and every ragged old article was brought to market. This led to some amusing scenes. One of our people bought a carpet from an old man, and paid the money, when the wife appeared. She seemed angry, and seizing the piece of carpet, carried it off triumphantly and hung it up on its place over the door of the kibitka. The old man looked rather forlorn, for he had to hand back the silver coins.[13]

All the members of the commission were adamant in their opinion that the people of this area, and particularly the Saryks, were to be considered as subjects of the amir of Afghanistan, Abdur Rahman. The Russians had therefore no right to claim the territory as an extension of their Turkoman conquest.

While in Penjdeh, Lumsden called on General Alexander Komaroff, the Russian Governor-General of the Trans-Caspian Provinces, and on Colonel Alikhanoff, the Governor of Merv. According to Simpson the British were courteously received and the conversation seems to have mainly centered on archaeological topics. The members of the commission must have been very familiar with Alikhanoff, since Kipling had been publishing the diaries of this officer in the *Gazette* and on October 13 the newspaper had reprinted the reaction in the *Times* to the suggestion that he would be appointed as one of the commissioners. Simpson asked Alikhanoff for his signature in Persian, which was reproduced in the *Illustrated London News*.

Up to this point in the campaign Wheeler and Kipling had depended for their coverage on the newsletters from their correspondents and had offered readers little other than the usual "cut and paste" pastiches and a couple of Kipling's translations. But with the mission in Penjdeh they must have felt obliged to come up with a deeper analysis.[14] This appeared on December 24 under the title "The Central Asian Question." The piece exhibits a thorough knowledge of how political instability within Afghanistan could be exploited by the Russians. The frequent use of semicolons and short sentences make for a histrionic style. The authors knew Simla would be reading.

They said that the problem facing the British government had to stated in the plainest terms :

> We are, in fact, face to face with a difficulty which must be met; and which, for all of us in India, has an overwhelming interest. Briefly stated the facts are as follows. The Russian outposts have been pushed up to the very frontiers of Afghanistan; and it is a moot point whether that frontier had not already been violated. Russia's agents are in Cabul, emissaries are working in Shignan and Wakkan; and if she is not yet prepared to advance on Herat, she has reached positions from which such an advance, if unopposed, can be made with ease.

The realm of Abdul Rahman was divided into three distinct districts: "Afghanistan proper, that is, the country between the Hindu Kush and Quetta," "secondly Afghan-Turkestan, or the country between the Hindu Kush and the Oxus; thirdly the Province of Herat." The Usbegs of Afghan-Turkestan had formerly been subject for the most part to Bokhara and Herat was the ancient capital of Persian Khorassan. They said the real question was "where should we draw the line beyond which Russia could not advance." Mistrust of the Russians and exasperation with the nonchalance of Home Government and "the mob" comes out clearly in the concluding paragraph:

> Russophobia is not a disease which we desire to see prevalent amongst Englishmen. On the whole, perhaps, we are inclined to be Anglophobists. We dread the ignorance of our countrymen at home, of our masters, the mob — on all matters connected with India and the East. We dread that indifference to danger in Asia, which will always accompany the occurrence of any storm in the Parliamentary teapot. Most of all perhaps, we have reason to apprehend with alarm, some mischievous blundering attempt, by soi-disant statesmen, to solve a problem, which needs the wisest counsels and the best energy, experience and intellect of the country.

Having made their presence known to both the Russians and the Saryk Turkomans at Penjdeh, the British were anxious to get to Bala Murghab

3. The ABC Reaches Its Destination

so that their winter camp could be set up before the onset of snowstorms. From Penjdeh, Lumsden proceeded up along the Murghab River, but the party was not able to cross over to the other side until it reached Meruchak. The fording of the Murghab on December 8 and the "tapa" at Meruchak furnished the theme of two lithographs published in the issues of the *Illustrated London News* on March 14 and March 21. Lumsden arrived at Bala Murghab on December 12, where he was joined by the other part of the force a few days later. The announcement of the completion of their journey appeared in the *Illustrated London News* on December 29, 1884.

Ridgeway's path to the south followed the ancient caravan route between Bokhara and Herat via Maimana. Owen described the march in the intense cold through a fertile yet uninhabited countryside in a letter to his wife dated November 29:

> Curious as you will think it, we have not passed a single village since we left Kuhsan. The reason being that all this country is overrun by hordes of Turcoman who loot everything they can lay their hands on. As far as I have seen at present there is not a single pass here which would stop the advance of the Russians.[15]

Owen's hospital once again began to fill up with patients as soon as the company reached Kushk. The journey must have been quite pleasant, as his diary notes waxed almost poetical in the descriptions of the countryside. His notes for December 6 can be given as an example:

> 6 Dec. Rouse at 6.30 A.M. march at 8 A.M. for Camp Kokchail. I had to see the Head of the Jamshidis and several big Khans before I could get away from camp which delayed me a good deal. We had a gradual rise up a valley composed principally of limestone rocks which were a mass of fossils. These defiles were all cultivated. At the summit the view was simply grand. A regular flat down picked out here and there with bits of bright red and yellow clay. The hills are covered in places with endless pistachio nuts and the juniper trees here are as big as firs on the Himalayas. In the valleys deep below are peaceful villages and hamlets with the herds of sheep and cattle from the same roaming on the hill sides. This view in Spring must be perfectly lovely. The sea of downs appears walled in by the distant mountains near Bala Murghab. Upon descending the slope one came upon masses of rare trees and after winding in and out a bit we reached our camp at Kokchail, a distance of 14 miles.

On the march Owen collected curios for the British Museum, sent rose seeds to Messrs. Sutton and Co. and considered the purchase of Turkoman carpets. When his wife mentioned in a letter that she was ordering new writing paper, Owen suggested she contact J.L. Kipling for a design.[16]

At least seven of Owen's letters written between Kuhsan and Bala Murghab must have been subject to Kipling's proofreading before appearing in the issues for December 9, 10 and 30. Owen's commentaries written en route to the winter camp assumed more and more the nature of travelogues. Durand's obscure references to Homer, Semiramis and Alexander the Great, displaying his knowledge of Greek, were replaced by Owen's picturesque sketches of the countryside and inhabitants. The accompanying maps acquired a remarkable attention to detail with mention of the tiniest hamlets and watering holes. A map in the December 10 issue even locates the area frequented by the illusive "Alieli" branch of the Turkoman nation.

The busy doctor attended as well to the medical needs of the locals. In London and Paris Owen had trained as an ophthalmologist and patients came from miles around for various eye affections. In the three months with the ABC he had registered about 2,000 patients. On December 13 Ridgeway's group met up with General Lumsden at Fort Bala Murghab. On December 17, Owen had his first Turkoman patient.

In Bala Murghab Durand once again took up his pen on behalf of the *Gazette* in Lahore. On December 20 he completed a report on the divisions of the Saryk tribe into five groups, concluding with a description of the women's silver jewelry:

Turkmen girl's cap obtained by Edward Durand from Saryk Turkmens in 1885. (Photograph courtesy of Lady Durand).

The women's ornament are curious things, ranging from the silver head-dresses of the little girls, which are at any rate wearable, to huge articles which the uninitiated would take for the latest designs in high church decorations. These they wear both on breast and back. A well-caparisoned woman, to judge by the ornaments one sees in camps, should be carrying about a stone in dead weight — pretty heavy handicapping that against the girls, if they ever indulge in dances. I don't think the girls themselves wear much (I mean jewelry of course) until they have taken that fatal ride, in a camel Kajawar, which comes to the pretty ones all as certainly as the terrible moment so dreaded by a bachelor friend of my own, who swore that the thought of that alone, had saved him from several proposals. The moment was the one in which you hear the carriage-door slam, and know that it's all over![17]

3. The ABC Reaches Its Destination

Durand must have shown Owen his Penjdeh carpets as well as the silver jewelry he had purchased for his wife and daughter. Both Durand and Simpon had completed a series of drawing and watercolors documenting the visit to Penjdeh. Owen would have been sick with envy. In a letter to his newspaper dated "Bala Murghab, Dec. 24," Owen described the wealth of Turkoman rugs already in the camp. Presumably Owen had John Lockwood Kipling, principal of the art school in Lahore, in mind, when he wrote:

> For the sake of our carpet industries and schools of art in India, it is to be hoped that many specimens here will find their way to India; for I feel that rivalry will be keen to reproduce such fine carpets.[18]

Owen noted, that is was difficult to acquire them, as the Turkomans were well-to-do.

Christmas Day found Owen traveling to a Jamshedi village with William Simpson, where the doctor operated on some women and was fed "a meal of some stuff like macaroni in a neighbouring kibutz."[19] The experience of passing Christmas on the edge of Turkestan is colorfully described by Arthur Yate, another of the able writers with the ABC.[20] After months on the march, the troops could finally relax and enjoy the fruits of their labor. Bottles of liquors transported from London were opened and glasses raised in honor of the queen. For the troops the climax of the feast was the serving of the plum pudding, which had arrived at Bala Murghab by special envoy via Teheran. Owen's newsletter to his newspaper (*Gazette* January 29, 1885) described the scene:

> On Christmas Day all the members of the Mission in camp dined together, and a very pleasant evening was spent. One of our members provided a splendid plum-pudding to which we all did justice; and the thanks of all of us are due to the kind heart of the lady who took the trouble to make it, and send it all the way from Teheran. After Mess, Sir Peter Lumsden, in a few well chosen and heart-felt words, proposed the health of the "Queen" and those "nearest and dearest to us."

The camp itself was strictly laid out on perpendicular lines radiating from the flagstaff and British ensign at the center with hospital, commissioner's tent, mess, lawn tennis courts and cavalry lines carefully arranged according to plan. Only the employment of circular Turkoman tents distinguished this camp from countless others in the Empire. After several months of continuous travel the members of the commission were grateful for a respite from cockcrow-rising. Lumsden wasted no time, however, in assigning his men their various tasks. William Merk and Captain Peacock departed on January first for Andkhoi and the Oxus River from whence they did not return until February 7. The remainder of the commission remained stationary but not inactive:

> In camp the survey officers were busy with their indoor work, and the political officers of the Indian section were employed in amassing information and drawing up reports on the Sarik Turcomans and the four tribes known as the Char Aimak.[21]

Photographs were taken of the area by Charles Griesbach in the course of his geographical survey and Aitchison set out in search of botanical specimens. Hunting expeditions were organized into the mountains to the south and east of the camp. The monotony of camp life was occasionally broken by the groups of Saryk Turkomans from Penjdeh who came to Bala Murghab in order to offer their carpets and silver work for sale.

The *Daily News* described this activity in a letter from Bala Murghab dated January 22, 1885 in its March 10 issue.

> A bazar has grown up close to our camp. The dealers are in tents, and it is curious to see the variety of articles for sale. On Sundays and Fridays there is a kind of fair, and traders from Maimana, Penjdeh, and other places bring in a varied stock of goods. There is still demand for carpets in our camp, and men may be seen daily walking about with such articles seeking purchasers. Prices for carpets are high—for good carpets very large sums are asked. Certainly some of them are beautiful articles. The wool is soft as silk, and in a few, part of the pattern is produced with silk. Carpets here are made so good that they last a life time. The colours are also very good, that is in the older ones, for aniline dyes have found their way even into Central Asia, and many of the colours now in the carpets are from that source, instead of the old materials which produced colours that lasted as long as the carpet itself.[22]

This idyll was suddenly interrupted on January 3, when the British experienced their first taste of a raging Central Asian winter storm. A company including Col. Ridgeway, Lt. Yate and Dr. Owen had planned to visit Penjdeh between January 5 and 14, but this had to be canceled due to the severity of the weather. The surveyors en route to the Oxus were particularly hard pressed by the change.

It seems, however, that Wheeler must have been rather exasperated with the lack of correspondence from Owen at this critical stage in the campaign. After Owen's reports sent from Bala Murghab on Dec. 26, 28 and Jan. 5 he had received nothing. Wheeler seems to have contacted Durand,

3. The ABC Reaches Its Destination

but Durand must have approached a colleague, Francis Drummond, about writing something for Wheeler. Drummond's newsletters appeared in the *Gazette* on February 3 and 9. His pieces are full of clever wittisms with Latin asides similar to Durand's, augmented with chatter about hunting, horse races, the weather and camp gossip.

In his diary for January 12 Owen wrote, "Drummond told me he was writing for the C&M" and the next day he "sent off a letter to C&M." Drummond's report published on February 9 was his last. Owen had been devoting most of his time to fulfilling his duties as the ethnologist for the commission. On January 19 he sent off a detailed article with illustrations on the "customs and habits of the Turcomans," which was published in the February 17 issue of the newspaper.

This hitherto unknown document can be counted among the most valuable products of the mission to Turkestan. An introduction about how readers in India might like to fill in details about the Turkomans not covered by the literature available to them in India leads into a long excursus on the absence of veils among the women, festivities and the recipe for the preparation of *pilau*, written with Owen's highly entertaining panache. Speaking then of the young Turkoman maidens, Owen writes:

> From early infancy till they reach budding womanhood, ever at their mothers' side, they soon acquire a proficiency in needlework; and as all the Turcomans wear, as a rule, embroidered garments of some sort or other, there is no lack of opportunity wasted.

Particularly instructive is Owen's description of how carpet weaving was taught:

> The mother of the family, or the grandmother, as the case may be, acts as the schoolmistress, and teaches the young girls what colours to place on the loom before them; each working member having a pile of coloured wools ready at hand. It is the mistress who reads the number of stitches, and by old practice knows exactly how and where the wools should be placed. The workers themselves cut the pile the proper length; and the fact that one rarely if ever comes across an uneven pile, shows how wonderfully accurate they become. It is not only in carpet manufacture, but also in crewel work that these people excel; but of the two, the carpet is to be preferred — as, both for colouring and for fineness of detail, it is far superior; the *sila* embroidery which is made here seeming to resemble Coventry work more than anything else.

The author then turns to the costumes of Turkoman girls, followed by a detailed description of the regalia of a married woman.

"Turkoman Ornaments plate I, (1) Married Woman, (2) Unmarried Girl and (3) Married Woman, Back." *Journal of Indian Art* I/7 (July 1886). p. 53.

To turn for a moment to the dress of the Turcoman maidens. First of all, all of them except the very poorest, wear a kind of silver helmet, with a red plume jutting out from the apex of the cone and set in a silver stem. The silver worn consists of small embossed facets of silver which are sown on to a silver or woollen cap of reddish colour. When the maiden marries she discards this cap as well as her other garments; and is at the time of the marriage ceremony dressed by the priest in the vestment of a married woman. At the same time she is presented by the bridegroom with a *rezaie* and a pillow covered with silk which is to form part of the "lit de noces."

The last section of the article deals with various pieces of Turkoman silver jewelry, illustrated by line drawings. There is a front and back view of a Saryk Turkoman woman in her full regalia as well as drawings of an earring, a breast ornament, a relic holder and the large heart-shaped back ornament known as the *ansuk*. The article contains the most detailed ethnographical descriptions of any of his newsletters and Owen probably intended it as a preparatory draft for his report on "the ethnography, arts, manufacture, trades and agriculture of the peoples through whose territory the Commission passed."

3. The ABC Reaches Its Destination

When Owen's newsletter arrived in Lahore, Kipling must have shown it to his father, who realized that this was exactly the sort of material he wanted for a journal he had founded in 1883, the *Journal of Indian Art*. J.L. Kipling shortened the text to deal only with the jewelry and published it anonymously in his journal.[23] The number of illustrations was expanded from six to 15. In addition to the views in the *Civil and Military Gazette*, the article in the *Journal of Indian Art* provided a portrait of an unmarried Turkoman girl, as well as illustrations of a coronet, another type of earring, two further types of breast ornaments, a shawl pin, a second ansuk or back ornament, a ring and a bracelet.

In a diary note for March 7, 1885, at Penjdeh, Owen wrote "I heard from Kipling about Turcoman ornaments, but I sent the letter on to Durand." Durand presumably had the draughtsman's original drawings in his possession. A comparison of the drawings of the married Saryk Turkoman woman in the *Gazette* with the versions published in the *Journal of Indian Art* reveals how Durand fleshed out the original drawings from Owen's draughtsman. Durand had earlier carried out an improvement of the draughtsman's drawings of the Bamian monuments for an article in the *Illustrated London News*.

William Simpson took full advantage of this unique opportunity to sketch the locality and to interview the people of the region. His description of their camp at Bala Murghab is particularly enlightening for the information it gives about the construction of the Turkoman tents:

> The encampment at Bala Murghab, where the members of the British Commission passed their Christmas, partly consisted, for the accommodation of the Indian soldiers, of Turkoman tents, which are peculiar in construction. They are called by the Turkoman people "alachuk," by the Persians and Afghans "khiryah," and by the Russians "kibitka." The lower part is formed of a series of cross pieces of wood, fixed together, so that, like the action of a pair of scissors at each crossing, they can be extended or contracted at pleasure, according to the diameter required. This part, with the framework of the door, is first put up and held together with belts made of wool. The crown of the tent has a circular piece of wood pierced with holes: into these holes are placed the ends of one or two long pieces of stick, and then the crown is erected, and held there by tying the lower end of the sticks to the top of the circular framework. Having fixed the crown with one or two of the sticks, sticks are then placed all round the tent, to support the roof. When this is done, the whole is covered with thick felts, which are strapped on with belts and ropes. A small piece of felt forms a hood to cover the crown; this can be moved by a rope, so as to make an opening on any side desired to let out the smoke or let in light. The advantage of the kibitka is the absence of the central pole, with a greater protection from cold than in a canvas tent, and fire can be made

in it with safety. It is approved by the medical officers for the hospital of the camp.[24]

The lithography of the camp in the *Illustrated London News* (page 279) depicts two Turkoman tents with peaked crowns covered by circular felts. A kilim has been placed before the entrance of the foremost tent and a patterned textile covers the door. Similar tents also are depicted in a lithograph in the *Illustrated London News* for April 11.

Arthur Yate related that Lumsden sent two Turkoman tents to London in February of 1885.[25] One was destined for the Foreign Office and the other was to appear in the Colonial and Indian Exhibition of 1886. The whole was covered from crown to foot with *namad* or felt. It was 16 feet in diameter and the trellis work interior was girded with a broad tent band some forty feet long. Owen's diary entry for February 10 reads: "The General is sending a capital kibitsa to England with the caravan which leaves tomorrow." In his *Gazette* article, Owen mentions that the kibitkas were "all made at Khiva" and "vary in price from 80 to 250 krams or 32 to 100 rupees."

Of great ethnographical value is a description of a Saryk family at Penjdeh. It reveals that the members of the Afghan Boundary Commission were seriously attending to their instructions to gather material about the peoples of the region.

> We have already described the felt tents of the Turkomans, called by the Russians "kibitkas." At Penjdeh, where the Sarik Turkomans form a large community, our Artist saw a highly ornamental residence of that kind. The roof of the kibitka in this case, it will be seen, is a dome; in this particular the form varies in the different localities. The sides are here ornamented on the outside with drapery, as well as coloured fringes and tassels. These are very tastefully arranged around the door, the door itself being formed by a beautiful carpet. "I managed," he says, "to get sketches at Penjdeh of some of the women and children, which I have introduced, and have made into the subject of 'Departing on a Raid.' The Khan, or chief, has his horse ready to mount; one arm caresses the horse on which his life may depend during the raid, while the other fondly embraces his wife. She, in the anxiety of the moment, turns to her child, who, with whip in hand, evidently wishes to ride his father's horse. At a kibitka behind, another Turkoman is bidding goodbye to some one dear to him. The dog looks as if even he knew what was going on, and is ready to start. The women's dress is peculiar; she wears a high hat, in shape like a Papal tiara, and her person is covered with large silver ornaments. The one on her breast is for holding charms.[26]

When Simpson visited a Jamshedi village on Christmas Day with Owen, he drew a portrait of Owen tending a woman with a facial wound.

3. The ABC Reaches Its Destination

"The Khan's Kibitka — Departing for a Raid." Drawing by William Simpson from the Afghan Boundary Commission album, The Marquess of Salisbury Library, fol. 67 recto. By permission of the Most Honorable The Marquess of Salisbury. The drawing appeared as a lithograph in the *Illustrated London News* on March 28, 1885, p. 318.

In a letter to his wife dated January 10 the doctor asked his wife to watch for it in the *Illustrated London News*.[27] When the *Illustrated London News* did not run the sketch, he was disappointed, but Simpson had not forgotten him. The portrait eventually did appear in the issue for June 13, 1885. Owen asked his wife to have it framed.[28]

Simpson gave a long description in the *Illustrated London News* of the operation, which Owen was performing:

> I went the other day with Dr. Owen to a village in the neighbourhood to see him operate on a young woman, who had fallen some time ago into the fire and burnt the right side of her face. It was healed up, but the shriveled skin had contracted and made the eye a hideous thing. The operation is one known as "plastic," the object being to take away the contracting power of the skin, so that the eye might be brought back to

"A Surgical Operation in the Murghab Valley: the Patient under Chloroform." Drawing by William Simpson showing Dr. Owen in a Jamshedi village. *Illustrated London News*, June 13, 1885, p. 602.

something like its original condition. For this purpose incisions were made above and below the eye, and the skin was separated; a portion of skin from the girl's arm was removed, and was placed on the space made by each incision; these I learn since have taken root, so that the wounds made will, when healed, be smooth and regular. A plan was adopted to prevent the eye from opening till the healing process is complete, and it is expected that it will then be restored to something like its former appearance. The operation was, of course, performed under chloroform. The girl did at times moan during the operation, and her female friends thought she was suffering; they called out her name soothingly, which was 'Gulsaman,' or 'Bosom Flower.' Afterwards, they were all astonished when the girl told them that she had never felt anything. This is the first time that such operations have been performed in this out-of-the-way region.

As it gradually became apparent that the Russians were unlikely to send their Commissioner, the British decided to move to a location that would offer better lines of communication to Persia and India. On February 15 the commission departed for Gulran, or Gurlin, ostensibly to guard the direct roads of approach from Badghis to the capital of western Afghanistan.[29] Ridgeway, assisted by Merk, Owen and Yate, remained at Penjdeh with an armed escort as a symbol of the British presence. The rest of the Commission arrived at Gulran on February 23. Two days later Simpson left for London. The assignment with the commission had kept him away from London for about eight months.

The response in the Russian press to the British expedition was: "It seems to us that the continued presence of an English detachment near our frontier, as well as the British munificence of Sir Peter Lumsden, may have an unfortunate influence on the minds of the too impressionable Afghans" (see Kipling translation, Appendix III.5).

4

Her Majesty's Troops Retreat

After the news of the failure of the meeting at Sarakhs reached London, critical voices began to be raised about the wisdom of sending a small British contingency into one of the more politically explosive areas of the world. The British had not forgotten their humiliation at the hands of the Afghans in 1842 and their alliance with the Amir Abdur Rahman was maintained only upon payment of an annual subsidy and with considerable supplies of arms. A letter from Mr. Stanhope, member of Parliament, in the *Times* of January 23, 1885, reminded readers that the situation of the Commission at Bala Murghab was rapidly becoming ridiculous as the Russian commissioner passed the winter on his estates.[1]

At the same time the question of the Afghan boundary had taken on a very different course with the arrival in London of Pierre Lessar, "a French engineer and geographer in the Russian service, who is sent here to discuss with our Foreign Office those very details of frontier topography which ought to be examined on the spot by the joint British and Russian Commissions."[2] Under a "smoke-screen" of diplomatic tactics which are not without parallels in modern history the Russians had sent an uncalled-for mission to London at the same time as they were pushing forward their outposts to Pul-i-Khatun and to Penjdeh.

Another letter in the *Times* on March 23 citing Lord Palmerston warned the British about the vagaries of Russian diplomacy.[3]

> The policy and practice of the Russian Gov't has always been to push forward its encroachments as fast and as far as the apathy or want of firmness of other Gov'ts would allow it to go, but always to stop and retire when it was met with decided resistance, and then to wait for the next

favourable opportunity to make another spring on its intended victim. In furtherance of this policy, the Russian Gov't has always had two strings to its bow — moderate language and disinterested professions at St. Petersburg and at London; active aggressions by its agents on the scene of operations.

The *Pall Mall Gazette* had fielded similar misgivings at the start of the campaign in an article titled "Hands off in Afghanistan"[4]:

But in the midst of all the negotiations and discussions concerning the new frontier, we must never for an instant lose sight of the axion which should govern all our dealings with Afghanistan. If Russia and England are ever to fight in Central Asia, the Power that can tempt the other to invade Afghanistan first is almost certain to win. The Afghans are ever the friends of the second comer, and their country is a death trap for invaders. In the present stage of the Central Asian question who leads loses, and the first who enters Afghanistan throws the game into the hands of his opponent.

Palmerston's predictions proved all too true for the following period. The eminent Hungarian professor Arminius Vambery had foreseen the outcome from the very beginning. In a paper published in the *National Review* of November, 1884 and in his book *The Coming Struggle for India* of 1885 he styled the whole affair one of the most ridiculous farces ever played in politics.[5]

Kipling's provincial rag expressed its misgivings the moment the ABC was announced. As the Indian contingent wound its way across the desert toward Herat, a notice appeared in the *Gazette* on October 8 with the following note: "A newspaper correspondent, at home, who had an unsolicited interview with Sir Peter Lumsden on the subject of the Afghan Commission, informs a contemporary that the work of the Commission has been practically settled at home"[6]:

Sir Peter Lumsden said that he "would concede nothing that has not or may not be conceded by the British Government." In plain English this must mean that Sir Peter has gone out with very definite instructions in his pocket, and that he has not been given the full powers that generally vest in the head of an important Commission. He also said that in the preliminary negotiations the British Government had expressed their willingness to allow the Russians to extend their frontier from Sarakhs to Pul-i-Khatun, some fifty miles further south, and consequently fifty miles nearer Herat. This concession, of which nothing is known in India, is very important, and will probably strike the key-note to the whole of the new frontier. Pul-i-Khatun lies directly on the 36th degree of latitude, and its cession would include all the debaeable [sic] country between this and Merv. It is perhaps safe to surmise that the Russians objected to our Commission altogether, and that their consent was only obtained by this important concession. As it is the delays caused by the negotiations are fatal to any chance of work this year. Sir Peter Lumsden arrived at Teheran on the 24th ultimo and expects to fall in with the Indian members of the Commission about the 6th November. It will then, as our London correspondent telegraphed on Monday, be too late to do anything; and they will have to go into winter quarters until the snow is off the ground again. But if everything is to be settled at the Foreign Office, as Sir Peter Lumsden's words seem to suggest, the members of the Commission might as well have stopped comfortably at home.

Although the communications were not mentioned in the official reports, Arthur Barrow's handwritten "Precis respecting Afghan Frontier from January 1884 to April 9th, 1885" gives some disconcerting details of the difficulties encountered by the British in Turkestan. Immediately after arriving in Sarakhs, Lumsden sent a report to London dealing with the unfriendly spirit of the Russians and the excitement which the delay provoked among the Turkomans. Upon learning that the British government had accepted the Russian version respecting the borders, Sir Peter tendered his resignation in a telegram of January 12, 1885. In this telegram and in another dated January 20, he mentioned that the commission was becoming burdensome to the country and that they were in a delicate situation with regard to the amir of Afghanistan and the local inhabitants. He therefore planned to move the camp from Bala Murghab to Gulran. The Russians in the meantime were claiming the whole Saryk tribe as a consequence of their supremacy over the Saryks at Yalatan. By February Lumsden was urging the breakup of the commission since all the negotiations with respect to the border were being carried out in London and in St. Petersburg.

A *Civil and Military Gazette* commentary for January 7, 1885, by Kipling boldly sketched the implications of the Russian advance for India (See Appendix I.1): "We may safely assume that Russia will annex, more or less formally and completely, every inch of ground in Central Asia." Once Herat was taken, the path would be open in the direction of India. Already Russia was seen to be stirring up resentment in the Raj:

> Paid agents of Russia — we seem even now, from time to time, to come across their track — would find a home in every native city, and at the court of every native chief. They would seek, and not in vain, to establish intimate relations with the various native societies, which, with more or less reputable objects, might soon become centers of disaffection. Everyone who felt

dissatisfied with our rule, who was impelled by some real of fancied grievance into a feeling of disloyalty, would be tempted to hold communications with the agents of a Power which might be destined to upset our Raj.

Through his translations Kipling kept a sharp eye on the Russian newspapers and was quick to pick up any unusual nuances or omission in the reportage. Despite disavowals from St. Petersburg, it was clear that Russia was taking advantage of the waverings within Gladstone's Foreign Office to undermine the position of the English in India. Speaking of the subjects of the Raj, he wrote: "The absence of active loyalty, even among the better disposed classes of the native community ... would make the disloyalty and lawlessness of the disaffected class, much more dangerous than it would be otherwise." He concluded by stating the "it is high time, to state clearly and emphatically, England's determination that the states of Afghan Turkestan, Usbeg though they may be, ought never to be allowed to fall under the dominion of Russia."

In a long article on February 2, the *Gazette* noted that "the St. Petersburg papers are having a lively time among themselves, as to whether the time had come for Russia to invade India, and make an end, once and for all, of the England's Asiatic Empire." The *Novoe Vremya* believed "that the little job ought to be taken in hand at once." The semi-official *Journal de St. Petersburg* continued to maintain the line that "the Czar has no present intention of even laying hands on Herat." In a letter in *Rus*, General Soboleff advocated invading India, "in order to compel England to quit custody of the Bosphorus and Constantinople."

In London the question of the Afghan Boundary Commission was suddenly relegated to the sidelines as the nation reacted in shock to the fall of Khartoum and the death of General Gordon at the end of January. A wellspring of anger at the inactivity of Gladstone while General Gordon fought for survival in Soudan almost toppled his government. In a translation from the *Novoe Vremya* of February 12, Kipling gave *Gazette* readers the Russian response: "The uncertainly regarding the fate of Gordon is at an end. The defender of Khartoum fell by the hand of an assassin on the day of the capture of the city by the Soudanese army." The *Novoe Vremya* noted that all the English newspapers, from the Radical *Pall Mall* to the Conservative *Standard*, expressed their outrage with cries "of the deeply insulted British vanity." These newspapers feared that "the failure of Wolseley's expedition will not only raise against England all the fanatical Musalmans of the Soudan and Egypt, but will react upon the Mussulmans of India." It was a question of "the prestige of the British name in Asia" (See Appendix III.5).

However, by the beginning of March, Gladstone had managed to deflect a party revolt by directing attention to Russian aggression in Central Asia. Simla felt it had finally been heard, when negotiations were undertaken to invite Amir Abdur Rahman to a grand durbar in India at the end of March. The *Illustrated London News* of March 7 reported that both Houses of Parliament had just dealt with the "sudden encroachments of the Russian military forces within the territory of Afghanistan immediately north of Herat." The matter was all the more insulting as this latest Russian advance had taken place in the "presence of the British Commissioner, General Sir Peter Lumsden, who has been kept waiting above two months for the expected arrival of the Russian Commissioner to perform the appointed task of surveying and delineating the proposed boundary."[7]

Due to renewed public interest, the *Illustrated London News* seized the opportunity to give expanded coverage to Central Asia and the Russian advances. The newspaper proceeded to elaborate on the geography of the frontier area and on the nationality of the peoples inhabiting the territory in dispute. Portraits were included of "several of the leading native inhabitants of Penjdeh, who belong to the Sarok Turkoman race, but are unquestionably subject of the Ameer of Afghanistan."[8]

A map in the *Illustrated London News* article demarcated the frontiers claimed by Afghanistan and the Russians. It indicated as well the location of the Tekke, Salor and Saryk Turkomans near Penjdeh in 1885. At the center of the dispute was the Saryk Turkoman settlement at Penjdeh. The Russians had drawn up their troop near to Sari-Yazi north of Penjdeh. A contingency of the Afghan troops under General Ghous-ud-din were garrisoned on the Aka Tapa to the south of the junction of the Kushk and Murghab rivers. Lumsden had met with General Komaroff and Colonel Alikhanoff there in December. Aka Tapa, meaning "White Mound" in the Turkmen language, was a large artificial mound about 100 feet high, which in past centuries had been surmounted by a fort. The main Afghan camp was pitched across the river, just to the west of the junction of the Murghab and Kushk rivers.

In a scrap published on February 25 (See Appendix I.4), Kipling calculated the length of time the Russians would need to amass its troops at Serrakhs:

> The Caucasus and Mercury Company have 19 steamers with an aggregate capacity of 20,000 tons. Messrs. Nobel Brothers have 12 large steel steamers, each big enough to transport 500 men. There are also a number of miscellaneous steamers; and it is reckoned that the shipping on the Caspian numbers over 1,500 vessels, of all classes. The passage from Baku

4. Her Majesty's Troops Retreat

to Krasnovodsk occupies 24 hours; so this section of the road to Herat would be easy enough. Say it would take three days to land 6,000 troops this side of the Caspian; which would be leaving an ample margin. From Krasnovodsk it is six easy marches to the railway; and it would take one day more to get to Kizil Arvat. Six trains could be run a day; and the first detachment would reach Kizil Arvat in about 8 days after embarking from Baku. The march from Kizil Arvat to Serrakhs would take three weeks; so in about a month's time the Russians could concentrate a formidable force at Serrakhs, from which place it is 13 marches to Herat.

Kipling noted ominously on March 5 (See Appendix I.5) that the Russian press had suddenly completely eliminated any references whatever to the Central Asian question: "while three weeks ago, every issue went more or less fully into the matter. The Dynamite explosions, the war in the Soudan, affairs in Lower Egypt, are all carefully followed by the journal which is silent on the—for Russia—all important topic of Afghanistan."

After having tendered his resignation as a protest against the diplomatic maneuverings being played out in London, Lumsden waited for a response and concentrated his attention on withdrawing the main body of his troops to Gulran. They left Bala Murghab on February 15 and arrived in Gulran on February 4. This site was strategically chosen as being within the disputed territory of Badghis, on the line of march toward Herat. Lumsden did, however, leave a British mission commanded by Captain Charles Yate at Penjdeh about five miles south of the Afghan position at Ak Tapa.

Gazette correspondent Charles Owen counted himself lucky to be included in this assignment as he wanted to continue his ethnographical investigation of the Turkoman tribes and perhaps acquire a carpet or two. On February 19 he wrote:

> Ridgeway who came in yesterday left this morning about 12.30 for Panjdeh. The General told me this morning that I am to remain here with Mark Heath and 50 sabres. I have been busy all morning arranging my hospital.[9]

The same day Owen sent off a letter to his wife in which he expressed his anxieties about being left behind to face the enemy while Lumsden retired to a position 80 miles to the south: "Let us hope all will pass over but I shall not be anxious to trust myself to the tender mercies of a Liberal Govt. again." At the same time any esteem Owen had for the commissioners was rapidly evaporating. In another letter to his wife he referred to Lumsden riding off to the protection of Herat like "an old woman" and to Condie Stephen as a cowardly "weathercock," whose only thought was currying favor with the Ministry or Lord Granville.[10]

In the weeks before his departure for Penjdeh, Owen ran through the markets bargaining for a few good examples of Turkoman carpets from the Saryk and Jewish merchants. On January 15 he wrote his wife, "I have bought one Turcoman carpet with bright vermillion and bright magenta ground" and in a postscript added, "I have been very extravagant today and bought a lot of Turcoman things in the way of one old carpet, at least 100 years old, and several other old pieces of sorts. Altogether I have relieved myself of 200/-." In a letter dated February 7, he said he was packing up his acquisitions and sending them off to Mortimer Durand at the Foreign Office in Simla via Quetta—five bales in all.

Arriving at the British camp near Penjdeh on February 22, Dr. Owen immediately set up his hospital, because he knew that building good relations with the Saryk tribesmen would be essential for their survival. By February 23 he was off visiting Sukti, Bairej and Allih Shah villages as well as catering to the needs of various Saryk leaders. On February 28 he wrote "I have managed to run up my patients to over 800 this month." On March first alone he treated 130 patients at the Afghan camp near Ak Tapa. His monthly tally had reached 2,018 by March 22, already exceeding his tally of 2,014 for December.[11] Owen observed in a diary note from February 23, "I find in operating on these rather (?) featured people that in many cases one ought to have a special set of instruments made as in many cases their eyes are so deep set and the aperture of the lids is very small."

In addition to his medical duties Charles Owen managed to keep up with his correspondence and his reports to the *Gazette*. His diary entry for March 7 is typical:

> I wrote to Mother, Drummond, Weir, Durand and Meeran Bux. I heard from Kipling about Turcoman ornaments, but I sent the letter on to Durand.... I have not been able to get any purdahs here yet, they are such enormous prices.

The Kipling letter about the ornaments was presumably either Rudyard's or John Lockwood's response to his article on the costumes and ornaments of Turkoman women.[12] By "purdahs" Owen was referring to the door rugs for the yurts. These were among the most valuable weavings offered by the Turkomans.

During most of March the events were allowed to smolder as diplomatic efforts at a compromise were carried on behind the scenes in London, St. Petersburg, Kabul and in Simla. An article from "The Silent Member" in the *Illustrated London News* for March 21, 1885, began with the statement attributed to Gladstone that "It has been agreed between Russia and England that no further advance should be made on either side." Also quoted was a telegram from her majesty's minister to Russia, Sir E. Thornton, dated from St. Petersburg, March 16, 1885: "The Russian Minister for Foreign Affairs states that the Russian troops will not advance from the positions now occupied by them, provided that the Afghan forces do not advance or attack, or unless in the case of some extraordinary reason, such, for instance, as a disturbance in Penjdeh. He also states that the strictest orders have been sent to the Russian commanders to avoid, by every possible means, a conflict or any incitement to a conflict, and that these orders will be repeated."

Encouraging news came as well from India. Editors filled their columns with the preparations for the conference between the newly appointed viceroy of India, Lord Dufferin, with the amir of Kabul, Abdur Rahman, in Rawal Pindi. The papers fantasized about the spectacle of the rough ruler from the hills of Afghanistan being introduced to the railway and the telephone. As a special distinction, the amir could look forward to being welcomed by H.R.H. the Duke of Connaught, the third and favorite son of the queen-empress. The truth of the matter was that the Russian advances threatened India, and the British desperately needed an alliance with the amir against Russia. The Foreign Office planned this state "durbar" for the amir in Rawal Pindi as a means of finalizing an agreement. The ruler of the Afghans could of course be assured of being munificently awarded for his cooperation, but at the same time the British intended to pull out all stops with a demonstration of their war machinery.

In Lahore, Wheeler worked to beat the other Indian newspapers with material on the upcoming conference in Rawal Pindi. Between February 3 and March 16, 16 articles and "scraps" on Afghanistan were published. A constant theme of these pieces is mistrust of Russia, the appearance of Russian agents in India and the importance of making a good impression on the Amir of Afghanistan. The longest piece (See Appendix II.17) is a biographical sketch of Amir "Abdul" Rahman published on March 11, 1885. Extremely well researched, it is augmented by various "cut and paste" items to fill up three and a half columns. On March 10 a long authoritative article on "Kandahar and Herat" was printed. Although anonymous, the phrases "we are bound," or "This is the policy we advocate" pointed in the direction of General Roberts. Wheeler and Walker decided that the young Kipling had gained enough experience, so that he could be sent to Rawal Pindi as one of the *Gazette* correspondents covering the meeting.

In addition to writing, arranging and digesting all of this, Kipling had to tend as well to the proofreading of Owen's newsletters from Turkestan. A couple of spelling idiosyncrasies make it possible to determine whether

Kipling or Wheeler was correcting the proofs. Wheeler preferred the spelling "Ameer" for the ruler of Afghanistan and "dawk" for the mail couriers in his contributions on the first and second page of every issue; in contrast Kipling and Owen always wrote "Amir" or "dâk." The newsletters appearing in the *Gazette* up to the one which was published on March 3, 1885 (See Appendix IV.27), used, with few exceptions, the spellings "Amir" and "dâk." In the ABC report for March 3, however, "Ameer" and "dawk" suddenly appear.

According to his diary, Kipling was stung on Feb. 24 in the eye by an ant and the next day he was blinded and couldn't see. For Feb. 26 he wrote: "Eye all right. W[heeler], said it wasn't and so lost my work for the day— served him right. Went to hospital... cocaine and was impressed."[13] Wheeler must have used the opportunity to make the point that he preferred the spelling "Ameer." Such editorial interventions reveal what a picky, miserable boss the young Kipling had to deal with. Wheeler applied the same principles to Kipling's newsletters from the Rawal Pindi conference, when Kipling's every "Amir" was published as "Ameer," especially in the frequently used title "To Meet the Ameer." After Kipling had recovered from the sting, the next ABC report slipped back into the "Amir" mode. Wheeler could obviously not check everything.

Distraught that his boy Friday would be leaving him, Wheeler demanded and received five further batches of translations, which were published after Kipling departure on March 16, 20, 21, 27 and April 3. In the first one, Kipling noted that the *Novoe Vremya* for February 16 had a piece on the reaction to a rumor that the Russian army had taken Herat. It had sent the Berlin and London stock exchanges into a dive. The newspaper commented, "If in Berlin there was alarm, in London there was almost panic" (See Appendix III.5). After reassurances from St. Petersburg to the "Bourse Masters" that "Herat is not taken, and no serious operations against it are contemplated from our side," stocks began to keep firmer.

The Russian newspapers were following Lumsden's progress closely, remarking that he "was making the population acquainted with English money." He was spending 160,000 roubles (£25,600) monthly, and that in "a thinly populated tract" (See Kipling translation, Appendix III.4). A translation (See Appendix III.7) from the *Novoe Vremya* of February 23 noted that "After the annexation of Merv last year, a deputation from the Sarrik Turcomans arrived there, and asked to be our subjects." The position which M. Lessar had harped on in London for the benefit of the British Foreign Office was once again reiterated: "We cannot agree to such a frontier. Once the ethnographic principle is considered just, every cession to

4. Her Majesty's Troops Retreat

Afghanistan of Turcoman land would be tantamount to depriving our new subjects of their pasturages. "

In a letter of March 16, 1885, Kipling's father, wrote Edith Plowden about his son's assignment: "Ruddy goes to Pindi as a special. He has started his pony and tum-tum [dog-cart] thither, and although a little nervous about his first big thing, I think he will do well. He has done some capital special correspondence."[14] It would have been one bundle of raw nerves that made its way in the tum-tum toward Rawal Pindi. Between March 9 and 20 Rudyard Kipling did not make one entry in his diary. Over the two pages for March 9 to 15 he later wrote in a large hand: "Here came in the Pindi Conference and my work thereat. Whereof I retain no remembrance."

After sending his first article from Rawal Pindi on March 21, Kipling hastened to Peshawar to await the amir. Noone seemed to know anything about the amir's schedule. When Kipling interviewed two Afghan Sirdars of the advance party, he was simply told, "The Ameer was a *Badshah* and could come when he liked." The author described the two talking loudly and quickly "squatted on their charpoys" and both wearing "the Tartar cap of black Astrakhan fur." A comment on their silver mounted swords and belts was "cornered" with the remark "that in *their* part of the world arms were the ornament of a man. Nevertheless Peshawar was a great city." Kipling remarked that "this somewhat inapposite codicil was thrown in, possibly to soothe the feelings of the degenerate white man who walks about with a cane." No longer under Wheeler's thumb, Kipling could allow himself a degree of literary freedom not possible in Lahore. Besides, James Walker had engaged two other correspondents to cover the more mundane aspects of the conference.

Kipling spent Sunday, March 22, to Saturday, March 28, in the city. The viceroy's careful arrangements were not going according to plan and it rained constantly. While waiting, Kipling sent off four newsletters to Lahore, including a brilliant piece on Peshawar, which he called the City of Evil Countenances (See Appendix I.10):

> Meanwhile, the City of Evil Countenances has become shrouded from sight by the incessant rain, and a journey to the Edwardes Gate means a mile-long struggle through soft oozy slim — to be undertaken only as a counter-irritant against the growing gloom of the evening....
>
> Under the shop lights in front of the sweet-meat and *ghee* seller's booths, the press and din of words is thickest. Faces of dogs, swine, weazles and goats, all the more hideous for being set on human bodies, and lighted with human intelligence, gather in front of the ring of lamp-light, where they may be studied for half an hour at a stretch, Pathans,

> Afreedees, Logas, Kohistanis, Turkomans, and a hundred other varieties of the turbulent Afghan race, are gathered in the vast human menagerie between the Gate and the Ghor Khutri....
>
> The main road teems with magnificent scoundrels and handsome ruffians; all giving the on-looker the impression of wild beasts held back from murder and violence, and chafing against the restraint. The impression *may* be wrong; and the Peshawari, the most innocent creature on earth, in spite of History's verdict against him; but not unless thin lips, scowling brows, deep set vulpine eyes and lineaments stamped with every brute passion known to man, go for nothing. Women of course are invisible in the streets, but here and there instead, some name-less and shameless boy in girl's clothes with long braided hair and jewellery — the center of a crowd of admirers. As night draws on, the throng of ignoble heads becomes denser and the reek of unwashed humanity steaming under the rain, ranker and more insupportable. A free fight takes place in a side gully and terminates, after a little turban pulling and hair snatching, in a gale of guttural abuse and the presence of a policeman, not as an arbitrator in the fight, but merely a dignified spectator of the *rixe*. What might have happened in other and happier lands across the border it is impossible to say.[15]

When the Amir still did not make his appearance, Kipling hired a modest "ticca gharri" on Sunday March 29, which conveyed him "as far as the historic walls of Jamrud, and from thence to the mouth of the Khyber," about two or three miles distant. Word had come through that the amir was approaching the border. The following is an extract from the sixth of Kipling's newsletters written on March 29. It appeared in the *Gazette* on April 1.

> His Highness the Ameer of Afghanistan is due this morning — no one seems to know at what hour. Meantime, the top of fort Jamrud is an elevated and decidedly airy point of vantage. The Four Winds of Heaven are fighting it out between them on the bastions, and each gust brings with it a douche of fine rain. The Khattak and Swat hills are swathed in mist. Only towards the north west and the Khyber, is the air comparatively clear. Along the undulating Khyber road runs a scattered line of the Ameer's camp followers, who have been dropping in all night and through a great portion of the previous day. Interminable files of camels, yaboos, coolies, and loud-voiced donkeys and flocks of sheep, stretch from the camp to the south of Jamrud, into the very jaws of the Pass and in the grey light of dawn, these resemble nothing so much as lines of black ants on a foraging expedition....
>
> *7 o'clock.* — The daylight has brought down the Scotch mist more densely than ever; and never did the Afghan hills look more rugged and forbidding than now. Jamrud has awakened the center of a little city, the population of which is increasing minute by minute. Still no news of the

4. Her Majesty's Troops Retreat 59

Ameer. He has left Ali Musjid. He hasn't. The rain has delayed him. He will be here in the evening. He will be in half an hour....

A young Afreedee of thirteen is keeping watch and ward over a bunch of picketed yaboos. The lad's garments are filthy, but he smiles and swaggers affably; displaying at his belt a Colt's revolver. Subsequent investigation shows that it is loaded and as clean as oil and rag can make. It belonged to his father who departed this life a year ago, the embryo cateran does not say how, and the weapon was handed on to the son. "Have you ever done anything with it?" The question is a somewhat brutal one, but the Afreedee regards it evidently in the light of a compliment. "Not *yet*, Sahib, but please God, I shall some day," he replies, with a cherubic smile, and swaggers over to his horses once more. A cheerful race these Afreedees....

8 o'clock.— Alarums and excursions. A dozen sowars and a European officer — all very wet — have come in from somewhere out of the mist and several bugles have sounded. The troop horses are being saddled, and the gloom is lifting a little....

10 o'clock.— One-two-three — twenty-one guns— the smoke hanging heavily at the mouth of the cannon; and by the time the last welcome is spoke, Abdur Rahman Khan, ruler of Afghanistan and its dependencies, has fairly set foot on British ground. For past ten minutes the field glass has shown him merely as a blot of blue on a small horse.... Behind him follow his cavalry, wild picturesque men on wild horses— to whose appearance it is impossible to do justice, while writing on the spot. No two sets of accoutrements are alike, *cela va sans dire*, if I except the regiment of Usbeg Lancers. These resemble Cossacks in every particular, down to the high-set saddle and the shaggy circular cap of hair. One or two of the officers carry the short-handled double thronged Tailor whips, and all, without exception, ride splendidly.... The riders represent every shade of Turanian and Mongolian blood, high cheek bones, oblique eyes, shaggy hair, flat noses, cavernous mouths.[16]

On March 30 the Amir finally reached Peshawar. Kipling had a hectic day. After observing the border crossing, he rushed back through the rain to Peshawar in his "ticca gharri." In his bungalow and at the railway station he managed to complete and send off a long two-part report about the welcoming ceremonies. After that he boarded the midnight train to Rawal Pindi. Four reports in three days plus arranging for travel. Kipling's statement in his autobiography that he had been shot at by a rapparee at the Khyber Pass has generally been received with a grain of salt, but given the pace with which he raced through March 29 and 30, the author can be excused for not mentioning it in his diary or newsletters.

Despite his gout and fatigue the amir decided to head for Rawal Pindi on the very evening of the day he arrived in Peshawar. Again the well laid plans of the viceroy were left in tatters by the end of the day. Kipling described the scene.

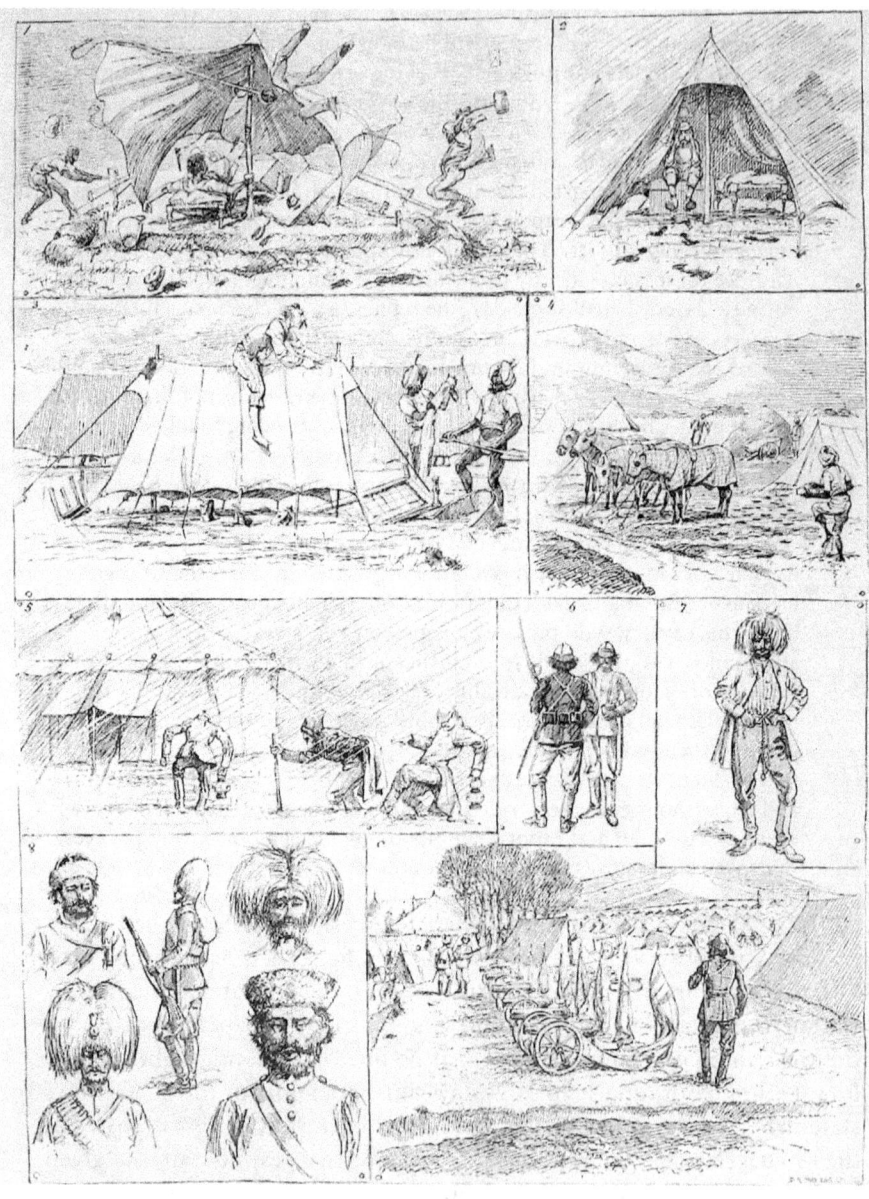

"Sketches at the Rawul Rindi Durbar, by Lieutenant Officer Shore, 3rd Punjab Infantry, 1. Camping on the Khanna Plain; a windy night. 2. Despair. 3. After three days' rain. 4. Horses standing in the mud. 5. Going over to the messtent. 6. Two of the Ameer's infantry. 7. One of the Ameer's cavalry. 8. Types of the Ameer's Army: one of the body guard. 9. The Ameer's screw-gun battery." *Illustrated London News*, May 16, 1885, p. 511.

4. Her Majesty's Troops Retreat

Monday night, half past eight; pitch dark and the platform of the Peshawar station, covered with the Ameer's horses, which are at the present moment entraining for Pindi. Unless you are actually on the platform, in serious danger of your life from flying heels and panic stricken horses, you will not appreciate the beauty of the situation. His Highness really starts to-night at eleven o'clock, more or less exactly, and before that hour strikes, seven hundred and fifty horses are to be cleared away somehow.... Neither Cabulies nor horses have seen a train before; but the former are adapting themselves wonderfully to circumstances. In the first place they are absolutely fearless; plunging head first, into the squealing, kicking truck-loads of yaboos, without a moment's hesitation.[17]

The spectacle of the head of the Afghan army himself, General Gholan Hyder Khan, driving horses up the ramps into the wagons made a deeper impression on the British than any military maneuver:

Hyder Ali, Commander in Chief of the ameer's army, has recognized the gravity of the situation and — think of Cs. in C. all over creation — is working like a navvy in the midst of his men. Three horses are down in a wagon of eight, and from the appalling noise inside, seem to be kicking each other to pieces. Hyder Ali, guided by a single lantern, dives into the tumult, directs, superintends, harangues and — from the tone of his voice — swears till the wretched beasts are set right. If one restive grey stallion could speak, he might even tell us how the Commander-in-Chief backed him, protesting and snorting, up the slippery gangway and into his fellows once more....

Ammunition cases, in red wood, home-made Martini-Henri rifles; tent poles, furs, food, samovars, hookahs, saddles two feet high, and every other sort of odds and ends, lie about in wild confusion. Everything is wet and clammy to the touch, and in the black darkness one stumbles across men and horses at every step. If the scene could be reproduced on canvas, it would be ridiculed as wildly impossible. Usbeg lancers and locomotives cheek by jowl; tartars and telegraphs, jostling each other; western civilization and eastern savagery, blended in the maddest fashion, and on the just and unjust alike, the ceaseless pitiless rain. No words in my power could do justice to the tableau.

Kipling had nothing but sympathy for the Amir, who was honked out of his comfortable divan, and torn from his "pipe of contemplation, and worst of all, just after the evening meal, about nine o'clock." Then he was compelled to discourse affably until the special train was ready. Kipling added in parenthesis, "(Fancy turning out into the wet, with twinges of gout in your left knee and an amiable smile on your countenance, at such an unearthly hour of night)." The whole business, he said, was a huge mistake.

"Gholam Haider Khan, Commander of the Afghan Army, with his Attendants."
Illustrated London News, May 23, 1885, p. 526.

Beginning with his fourth newsletter published on March 31, Kipling's status was raised from "our own Correspondent" to "our Special Correspondent." Perhaps this was Walker's suggestion, so as to distinguish Kipling's contributions from those of two other *Gazette* correspondents. James Walker attended the conference and probably had a hand in Kipling's arrangements in Peshawar.

Kipling must have burned with annoyance at Wheeler's attempts to make his mark on all the Rawal Pindi reports before they were published. In his diary Kipling wrote consistently "Amir"; in the *Gazette* the word appears consistently as "Ameer." Kipling writes "Peshawaur," it appears as

"Peshawar," his "Jamrood" becomes "Jamrud." At least Kipling's spelling of the name of Afghanistan's ruler as "Abdur" was allowed to stand. Up to the appearance of Kipling's first report, the *Gazette* had always referred to him as "Abdul."

Meanwhile, back in Penjdeh, Dr. Owen continued to build up his good relations with the Saryk, investing at the same time in a few more carpets. The political horizon, however, grew increasingly bleak. He wrote his wife on March 12:

> The General has a great idea of throwing himself into Herat at once but he is such an old woman that he will probably do it. If only the home Govt. stick out that they intend to go to war Russia is bound to cave in but at present there is delightful uncertainty about it. If we do fight George [his brother] will no doubt have to come I should say as there are 60 guns at Hussein Abdul and probably Le Mesurier will have to be there. I heard to-day from Gulran and Durand tells me that Peggy is all right as well as her pups but he say the place is awfully dull. Candie Stephen hooked it off to Meshed as soon as the big camp reached Gulran. He was in such a funk that we should all be smashed up that he thought he would make tracks as soon as possible. He nominally went to arrange a postal service but we all know what that meant. Lord Granville telegraphed to the General the other day and said he quite approved of his arrangement. Rather a joke when it was Ridgeway who did the business and *made* the General with the greatest difficulty sit up. So poor Ridgeway gets no thanks for all his trouble. The best of it all is that the General does not see how he ran the chance of being ruined for ever if he had acted on his own ideas. Stephen is such a [illegible] and weather cock that it is most unpleasant. He has no idea of sticking up for his country and only of currying favour with the Ministry or Lord Granville.

On March 15 he packed up his carpets and sent them to Col. Ridgeway. Owen was homesick. In a postscript to a long letter on March he remarked, "I dreamt of you last night and you were so loveable that there was an awful explosion. You can guess what I mean."

On the occasion of the Persian New Year (Nauroz), the British under Captain Charles Yate were invited by the Saryk Turkomans to a two-day horse racing meet on March 21 and 22. The captain's younger brother Arthur captured the scene:

> It was decided some days ago to get up some sports amongst the Turkomans (Saruks), and to leave them to manage it in their own fashion. Accordingly, all the headmen of the different sections were invited to the British camp on the 19th, and they were asked to draw up a programme of their own. 1000 *karans* (= about £33, 6s, 8d.) was the sum placed at

their disposal for the prizes. It was agreed that this was too much to spend in one day, so it was unanimously decided to have a two days' meeting.[18]

The prizes for horse races ranging in distance from 500 to 3,000 paces were agreed upon. In addition there were to be wrestling and shooting matches. The total for the prizes amounted to 276 *karans*, leaving 50 *karans* for casual prizes and 176 *karans* for extras.

Once the races began her majesty's subjects were amazed by the intense excitement and confusion "that would shock the proprieties of British frequenters of the turf."

> At an early hour on the morning of the *Nauroz* ... the Saruk headmen began to assemble at the British camp, and before 9 o'clock all rode down with Captain Yate ... to the ground, where the various distances had been marked out in a straight line from the winning-post by little heaps of sand. The first race brought four horses to the post, and the second and third three each. The jockeys were all boys, showing that the Turkoman fully understands the advantage of putting up a light weight. Some thousand odd Turkomans were assembled, sitting and standing in the double or treble rows close to the winning-post, or rather heap, opposite to which were seated in state all the *katkhudas* or headmen, with the *khalifa*, the *kazi*, and a number of *saiyads* and *mullas*, all of whom rank high in the order of precedence by virtue of their religious calling.

The details of how the start signal was given remained a mystery to the British. Once over the finish line, the winner galloped over to the *Gul Bator* to receive the prize money and then "waving this over his head, he then cantered his horse out to the end of the line of spectators, and then turning, galloped back again at full speed to the winning-heap, accompanied by the owner and number of his friends or backers, all shouting and yelling like fiends."

Even more mysterious were the "rules" of the shooting-matches, with which Arthur Yate was personally involved:

> No idea of targets, much less of butts, ever entered their minds. In about two minutes the knuckle-end of a old bit of bone was stuck up on a bit of stick about 4 inches above the ground and some 120 yards from the firing-point. Then forth-with all the *mirgans* commenced firing indiscriminately; no roll, no calling out of names, no naming the man to fire. Every man just lies down on the ground, plants the two-pronged iron rest attached to his gun in the ground, and the moment the smoke clears sufficiently to let him see the object, takes aim and fires. The first man hitting the bone was to get the prize. How the men setting up the mark were

4. Her Majesty's Troops Retreat

not shot is a mystery. Hardly were their hands off the bone, than bang went a gun and a bullet whizzed within a few feet of them, not to mention all the small boys waiting to run in and hunt for old bullets. Bang! Bang! goes on the fusillade, only a cessation at times for loading. At last a man hits the bone, up he jumps with a shout, tosses his cap in the air, and rushes off for the prize. I shall not easily forget my dilemma ... when three men, each claiming to have hit the mark, and each backed up a crowd of friends, rushed at me and thronged around me, each clamouring in louder and shriller Turki than the other. With some difficulty I induced the three claimants to divide the 20 *karans* between them.

After the shooting came the wrestling and races for camels and mules. The English found that their exercises at tent-pegging and lime-cutting found little enthusiasm among the spectators. At the conclusion of the day, there was a liberal sharing of food, drink, music and singing between the "Sahibs" and the Saryks.

The second day of the Penjdeh *gymkana* had to be postponed. Ominous rumblings were being heard from the north. Exactly at *Nauroz* on March 22, General Komaroff and Colonel Alikhanoff advanced to within 18 miles of Ak Tapa. The Saryks were seen to be nervous. Colonel Alikhanoff was said to have visited Ak Tapa in disguise. By March 25 the Russians were camped in force within sight of Ak Tapa. Alikhanoff sent daily threatening messages to the Saryk elders. On March 26 Captain Yate held a meeting with Komaroff's chief of the staff and requested an explanation. He was told that the negotiators in London had set the line of demarcation at the Kushk river. Captain Yate was hardly in a position to dispute this. Communications to St. Petersburg were much faster than to London. Owen wrote to his wife "Yate is no good, he is a perfect babe in diplomacy" (February 27). The British could only tighten their belts and hope for the best. On March 29 Yate met with the Russians for a "champagne luncheon" at which Russian demands for the immediate evacuation of Pul-i-Khisti were tactfully deflected. Owen's notes let us in on the tidbit, that nearly all the correspondence with the Russians was actually written by De Laessoe and himself, as Yate did not know a word of French.[19]

All hopes for a peaceful settlement were bitterly shattered on March 30 by the announcement that the Russians had advanced to Pul-i-Khisti and that they had launched an attack on the Afghans stationed there. The Afghan forces consisting of 4,000 men with eight guns were quickly overwhelmed, resulting in the loss of 500 soldiers, the whole of the artillery, two standards and the entire camp provisions.

The Russian version of the attack was given in the *Illustrated London*

News for April 18, based on a telegram from General Komaroff published in the *Official Messenger* of St. Petersburg:

> On the 25th ult. our detachment approached Dash-Kepri, on our side of the Kushk river. When near the bridge, we found an intrenchment occupied by the Afghans. In order to avoid a conflict, I stationed my troops at a distance of five verats from the Afghan position. On the 26th ult. negotiations were commenced with Captain Yate. When the Afghans were convinced that we had no intention of attacking them, they daily drew nearer to our camp. On the 27th, they dispatched against our company intrusted with covering a reconnoitering party, three companies with a canon and some cavalry. Their audacity and arrogance were increasing little by little until the following day, when they occupied the height which commanded the left flank of the camp. They commenced to throw up intrenchments, established a cavalry post to the rear of our line and placed a picket at gunshot distance from our ford. On the 29th, I sent to the commander of the Afghan detachment an energetic summons, giving him till the evening to evacuate the left bank of the Kushk and the left bank of the Murghab as far as the mouth of the Kushk. I received a reply from him, that acting upon the advice of the English, he refused to retire behind the Kushk. I then sent him a private letter, couched in amicable terms. On the 30th ult., in order to support my demand, I marched with my detachment against the Afghan position, still counting on a pacific issue of the difficulty, but the fire of the Afghan artillery and the attack of their cavalry compelled me to accept the combat, the results of which are already known.[20]

Alikhanoff's version given years later was that "the Afghans were mounted on stallions, which were restless, and one of their carbines went off by accident or design and wounded one of the horses of the Cossacks. An officer rode up and reported this to me and I replied, 'Blood has been shed, we must now get to business.' Upon this the Cossack cavalry screen withdrew and the dismounted Cossacks opened fire."[21]

A map prepared by Captain Charles Yate and published by Percy Sykes in his biography of Sir Mortimer Durand gives the layout of the battlefield.[22] The main Russian camp was pitched to the west of Yarim Tapa. The line of the Russian vedettes was set up directly opposite the Afghan vedettes along the Kushk river. The attack was commenced at 6:30 A.M. by the Tekke levies hurling themselves at the Afghan south flank. When these fell back under Afghan fire, the Russian infantry opened fire and advanced through the center of the line. Afghan resistance, particularly of the Herati Horse, proved to be very stubborn, but General Ghous-ud-din Khan was wounded. To the north of his position, Russian Cossacks overcame two companies of Afghans, who were killed to a man in the trenches. With the powder for their muzzle-loading weapons wet from the morning drizzle, the ill equipped Afghans didn't have a chance against the Berdan rifles of the Tekke recruits and the Cossacks. Then began a mad rush over the Pul-i-Khisti bridge and across the river. The battle was over within 45 minutes.

The *Official Messenger* of St. Petersburg then went on in its April 9, 1885, issue to describe how General Komaroff dealt with the English.

> When the fighting was over, General Komaroff returned across the Kushk to his former position. When some British officers, who were eyewitnesses of the engagement, but had not taken part saw that the Afghans were beaten, they asked the Russians for protection; but unfortunately the convoy which was immediately dispatched by General Komaroff was unable to overtake the Afghan cavalry, who, in their flight, had carried away the British officers with them."

The Afghans suffered an ignoble defeat and the Saryks at Penjdeh submitted without resistance to their new rulers. As for the representatives of the British crown, they escaped, in the words of Captain Yate, "only by the skin of their teeth." In contrast to Komaroff's account, Captain Yate maintained that Governor Alikhanoff had set a bounty of 1,000 kram on each of their heads. The mission was only able to evade capture with the assistance provided to them by the Saryk Turkomans. Owen captured the day in his diary:

> 30 Mar. I was having my tea in the early morning when at 20 to 7 I heard the sudden sound of furious firing at Ak Tapa as well as guns being rapidly fired. Of course one jumped up and dressed at once as we knew full well how serious the result of the action at Ak Tapa would be if the Afghans were driven back. The fight continued for 35 minutes and as the sound of firing seemed to get more distant we naturally thought at first that the Russians had been driven back. There was immense excitement among the Turcomans who crowded across the maidan in the direction of Ak Tapa. Soon after 8 A.M. I saw masses of men coming back from the direction of the Afghan lines and news was brought to us while we were having a scratch breakfast that the Russians had occupied Pul-i-Kishti. The Afghan forces drew up opposite our camp and for some time we were anxious as we did not know what the temper of the troops would be like. The Naib Salar sent in to ask which road he should retire by. At the same [time] we asked Yalantush Khan to come in, which he did leaving some of his sowars to guard our camp. Ak Mahommed, Zimam Islam and Multah Khan and other leading Sarghs(?) came into camp and were told to keep quiet. A letter was sent to the Russians offering my services, and it was not till about 11.30 that (illegible) returned with no reply but stating

that Alikhanoff had offered 1000 Krans for our heads. He advised us to be off as soon as possible.[23]

Captain Yate first informed the Turkomans that it was his intention to remain with them and he sent a message to the Russians, demanding an interview. Instead they sent the boots of General Ghous-ud-din as a present from Colonel Alikhanoff. An order for packing and marching was issued, but to calm their Saryk allies, the British took pains to not give the impression of haste. Yate could thank the good impression left at the recent *Nauroz* festivities and Owen's busy hospital "kibitka" for being left unmolested.

The British were barely on the road, when a torrential rainstorm hit. The downpour prevented the fleeing company from crossing the flooded Kushk river to meet up with a cavalry detachment of 50 men under Captain Heath stationed at Kila-i-Maur. Traveling by day and night through the driving rain and snow and soaked to the flesh, Captain Yate and his men finally reached the British camp at Gulran on the fourth day after the attack at Pul-i-Khisti.

5

England and Russia Face to Face in Asia

A telegram from Gulran about the events of March 30 did not reach London until April 7.[1] The official announcement of the defeat was made on April 9. On April 18 the *Illustrated London News* featured a long editorial in which the specter of war between Russia and England on the northern frontier of Afghanistan was raised.[2] The violent outrage excited indignation and calls for retribution: "It looks very much like a wanton breach of faith and a gross insult." The general consensus was "Grattez le Russe et vous trouverez le Tartare." Stories about Russian plans for the invasion of India were revived.

The essay titled "Russia and England in Asia" expresses the English confidence in their mission in improving the lot of the peoples of Asia:

> We feel concerned for the credit and influence of that general movement of civilisation, proceeding from modern European Christendom, which is at length finding its way into Asia, and which promises, if it be not untimely checked by the ambition of military conquest and by the vices of Imperial despotism, to afford the means of raising the Asiatic races of mankind to a higher standard of social life. Let us at once declare our conviction that Russia, as well as England, has evidently a genuine mission to perform in the improvement of the condition of Asia.

In reviewing Russian advances to the East, the paper printed another description of the divisions of the Turkoman tribes, which included some further ethnographical details. They are said to be from Simpson but it is more likely that they were "lifted" from Vambery:

So far, Russia had only had to deal with the Turkish and other semi-civilised inhabitants of the old Khanates, who are not a warlike race, but effete, cowardly, and lazy, and were ruled by contemptible monarchs. It was very different when Russia was obliged to undertake the task of taming the plundering, man-hunting, merciless Turkomans of the Kara-Kum Desert, whose perpetual yearly raids for pillage and for procuring slaves had so long made desolate the borders of Persia. There are several families of these; we shall only mention a few of the principal of them. The Yomuts are a very large family; they live principally to the east of the Caspian, from which they extend to near Khiva. The Goklans are also numerous, and their aouls, or collections of tents, are along the Gurgan river, on the Persian frontier; some of this tribe acknowledge the sovereignty of the Shah. The Tekkes are classed under three heads—the Merv Tekkes, who dwell near or about Merv; the Akhal Tekkes, who were the tribe which defended Geok Tepe, and were conquered at last by Skobeleff; and the Atak Tekkes, another branch of this tribe, on the Persian frontier; their aouls are near to a range of hills which separate Khorassan from the desert. This range is called Atak, which is said to mean "on the Border." We are told by our Special artist, Mr. Simpson, who has lately gained much acquaintance with some of these wild folk, that in the language of the Turkomans, "khalk" is the word used for a tribe; a subdivision of the khalk is the "taife," horde and the horde is formed of "tires," which may be something like the chan, or family. Their government is of the primitive patriarchal form, all matters being left to the decision of the "Ak-Sakkals," which term means the "white-beards," or the elders. It may be supposed that their laws would be of very loose nature, and liable to many changes, but "Deb," or custom, is the great authority with them; it is the guide which rules their conduct, and is the basis of whatever law and order there may chance to be in Turkestan. The Turkomans are Sonni Mohammedans, and have the moral code of the Koran as a guide. They are religious according to their own views on that subject; and a strange aspect of this existed in the old raiding days, examples of which might be given as having taken place in other parts of the world. When a raid was about to start, the Mollahs were in attendance, and pronounced a blessing, wishing it, in the name of Allah, victory and success, and that it might return with ample spoil and a multitude of slaves. The law of the Koran is that no Mohammedan can hold another in slavery. Kaffirs, or unbelievers, may be made slaves. This being the case, some have supposed that the Sonni Turkoman considered the Shiah Persian as no better than a Kaffir, and worthy only to be a slave. But it is easy to suppose that Deb, or custom combined with self-interest, had a stronger hold on the Turkoman mind than the teachings of the Koran.[3]

The editorial concluded with a re-evaluation of the value of the Russian acquisitions in Turkestan and compared them to what England might gain by annexing the Sudan:

5. England and Russia Face to Face in Asia

> We have brought our historical review down to the "complication" which arose last year from the nearness of Merv to the undefined frontier of the Afghan territories. We consider that, until the question of an actual encroachment on the recognised or reputed Afghan frontier had arisen, there was nothing done by Russian, in the matters above related, which ought to be resisted or resented by the English nation. The hope was expressed that the emperor Alexander III might make some efforts at reconciliation after the breach of peace and that some apology and compensation would be made to the Emir of Afghanistan.

Although the editorial clearly represented the view of the Liberal government under Gladstone, it appears not to have been sufficient to sooth the wrath of the British public. On April 27 Gladstone asked Parliament for a vote of credit for war preparations. He had already called out the Reserves in view of a conflict with Russia. England seemed to be on the brink of another war.

News of the Penjdeh defeat immediately put a damper on the proceedings in Rawal Pindi. Due to the precarious nature of telegraph communications in North West Afghanistan and Persia, the Amir had probably been informed about the fate of his forces on March 30 long before the reports filtered through to the ears of the Viceroy of India, Lord Dufferin. Sir Mortimer Durand's version of breaking the news to the amir was that, "We received the news about dinner time, and I drove at once to tell him of the slaughter of his people."[4] Kipling may have had an inkling of the disaster when he wrote in his diary for April 2: "Wild excitement for nothing. Knocking about all over the place and wrote another special."[5]

Kipling's special written on April 2 gave, however, no hint of the Penjdeh disaster. The main theme was that the weather broke and "Pindi awoke this morning in a flood of brilliant sunlight." At 3 P.M. the amir visited the viceroy for 45 minutes. His Royal Highness the Duke of Connaught first attempted to return the visits of various native princes, but finding the roads unpracticable, "contented himself with miscellaneously perusing about Pindi." Kipling's April third newsletter confined itself to descriptions of the native princes and to changes in the program. It would seem that India's new Viceroy, Lord Dufferin, had issued strict instructions about reporting on the defeat. Not until April 5 did Kipling begin to give a hint of the soup the British were in. Kipling gave voice to his frustration with the censorship in a newsletter published after the conference on April 14 (See Appendix I.23): "Lord Dufferin — moved surely by the spirit of bitterest sarcasm — is said to have complained that affairs of State, political and military movements and the like, are too hastily made public and bruited abroad — a state of things which he is determined to put a stop to." Kipling and Owen were of like mind as regards freedom of the press. Due to the miserable weather, the grand durbar set for Saturday, April 4, was postponed until Wednesday, April 8.

The amir proved himself, however, a shrewd man who was not to let a minor battle on the furthest corner of his realm spoil the entertainments. Kipling described the scene on April 5 (See Appendix I.17):

> Sunday has been devoted to discussing the chances of war, and since the one invariably entails the other, unlimited abuse of Mr. Gladstone and all his works. Besides this there is nothing else to do. The weather, as a matter of interest, has been played out long ago, and we view it now with the calm despair born of quagmire tents and soaked garments. In the Viceroy's camp there reigns a holy peace, and as with us — melancholy resignation. Things are at a dead stop all round, and if Monday brings us rain once more — as from the appearance of the sky it most certainly will — we shall have to halt this funeral procession for another four and twenty hours at least.[6]

The maneuvers set for April 5 had to be eliminated from the program. The viceroy's company despaired, but Kipling reported that "both Abdur Rahman and his following are having a delightful time, and are not in the least hurry to move on." Without any ceremonies to report on, the author turned his attention to the amir's camp.

> The Usbeg lancers, in their mustard-hued coats, shaggy caps and strange accoutrements, would make an artist's fortune. So would some of the interiors of the tents, where rich carpets, quaint Persian aftabas, turquoise-studded brow and breast bands, Russian Samovars, orange peel and slices or red raw mutton lie about in picturesque profusion; everything being toned down by dirt and use from its original brightness and purity....
>
> One further peculiarity of these interesting savages is worth recording. They blush like girls; the blood showing plainly under the fair skin. Those anxious for a novel sensation, I would recommend to compliment an Usbeg on his martial appearance, and to stand by while the burly giant looks down on the ground; plays with his lance sling and becomes tricked into confusion.

On April 6 Kipling began his report with another commentary on the weather (See Appendix I.18):

> At last we seem to have started work in earnest and the gloomy forecasts of yesterday have been but partially fulfilled. To be sure the sky is as black as ink all round the horizon, but the clear patch of blue in the centre, and

5. England and Russia Face to Face in Asia

"Usbeg Cavalry. The Amir's Escort, Rawal Pindi, March 1885." Photograph by John Burke. (British Library Photograph 473/25, by permission of the British Library)

> the restless winds, promise April showers at the utmost, and not the steady wet to which we dwellers in tents have become so painfully accustomed. In an hour or so, the grand Review of troops in camp will begin. Meantime, carriages and riders are already beginning to assemble by the three huge sheep pens which mark the spots whence the Viceroy, the Punjab Chiefs and the common folk, are to view the ceremony. Of decoration, beyond the naked pole to the saluting base, there is no sign — the army here gathered together is to march by with no scenic accessories, beyond those of gloomy skies, wind-shaken woods in the back ground and the shrill whistle of the iron horse in front.

The Grand Review of troops finally took place about 9, even though it had to be reduced to merely a march past, without maneuverings. This was followed by the viceregal salute before "an assemblage which includes half the best known men in India, and a fair sprinkling of the great ones of the earth":

> 11 o'clock or there abouts. The guns have fired, the horses have protested, and His Excellency, Earl Dufferin, Viceroy and Governor-General of India, and His Highness, Abdur Rahman Khan, ruler of Afghanistan and

"The Saluting Point, Khanna Plain, Rawal Pindi, 1885." Detail of photograph by John Burke. Viceregal party and escorts drawn up on horseback at the saluting point. Abdur Rahman is at the center of the group, the Viceroy two horses to the right. (British Library Photograph 473/16. By permission of the British Library)

> its dependencies, are riding side by side to the saluting point. The Viceroy is in plain clothes, with a star on his breast. The Ameer, like Alice Fell, is clad in duffel grey, with a gold embroidered black belt, long boots, and the tartar cap of grey Astrakhan fur. He is riding a small bay pony, and looks burlier and more thick set, than ever. With these two, ride a miscellaneous escort of English and Afghan officers.[7]

The following day, Tuesday, April 7, another review took place and Kipling, tiring of the mélange, wrote "As far as the excellence and appearance of the regiments go there is nothing to [be] added to what was recorded yesterday. We have the same regiments paraded before us in different formation and the grand stand." Photographs were taken, details of an agreement were finalized and everyone made themselves ready for the "last act of the great drama," the State Durbar.

Kipling aroused himself from the lethargy of endless parades and horse races and rose once again to the occasion (See Appendix I.20):

> The Viceregal dais was in the centre of the cross-piece of the T, and was guarded by eight of the Body Guard, and the usual cohort of resplendent mace bearers and *chobdars*. Three silver chairs, one for the Viceroy, one for the Ameer on the right, and one for the Duke of Connaught on the left, were disposed on the dais; seats for Brigadier General Gordon, on

special duty with the Ameer, our Lieutenant-Governor, the Lieutenant-Governor of the North West Provinces, the Commander-in-Chief in India, and the Maharaja of Pattiala being reserved below. Everybody who has attended a durbar — and in India who has not — will understand what an imposing array it all presented — would realize how the intense sunlight lit up velvet and brocades like jewels; and jewels like stars — how the air was thick with perfumes of attar and sandal wood — how the huge pierced emeralds and rubies clanked and tinkled as our Punjab pincelets turned their heads — how the great guns boomed and thundered outside: and how, ever and anon, a wearied elephant would trumpet in response to the artillery; and lastly, would know far better than I could tell him of the sea of impassive British faces turned doorwards to the glare without; and can hear the undercurrent of whispered comments and questions, as one by one the planets of our firmament wheeled into position in the shawl covered chairs arrayed for them.

The one sour note was the behavior of the women attending the durbar:

To allow them at all is a mistake for many reason; and though it may seem a brutal and ungallant remark, they seriously impair the effect of a public ceremony in oriental eyes. There is — it has been said over and over again — but one way in which an Asiatic regards a woman, and that way is the reverse of complimentary. Wherever men meet together, her presence is an intrusion and an impertinence to his mind; and when men meet in solemn conclave, something a good deal worse.

Kipling later elaborated on the theme in a separate "scrap" on the front page of the April 13 issue (See Appendix I.21).

After the presentation of an array of magnificent gifts, the amir unexpectedly made a speech, which had to be hastily translated on the spot. Lord Dufferin then presented the amir with a sword of state embellished with gems, with which the amir said he would "strike down any enemies of the British Government." With this another chapter of the Great Game snapped shut.

Kipling lingered a few more days in Rawal Pindi to see the Amir off and was pleased he had, because he was able to witness the visit to the Rawal Pindi arsenal, which "seems to have interested him more than any of the various military demonstrations." Despite his gout he descended the steep stairs to the powder magazine. While minutely inspecting all the piled barrels, cases and rifles, he "lost all his reserve and chatted as freely as any sight-seeing T.G. on his way through the world." As a finale the amir ascended one of the bastions of the fort "from thence surveyed the country below." April 15 found Kipling back in Lahore reporting on the visit

"The Viceroy, Amir and the Duke of Connaught, Rawal Pindi, 1885." Detail of photograph. The four main figures are, from left to right, Sir Donald Mackenzie Wallace (private secretary), the Duke of Connaught, Abdur Rahman Khan and Lord Dufferin. (British Library Photograph 473/26, by permission of the British Library)

of the viceroy to his city (See Appendix I.24). After submitting a second installment about the visit, completed on April 17, Kipling was off to a well-deserved rest in Simla.

Kipling spent almost a month away from his office desk on this assignment. A letter from John Lockwood Kipling to Edith Plowden dated March 16 mentioned that Rudyard had started "his pony and tum-tum" direction Rawal Pindi. Kipling's first newsletter from Rawal Pindi is dated March 21. The next six days he was in Peshawar. On March 29 he took a carriage up to Jamrud, rushing back by rail to Peshawar and then to Rawal Pindi the next day.

Between March 31 and April 11 Kipling covered the events at the conference. On the day of the state durbar Kipling made a final note in his diary: "Wednesday 8 April: Two and a half columns about the big Durbar; Luckily got a good sleep last night and am fit for anything. Pindi Club crammed. Nothing but cannon all day and half the night." It seems that not only the Afghans were taking full advantage of her majesty's largesse.

5. England and Russia Face to Face in Asia

Returning by rail, he arrived in time for the viceregal visit to Lahore. From April 9 to 29 Kipling made no entries in his diary.

Kipling's experiences at the conference later served as the basis for a story in the first *Jungle Book*: "It rained heavily for one whole month, raining on a camp of thirty thousand men, thousands of camels, elephants, horses, bullocks and mules all gathered together at a place called Rawal Pindi to be reviewed by the Viceroy of India." In his diary for April 7 Kipling wrote about the "phantasm of hundreds of thousands of legs all moving together have stopped my sleep altogether."[8] He also wrote a short story, "The Amir's Homily," describing the amir as governing "not as he would, but as he can, and the mantle of his authority covers the most turbulent race under the stars."[9] His experiences with Russian duplicity were to remain with him for the rest of his life. In addition to the many expressions of congratulations, Kipling got a pay increase thanks to the *Gazette* assignment. On July 30, 1885, he wrote to Edith Macdonald from Simla:[10]

> I'm here at Simla with the Mother and Trix as Special Correspondent for the Civil and Military Gazette. I told you that for my work at the Durbar they raised my screw to £420 English or £35 a month. For that sum I try to give my paper as near to £40 a month of editorial notes; reviews; articles and social Simla letters.

Kipling's diary for 1885, incidentally, is one of the few manuscript witnesses of his youth in India. He left it behind in the offices of the *Civil and Military Gazette* when transferred to Allahabad. Kipling would certainly have destroyed it, if he had ever been able to get his hands on it. The diary is now at Harvard University. Not one single letter of Rudyard Kipling survives from the first half of 1885.[11]

On his return to Lahore, Kipling took it upon himself to gradually withdraw from his heavy editorial duties. Wheeler and James Walker understood Kipling's frustration and sent him to Simla for six months to cover the social season. Kipling's reputation as a Central Asian expert and as a writer preceded him. Walker arranged for invitations to viceregal dinners. The fact that the son of Lord Dufferin fell in love with Rudyard's sister Trix confirmed the ascent of his bourgeois family into the ethereal realms of upper crust Raj society. Kipling's close association with Sir Frederick Roberts, the future commander-in-chief of India, dates from this period. It must have been difficult for him to come back to Wheeler and his miserable office in Lahore at the end of the season.

Kipling's last major assignment of the year was the *Quartette*, the 1885 Christmas annual of the *Civil and Military Gazette,* with contributions by "Four Anglo-Indian Writers," namely Rudyard Kipling, John Lockwood

Kipling, Alice M. Kipling and sister Trix. Plagued by health problems, Wheeler took a leave of absence in the summer of 1886 and a journalist with whom Kipling had more sympathy, Kay Robinson, took over the newspaper.[12]

William Simpson must have been extremely surprised to learn of these developments when he arrived back in London at the end of April. In his account in *Harper's Magazine* he described his departure from Gulran:[13]

> As it appeared that everything connected with the boundary was uncertain, and the coming of the Russian Commissioners seemed as far off as ever, I determined to return home; so toward the end of February I recrossed the Heri-Rud, and came back by way of Meshed and Shahrud to Astrabad. At Bunder Gez, the port of Astrabad on the Caspian, there is a line of steamers, which brought me to Baku, and there I was again on the route by which our party travelled on the outward journey in September. The Caspian and the Black seas are connected by the railway from Batoum to Baku; from Batoum steamers run to Odessa. By this line of communication I returned to Europe, after an absence of about eight months.

In Berlin Simpson had been invited to court to submit his drawings to the inspection of the princess imperial of Germany and Prussia. His reception in London was equally auspicious. Invitations to visit both the queen and the prince of Wales arrived on his doorstep. This period must have marked for him the culmination of his career.

The British public began to gain an inkling of the true course of events in Afghanistan when an anonymous letter was published in the *Times* on May 25, in which the British retreat from Penjdeh was described:

> Long before this reaches London it will be known that the Russians and the Afghans have fought at Penjdeh, and that we escaped from the latter place by the skin of our teeth. The action commenced on the morning of the 30th of March, and was over in about 45 minutes. The Afghans were driven back and lost heavily. They formed up outside our camp, and we were for some time anxious as to whether they would attack us or not. Luckily for us they never attempted it. We had the leading Turcomans in camp with us, and they were sent with a letter. On their return without an answer, they told us that Alikhanoff had ordered them to attack us, and, when they refused, had offered 1,000 kram for each of our heads. We then thought it time to be off, and accordingly left Penjdeh about noon on the 30th. We proceeded in the blinding rain for some time along the same road that the retreating Afghans had taken, and then turned off into a desert, which is called the Chul, and made for Kila-i-Maur, where our

5. England and Russia Face to Face in Asia

> detachment of cavalry was. We marched all day and till midnight, when we reached the ford close to Kila-i-Maur. The Kushk river was in flood; we could not cross it, so waited till 4 30 A.M. lying on the wet ground, and defending ourselves from the snow as best we could. We had sent off a messenger early in the day to the cavalry to inform them of the way we were coming; but no answer was received, and it was not till the next morning, when we went over the hills to strike another ford, that we met a man who had been sent out to hunt for us. We forded the river and found our cavalry about 8 30 A.M., and after giving a little grain to our horses we started all together about 10 30 A.M. for Chaman-i-Baid, having travelled over 40 miles in about 36 hours.
>
> The whole country was under water, and our mules and camels came to terrible grief. We tried to cross the river, but were unable to do so, and after marching all day, we camped on the side of the river, and our stores and baggage, which we had previously left, were on the opposite side, so we had to do without any food for ourselves and our horses.
>
> The next morning saw us on the march again to Islim, leaving an officer and a guard behind to bring on stores and baggage if he could get them across the river. We halted at Islim for three hours to pick up some supplies, meeting some Akhal Turcomans on the road whom the Russians had sent out to look for us. We kept them with us till we left Islim, and then marched the same day to some 11 miles nearer Gulran. We grazed our horses and tried to get some sleep in our dripping clothes and tents, and went the next day to Gulran, which we reached about 6 30 P.M., being soaked through to the skin with rain on the road. The night we dined with Sir Peter Lumsden and halted the next day, during the whole of which it poured unceasingly.[14]

Lumsden had already made preparations to move his troops to Tirpul near the Iranian border. The forces at his disposal could not have halted a determined Russian advance and the faith the Afghans had in the British military prowess was quickly evaporating. Tirpul offered as well better lines of communication with London. The anonymous writer to the *Times* then described the move over the pass in the midst of a violent rain and snow storm.

> Our position was a critical one, as the Russians, Turcomans, and Afghans were all against us. The distance from Penjdeh to Gulran is about 125 miles, which we traversed in about 72 hours. The whole time at Gulran it rained hard, but, in spite of the downpour we decided to cross the Chasma Sabz Pass to this place, *en route* to Tirpul, where the infantry and heavy camp had previous gone. We had not proceeded far up the Pass when the wind rose and the dry bed of the stream began to fill, then to rise in flood. The road is a difficult one at any time, but in this weather it was well nigh impassable. On reaching the top of the Pass the wind blew

so fiercely that we were almost blown out of our saddles. The General, myself, and a few others reached this place about 12 30 P.M. A howling, bitter wind was blowing, and we tried to get under a hill for shelter, but in vain — rain, rain, rain kept pouring down, and the biting blast froze the blood in our veins. We tried digging holes in the earth to get out of it, but nothing answered, and we soon saw that we were in for a fearfully rough time of it. Our baggage could not possible come in with the drivers and mules more dead than alive, and an attempt was made to pitch a tent, but this took some hours, and it was blown down again as soon as erected. All the men in camp were perished and shivering from the intense cold, and I was busy doing all I could for them till mid-night. As ill luck would have it, some stores that had remained in this camp had been sent away, and some of us were without food or fuel. At night I managed to get a shake down in a small pal (native servant's tent) with four others, and we huddled together to try and get some warmth, as we were drenched to the skin and had to sleep on the mud, as it was. You can imagine the horrible time we had to go through. About midnight it came on to snow hard, and we became most anxious about our men in camp, for we knew that many men and animals must meet their death, exposed as they were in the Pass throughout this bitter night. The wind was so strong that of the three or four tents pitched that night most were reduced to rags before the morning. The General and most of the cavalry went on to Tirpul the next morning, leaving Captain Yate, Mr. Wright, the Nawab, and myself here to bring up the remains of the party and baggage as soon as we could get along.

Ever since we have been here and up to the present time we have brought in some 24 bodies, and only a fraction of our kit. To make it worse and to add to our misfortunes, all our baggage had been looted, and I am left with only my bed and bedding; everything else has been taken, even to my ink-pot, pince-nez, compasses, thermometers, eye instruments, carpets, silk embroideries, photography frames, stamps, envelopes etc., not even so much as a comb being left me. Of course, the whole place is thoroughly demoralized, and our other troubles are sufficiently critical without such a fearful addition as this. All the prestige we ever had here is gone, and, as far as I can see, Government care no more whether the whole Commission is wiped out or not. We have not a friend in the country, as the people see that we talked a great deal but have nothing to back it up with when the time of trouble comes.

I had the first decent night's sleep I have had in a bed last night since about the 27th of last month. Of course one is thoroughly knocked up with all one's troubles and hardships, and one can see nothing good ahead. How will it all end, and shall we get any compensation from Government for our losses, or thanks for our hard work?

In his book *England and Russia Face to Face in Asia: Travels with the Afghan Boundary Commission*, Arthur Yate described how 24 men died in the freezing cold and the baggage was strewn all over the country. The Persian muleteers and camel drivers looted the kit. Medals of the sowars of the 11th Bengal Lancers were cut off the tunics. Arthur Yate reported "that the inhabitants of all the country round had promptly swarmed to the scene of the disaster and looted all they could lay hands on."[15] Owen's hospital was completely plundered. His surgical, meteorological and eye instruments were all taken. *The Graphic* included a picture of the devastation at Chasma-Sabz on the morning after the storm of April 4 in its June 6 issue.[16] The crossing to Tirpul had disastrous consequences for the morale of the company.[17]

Holdich spoke as well about the "shamshir" that hit the ABC, "the blizzard of the north that occasionally wraps up men and animals in the cold embrace of blinding, freezing hurricane, and leaves them helpless on the open steppes."[18]

> It was not long before the gusts gave place to a wild, fierce shriek of blizzard and snow, darkening the air and blinding the eyes with its fury. It is impossible to give any adequate idea of the strength of the icy "shamshir" blast. Horse and mules would not face it, and man could not. The rule of the road, when it passes, is to stand fast and make the best of circumstances till it is gone. If it freezes the life out of a man before going, that is but a matter of detail; it would be frozen out, anyhow. Here it caught the caravan in the rear, and might have assisted to blow them over the brow of the mountain on to sheltered slopes on the far side, but for the melting process which set in on the hillsides under the influence of snow and sleet. In the space of a few minutes the mountains ran down to the plains in rivulets and streams of mud.

In a letter to his wife dated April 17, Charles Owen expressed regret at the loss of "all my nice things" and owned up to the anonymous letter in the *Times*:

> I expect before long you will get a letter of mine to the C & M quoted in the London papers as it gives correct account of the Panjdah [... ders?]. Of course I could not give all official secrets to the public but I sailed pretty close to the wind. I count over the loss of my kit and my instruments etc. latter I am lost without and feel inclined to chuck up work & go.[19]

Wheeler must have distinctly felt the pleasures of Schadenfreude when he passed on Owen's letter to the London newspapers. On June 30, 1885, Owen wrote to his wife: "I am sorry that letter of mine was put in the Times as everyone spotted it but it does not much matter now. I expect they will make some remarks from India but as it was a private letter they can only do that and nothing else."[20] Owen was particularly annoyed when some Indian journals picked up his anonymous critique as well, but he received compliments as well. His diary for May 26 contains the remark: "Heard from Wheeler about my report of Panjdeh. He notes that it is the best letter he has read since he has been in India."[21]

The mood of the camp was very dark indeed, and all three ABC commissioners came in for some bitter words from Owen: "The General has an idea of moving on Herat, but if he does we shall have a bad time of it, as the whole country is now against us.... The General is a silly old man and tries to make out that the Russians will cave, but I should like to know what will happen if the Government says they do not intend to move."[22] He told his wife, "he will not look ahead and see what is before him, nor will he act in the slightest on his own responsibility." The "crusty" general had even called up Ridgeway on the mat: "Old Lumsden has shut up Ridgeway's writing for the Times so that is why the letters home ceased." Telegraph lines to London had been broken down for nine days.

In other letters he expressed his opinion of the two deputy commissioners as well: "That skunk Condie Stephen is just going home — just as well as there isn't a soul hardly in camp who would speak to him now."[23] As for the commissioner who had waited until the spring before making his appearance Owen said, "Old Colonel Stewart who joined the camp when I was at Panjdeh is a queer old stick; he goes by the name of Mock-Turtle or soup Stewart and he looks his name."[24] In another letter he added, that one could always butter up Stewart by getting him to talk about his traveling through Persia disguised as an Armenian merchant, but he doubted anyone could have believed in his cover for more than two minutes.[25]

Owen's views on the charade in Rawal Pindi were just as sharp: "From all I can hear they have made a mess of the Amir's visit to India, loaded him with money and taken no guarantee from him. If we fight Russia it can only be with British troops and not with Afghans but the worst of it is that our British Regiments require such a lot of impediments to move that where we could move one Russian could move 3."[26] He could however register his pleasure that "I have had several complimentary letters from India about my letters to the C & M, or as we call it here the Swiveller."[27]

Since he had been involved with the heavy camp preparing the ground on the Persian side of the Heri Rud, survey officer Holdich could give a more dispassionate account of the disaster, which attended the move of the cavalry and light camp from Gulran over the pass called Chasma Sabz to Tirpul. He said that more than 20 men as well as many mules and all the dogs perished, but the immediate effects of the misadventure soon wore off once the brightness of a clear morning broke on them. Holdich admitted that "there was some looting, of course, but not much" but he was surprised how the memories of the camp-followers were awakened when the question of compensation arose.[28] It was the old story of the stiff upper lip of the British bureaucrat.

Sir Peter Lumsden made preparations to return to London as quickly as possible but his plans were frustrated by the resentful attitude of the Afghans, who boycotted him and his officers and delayed their mail. He had already heard that their camp in Bala Mughab had been burnt by the Afghans.[29] The commissioner had experienced a similar dangerous situation in Afghanistan in 1857, when he and his brother Major Harry Lumsden were kept under house arrest for a year in Kandahar during the Indian Mutiny. Treated with indignities while in custody of the Afghans, he and his brother were only allowed to return to India after the tide of the war was turned on the plains of Hindostan. At a moment when the prestige of England in Central Asia stood lower than ever in the annals of history, the commission could do little but await the response of the government to their precarious position. The Russians, however, seemed content with the occupation of Penjdeh and there was no sign of any further advance southward in an attempt to take Herat.

The order from the home government to return to England without delay reached Tirpul on May 8.[30] General Lumsden and his aide-de-camp, Capt. Barrow, left the next day. In contrast to Simpson's leisurely voyage to London in first class railway coaches and on steamships filled with tourists, Lumsden and Barrow had to ride all the way from Herat to Astrabad, often on the vilest horses. For days they never had a chance of changing their clothing. In Astrabad they were delayed for two days waiting for a ship. From Batumi on the eastern end of the Black Sea they sailed to Constantinople, where they were delayed for another two days by suspicious Turkish officials. Reaching Vienna on June 4, Lumsden had the misfortune of speaking too openly with a reporter of the *Times* about the policy of the government in Afghanistan, so that his negative comments were featured in the issue of the *Times* which appeared the following day.[31] Particularly cutting was his comment that he had the impression Gen. Komaroff's word was believed before his. The Russians "knew they were dealing with a Government which did not mean to fight either, so they played a game of diplomacy and bluster, and won it.'" On June 6 he arrived in London.[32]

Major-General Sir Peter Lumsden, the Chief of the Commission for examining and settling the north-west frontier of Afghanistan, arrived in London at six o'clock last Saturday evening. He was met at Charing-Cross station by a large number of friends, including Lord Chemsford, Lord Strathnairn, Lord Napier of Magdala, Field-Marshal Sir Peter Grant, and other officers of distinction, and was loudly cheered on alighting from the train, and by a crowd outside the station.

By this time, however, the border question had been as good as settled. Lumsden's political assistant, Condie Stephen, had returned somewhat earlier to London and in announcing his arrival the *Illustrated London News* had released the following commentary in the issue of May 16:

The statements of Ministers in Parliament on Monday last, with respect to the settlement of the dispute with Russia, show that the Afghan frontier question is in a fair way of being disposed of by direct negotiations between the Cabinets of London and St. Petersburg. Earl Granville and Lord Kimberley have examined the topographical details in a conference with M. Lessar, the special agent of the Russian Government, and have substantially agreed with him in a "delimitation" which is perfectly satisfactory to the British Government, to Lord Dufferin and the Council of India, and to the Ameer of Afghanistan. It only now awaits the conclusive acceptance of the Russian Government.[33]

The course of the negotiations was greeted with less warmth by the members of Parliament. Whatever his feelings about his reception, Lumsden must have been satisfied with the thought that he may have contributed to Gladstone's fall from office. Only a few days after his comments about the treatment which the commission had received appeared in the *Times*, Gladstone's government was unexpectedly defeated during a vote on the budget on June 8.

Simpson's rewards were of more material kind. Returning to England before the rest of the members of the Commission at a time when the border conflict was at its apex, he had been courted by both royalty and the government. In his autobiography he discusses this moment in his life:

The action of the Russians at Penjdeh, which so nearly led to war, seemed to have given the Queen a great interest in the locality, for at the end of May I received a message from Sir Henry Ponsonby that I was to come to Balmoral, where Her Majesty was, and bring my sketches with me. I started on the 1st of June, and arrived at Balmoral next day. Sir Henry told me that I was to remain two nights in the Castle. I had my meals with the suite. In the evening, just as dinner was coming to a close, a message came in from the Queen asking if my sketches could be shown at night. I said "Yes," and went to my room to bring them. I was taken into the drawing-room, where the Queen sat with some ladies. One was the Marchioness of Lorne, and another was the Princess of Leiningen. I had with me some silver ornaments which I had brought from central Asia, as well as child's cap I had brought from Penjdeh. These were first looked at, and the Queen appeared to be delighted with the jaunty look of the little cap, for she held it up as high as her hand could reach, and called the attention of the other ladies to it. Her Majesty looked carefully over all the drawings, while I stood at the table and gave explanations of each....

About a week after I was called to Marlborough House to show my sketches of Central Asia to H.R.H. the Prince of Wales. The Princess of Wales and one of her daughters, with Prince Victor and Prince George, also came in to see them. This was in the Prince's own room. I took the silver ornaments with me on this occasion also, and the ladies were much interested in them. One of the ornaments, which is worn on the breast, I placed on the breast of one of the Princesses to show the manner it was worn on the Afghan frontier. It was much admired. I had lost the small medal of the Prince's visit to India which he had given me in the Terai. It had dropped off the chain on which it hung in one of the marches, the third beyond Meshed, during my expedition, and on this visit to Marlborough House the Prince most kindly gave me another to take its place. I was invited to stay to lunch on this occasion.[34]

One of the last references to the Afghan Boundary Commission was a brief notice in the *Illustrated London News* of June 27 about a lecture presented to the Royal Geographical Society:

Sir Peter Lumsden's lecture to the Royal Geographical Society, last Monday evening, on the country of the Murghab, the Kushk, and the Heri-Rud, north of Herat, recalled many of the descriptive notices of that topography which accompanied the Sketches of our Special Artist, Mr. William Simpson, during his sojourn there with the Afghan Boundary Commission.... The British Commission is now encamped near Herat, and is being consulted by the Ameer's Government about the fortifications of that city.[35]

It remained only to publish on July 6 two of Simpson's sketches, which must have been remaining in the files.[36]

6

Forging the Boundary

The members of the commission who remained in Afghanistan were all but forgotten. On May 18 the commission moved from Tirpul to Sinja, where Col. Ridgeway was to supervise the improvements for the defense of Herat. The thunderclouds of war gradually cleared over the summer. Russia set aside its plans for invading Afghanistan for another century. On September 10 a protocol regarding the course of the boundary between Afghanistan and Russia was signed at the British Foreign Office in London. Twelve officers were told off for the demarcation party headed by Sir West Ridgeway and his assistant William Merk. The group consisted of three surveyors—Holdich, Gore and Talbot,—three politicals—Durand, Charles Yate and De Laessoe—and two men from the intelligence branch—Maitland and Peacock. Charles Griesbach and Owen counted as scientific experts. Nawab Mirza Hassan Ali Khan came as interpreter and manager of the mess. In addition there was a small escort of the 11th Bengal Lancers under Major Bax and Lt. Drummond, and Captain Cotton led the 20th Panjab Infantry. The rest of the Indian section of the ABC returned to their point of departure during December 1885 and January of 1886.[1]

On November 10 the demarcation party under Ridgeway met with the Russian commissioners Colonel Kuhlberg and Pierre Lessar at Zulfikar. In a letter to his wife Charles Owen described their first reception in the Russian mess four days later:

> The English mail came in this morning with your letter of 9th Oct. and it found me a most dyspeptic wretch for I had not recovered from a huge entertainment given us by the Russian Commission last night. They did the thing very well. They received us in full dress and seemingly every

Russian officer has at least a dozen orders and medals. We were ordered to go in undress which was of course a hideous mistake however there was no help for it so we made the best of our awkward predicament. I had rather a treat of it for I was between a Russian who could only say Bon Sante and a man who could speak Persian. So I had to do the Persian business which is rather a bore when one wants to enjoy the evening. Liquors were flying all over the place and everybody would insist on drinking one's health a dozen times over which was fatal. My brother guest only knows German so I was out of that and handed him over to someone else. The Cossacks sang glees outside all the evening. They had turned one of the huts into a Mess Room and had brought in evergreens to hide the ugly walls, had sported the Russian colours all over the place and had swords and bayonets and crossed daggers stuck here and there. The more we see of Colonel Kuhlberg the better we like him. He is a gentleman which is a great thing. Lessor is as sharp as a needle and lies like a fiend and all the time looks on you with a pair of benevolent eyes as if the whole thing was perfect gospel. Lessor wears about 20 orders. They give them away apparently to everybody. They have however 30 orders to give away from instead of 3 as in England. They lit up the road to their camp with huge bonfires. It was midnight before we parted and the consequence of drinking sweet champagne was that I had a bad night of it. They all dine with us tomorrow night and we are busy preparing for the struggle. The boundary work will not be commenced again till the day after tomorrow when the survey party will be off.[2]

On November 12 Ridgeway and Colonel Kuhlberg of the Russian Commission set up the first border post at the Zulfikar Pass. Durand sent a sketch of the fixing of the site to the *Illustrated London News*, which appeared on January 9, 1886.[3]

Then began ten months of surveying and endless bickering about the course of the boundary between Zulfikar and Khwaja Salar.[4] The Russians were accused of stalling, because they were getting triple pay. Ridgeway refused to make any decisions on his own and referred every problem to the amir or London. The troops grew seedy and were caught eating opium and stealing. It rained incessantly making fords impassable. Tent poles broke in the middle of the night. At the banquet for her majesty's birthday on May 22 Ridgeway appeared in evening dress, even though he knew Col. Kuhlberg and all the Russians would be coming in full dress. The Afghan escort prevented villagers from visiting Dr. Owen. Holdich forced Gore and Talbot to do all the survey work, while he took it easy in camp.[5] The whiskey supply was exhausted.

The ABC officers desperately competed with each other in trying to acquire a few Turkoman rugs from the rug merchants who occasionally visited the camp. In a letter to his wife dated Dec. 21, 1885, Owen wrote:

Setting of the first border post at Zulfikar with West Ridgeway and Col. Kuhlberg. *Illustrated London News,* January 9, 1886.

6. Forging the Boundary

"I managed to get hold of a very nice door purdah at Kila Maur but as for here I have not been able to lay my hands on any good carpets as the Russians will not allow the Panjdeh Turcomans up here."

As the mission moved eastward, various other types of Turkoman rugs made their appearances. In the course of an account of the Turkomans around Andhui Arthur C. Yate came to comment on the quality of Saryk weavings in comparison with those of the Ersari:

> Like the Tekkes and Saruks, the Ersaris are great manufacturers of carpeting; but to my mind the articles they turn out are decidedly inferior to those produced by the two former. Both for taste in colour and for soft velvetiness of texture, the Saruks, I think, easily bear away the palm. The Tekke colouring is too vivid; but it must be admitted that the texture of their best productions is wonderfully close and beautifully soft. They seem, however, to produce a large quantity of inferior articles; and this may be attributed to the fact that the Russian annexation of Merv has opened the markets of Europe to the Tekke industries. Almost every carpet from a Saruk loom that I have seen has been good of its kind.
>
> In the meantime the Commission is making very creditable progress towards spoiling the markets. I believe I am not exaggerating if I state that for the purchase of horses, carpets, and jewellery not less than Rs. 10,000 have flowed from the pockets of the Commission into the coffers of the Saruks of Panjdeh. In this sum I do not include the ordinary everyday trifles of every description, food, dress &c., that are purchased in the camp bazaar by all ranks and classes.[6]

With respect to this collecting activity, one of the youngest members of the ABC, Lieutenant the Honorable George Talbot, the sixth Baron Talbot de Malahide, can serve as an example. The Talbots had been the lords of Malahide Castle outside Dublin since the twelfth century. Despite his ancient titles, Lt. Talbot did not frequent the august circle around the three commissioners and Col. Ridgeway, but trekked out in the middle of winter, alone or with an assistant, to map out the course of the Oxus or the exact location of the Buddhas at Bamian. In his diary note for December 1, 1885, Owen wrote:

> News from Talbot in yesterday. He had experienced a rough time of it and with little success. Have to ascend peaks of 5000ft for simplest kind of work. This means 2000ft of snow at present. They have measured height of idols at Bamian. One is 120ft and the other 170ft."[7]

Of the rugs that Lieutenant Talbot purchased on the northern border of Afghanistan and brought back to the family's ancestral home at Malahide Castle outside Dublin, one was an ensi. It is significantly not a

Saryk but a Tekke door rug. The panel expresses the Turkoman conception of the world as composed of earth, the temporal space and the sky. At the base are masses of flowers. In the central section is a rising column crossed by a horizontal field. At the top is a single "mihrab" said to signify the bridal litter. The central field is crossed by a vertical pole and a wider horizontal panel with the *kotchak* pattern.[8] All along the outer edge repetitions of the horizontal double-rams horn motif on white ward off evil.

Lord Talbot's small Saryk main carpet is a superb example of its kind. The piece is almost square in shape (48 × 41 inches) with a purplish-brown color. There are three rows of Saryk güls (or sary göls). The main border features the so-called "naldag" motif. Natalia Nekrassova at the Toronto Textile Museum supplied the following analysis of the carpet. The technical terms she uses for the patterns are taken from the *Carpets of the Peoples of Central Asia* by V.G. Moshkova.

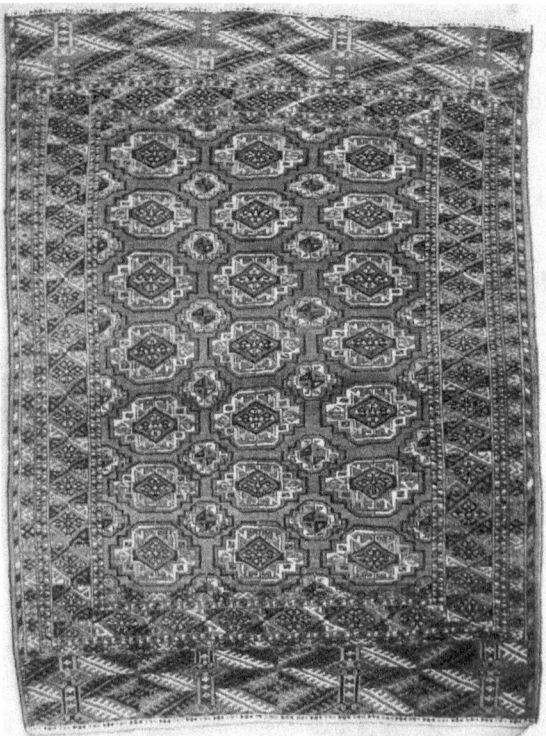

Saryk Turkmen Carpet acquired in 1885. (Collection of the Honorable M. G. Talbot de Malahide; by permission of the owner)

The rug shows a typical composition of a main Saryk rug. The wide central field is decorated with three rows of *sari* or *pendeh guls*—the distinctive elements of main Saryk rugs; seven guls in each row. The additional element used here is a *chuval gul*. Two rows of *chuval guls* are disposed between the rows of the main pattern; rows of halves of the *chuval guls* side with the border.

The border is not too wide and forms one-third part of the rug's width. Such width of a border used to be considered as evidence of the good age of a rug, not later then the 1870's. The border consists of five strips, the main of which shows *naldag* pattern, quite usual for Saryk rugs. Minor borders are decorated with variants of *khamtoz* and *gochak* patterns typical for the rug production of the whole Pendeh oases. The rug has two wide additional borders on the ends—elems, decorated with a variant of *kelleli* pattern, used by Saryk and Tekke weavers for this part of composition.

As far as one can judge by looking at the photograph, the color scheme of the rug consists of six colors: two shades of red, two shades of blue, brown and white. White details seem to be of cotton.

The most passionate "carpet knave" of them all was certainly Dr. Charles Owen. Although he had nowhere near the income of Sir West Ridgeway, who brought along his own Paris trained cook, or the wealthy Dane De Laessoe with his whole slew of servants, Owen nevertheless managed to send at least seven shipments of carpets and silk to his wife in England and to India.

Owen was overjoyed to receive a letter from General Sir Frederick Roberts offering him an appointment as surgeon to the commander-in-chief India. He immediately contacted his wife in England about making arrangements for the move to Simla. He sent off two bales of carpets to James Walker in Simla for their home, contacted former servants in Jaipur and ordered new visiting cards. Their greatest expense, he told his wife, would be a piano.[9]

He soon found, however, that intrigues in the India Foreign Office were hindering his appointment. After months of planning, he was devastated to learn that he was being given the civil surgeoncy of Simla for four years rather than a place on the staff of General Roberts. He noted in his diary: "Quite broke over it as I fancy all my people will think I have disgraced myself."[10]

This final period of the ABC was later described by three members of the commission. Thomas Holdich's book *The Indian Borderland 1880–1900*, offers an overview of the period, even if Owen said Holdich tended to see things through rose-tinted glasses. The Yate brothers Charles and Arthur both compiled their correspondence with various newspapers soon after the end of the ABC. Captain Charles Yate, who witnessed the affray on March 30 at Pul-i-Khisti, published *Northern Afghanistan or Letters from the Afghan Boundary Commission* in 1888. A year earlier his brother Arthur collected the letters he had written to the *Pioneer*, *Daily Telegraph* and other journals for his book *England and Russia Face to Face in Asia: Travels with the Afghan Boundary Commission*.

However the most colorful and personal account of the trials and tribulations by far is preserved in the unpublished letters, diaries and newspaper articles of Owen. Very little escaped his sharp eye, whether it was

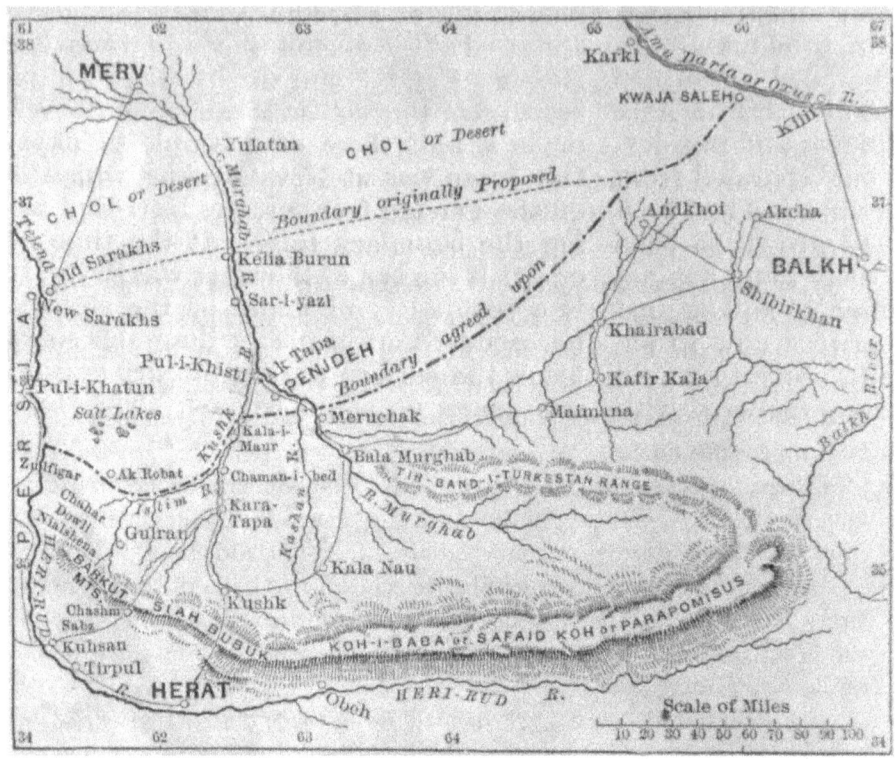

"The New Russian-Afghan Frontier." *Harper's Magazine* 72, 1886, p. 602.

the vanity of Col. Ridgeway, the "fearfully lazy" Thomas Holdich or the "navvy hairy monkey" St. George Corbet Gore. Even his fellow *Gazette* correspondent, Edward Durand, did not escape criticism. Durand had been granted permission to return home directly via Russia, rather than returning first to India, although if any one else had asked, the request would certainly have been refused.

One has the impression that Owen was suffering from cabin fever. He complained about Arthur Yate getting sensitive political material for the *Pioneer*, which he, Owen, did not have access to.[11] As for the elder Yate—"he splutters and talks with his mouth full and when he is eating you can hear him a hundred yards off."[12] Bax was "an awfully mean fellow," who thought only of himself.[13] De Laessoe spent an awful lot of money and "I don't believe he sends his wife a farthing."[14] The wretched Walkers did not answer his letters. Cousin Jessie Ilbert could not get along with the wife of his former commander, Lady "Bobs." His servants lost or broke something every day.[15]

6. Forging the Boundary

For Captain Cotton of the Panjab Infantry and the Honorable Milo George Talbot, however, he had nothing but praise. Owen wondered how Talbot endured the cold rough terrain he was assigned to survey and he recorded Talbot's measurements of the Bamian statues. The most high born of any of them, yet Talbot avoided the petty rivalries of rank at camp. When his fellow surveyor Gore fell sick, he tended him like a nurse.[16]

Owen doggedly persevered with his newsletters to the *Civil and Military Gazette*, although the monotony of camp life made it increasingly difficult to find anything new to say. On August 6 he received a letter from Wheeler, who announced that he was going home for four months. A London journalist, Kay Robinson, would be officiating for him. In a letter to his wife dated March 23, 1886, Owen asked his wife to check out a piece in the *Gazette* that was probably written by Rudyard Kipling: "You will see a good skit in the C&M on the camp exercise which will amuse you. Kipling must have written it for it reminds me of his style."[17]

Growing weary of the bickering and expense of maintaining the demarcation commission, the home government finally informed St. Petersburg that the mission could not be kept in Afghanistan past September 15. Negotiations over the disputed Kham-i-Ab boundary were to be carried on by the Russian and British foreign offices in consultation with the Amir. Although Kuhlberg kicked up a fuss, the last protocol was signed on September 14 and the camp broke up the next day direction Kabul. Durand set off for Merv and Askabad, while everyone else turned south.[18]

Going over the Hindu Kush pass, the mission reached the new Aliabad palace outside Kabul on October 15. The sight of palaces and civilization after two years of life in tents and kibitkas made an indelible impression on the men. Owen had taken part in the vengeful destruction of the capital in 1880, so he was amazed at the difference.

> The house which was placed at your disposal is an old fort which has been thoroughly done up for the occasion, newly painted and furnished. Lamps in the garden and in every room. Tasteful curtains of brown lined with scarlet. Before the General [Amir Mohd] left he presented a supply of sweetmeats which were brought in trays and the trays when laid out covered the whole of the courtyard. The Commr's. suite of rooms at the top of the house are tastefully furnished and there are a large number of handsome Persian carpets. There is khansama. Breakfast for all was provided by the Amir and many excellent dishes were provided which we did justice to. The fruit was magnificent. A fine durbar tent is erected in the garden and the place is guarded by the Kabul police whom one meets at every corner.[19]

Owen noted that there was a large bazaar close to the place in which everything could be bought. The Amir had made immense improvements round Kabul with good roads in every direction.

The officers were shown around all the gardens, bazaars and palaces of the city and met all the Afghan dignitaries who had accompanied Abdur Rahman to Rawal Pindi. On October 21 the mission had an audience with his highness in his new Harem Serai palace, which rivaled those in Istanbul for luxury. The Durbar Hall itself was 180 feet long and about 70 feet wide with 16 columns:

> After the Durbar and breakfast these [women's] apartments were shown to us and it was perfectly astonishing to see the luxury and comfort with which they have been fitted up. The rooms are double, the outer one lofty and well lit by many windows and the ceiling is similar to that of the Durbar Hall. The walls are hung with huge mirrors reaching almost from ceiling to floor. The windows are draped in damask and thick curtains and the carpeting is of (?) or velvet embroidered with gold. Fine crystal candelabra standing some 6ft height are in the middle of the outer room and one or two chairs of crystal with velvet cushions. This is evidently the day apartment and opening out of this are the sleeping apartments in which are handsome English bedsteads of brass and iron. Chromo lithographs of all kinds. Innumerable are the recesses in the wall which are closed by glazed frames and at the time of our visit were full of every kind of china and glass of European, Chinese and Japanese patterns. The rooms are all heated by hot air apparatus so as to maintain an equable temperature during the winter.[20]

At the durbar the Amir commenced a conversation, which he "carried on for more than two hours on every possible subject," emphasizing in particular his friendship with the British government. Owen spent the evening completing one of his longest newsletters, which filled a full three columns for November 2.

The final grand durbar took place on October 23 in the mess room of the Aliabad.

> After some little time spent in the interchange of compliments the Dabir-i-Malik presented a letter from the Amir for Lord Salisbury which was handed to Sir West Ridgeway. This letter contains 10 points referring to the state of Afghanistan and the information contained is of a secret nature. Ridgeway said he would take every care of the letter for which he gave a receipt and would personally give it to Lord Salisbury and also explain the contents to Lord Dufferin. The letter was enclosed in a handsome Kaniab(?) bag. After a long interval a messenger came to the Amir with presents for the Mission but first of all a tray was brought in on

which were two jeweled Orders of the Chivalry (Bahadur) of Afghanistan, the highest badge of the Order set in diamonds was given to the Commr. and the next grade to Lt Col Bax. All the B.O. officers were presented with gold badges of the Order and as well Kazi M. Aslam. Silver badges being given to the Native Attaches. Ridgeway acknowledged these in a suitable manner and the presents were shown, each officer being presented with a trayful of handsome articles. The Durbar then broke up and the members of the Mission left for their tents to don the new Order before visiting the Amir. About 11.40 a.m. a move was made to Baber's garden where the Amir was.[21]

Ridgeway reminded the Amir, that "no B.O. was permitted to wear Orders without the special permission of Her Majesty, but he would lay the matter before the Queen and trusted that Queen would be pleased to grant it." In the afternoon there was a parade of Afghan troops, which was inspected by the Ridgeway. At a final 5:30 durbar, Owen was handed a letter from the Amir "in which His Highness thanked him for all he had done for the people of the country."

Two days later the camp was on the road to the border. From Camp Rozabagh Owen filed his final last ABC report on October 27. In his diary he noted that "on the top of Latabund there is an iron cage with the skeleton of a man in it — Amir's mode of punishing thieves when caught." An Armenian, whom Owen met at Jellalabad, told him that the Amir was hated everywhere and some day his army would turn on him and then it would all be over.

On October 31, the British reached Jumrood, where a year and a half earlier Kipling had watched the approach of Abdur Rahman Khan from the elevation of the fort through a field glass "as a blot of blue on a small horse." Colonel Waterfield, who had welcomed the Amir *en route* to Rawal Pindi, was on hand to greet the mission. The next day everyone was off to Lahore.

7

The ABC in Lahore

The *Civil and Military Gazette* that Owen came back to in 1886 was quite different from the one from which he had received his assignment as an ABC correspondent in 1884. Wheeler had obtained a leave of absence to return to England for four months in the summer of 1886 and Kipling finally felt he had some breathing space with the new editor, E. Kay Robinson. Before departing, Wheeler had indicated to his employers and to Robinson, that Rudyard Kipling was "averse to routine." Kipling reacted with fury and wrote to Robinson on April 30, 1886:[1]

> Allen [another co-owner of the *Gazette*] said the same thing and then I sat tight, he being a full mouthed man and one [of the] owners to boot. Now I'll speak distinctly as the drunkard said. The whole settlement and routine of the old rag from the end of the leader to the beginning of the advertisements is in my hands and mine only; my respected chief contributing a blue pencil mark now and then and a healthy snarl just to sooth me. The telegrams also and such scraps as I or my father may write are my share likewise, and these things call me to office half one golden hour before, and let me out, always three quarters, sometimes a whole hour behind, my chief. My Sabbath is enlivened by the official visits of the printer and my evenings after dinner are made merry by his demands. So much for the routine to which I am averse. Of the scraps it is no profit to speak. They are pasted into a book with the days marked over them and are ready to be shown up the next time I have the "aversion" brought officially to my notice.

It was furthermore not true that he was writing his "skits" in office hours. He said that all his "rhymed rubbish" and other literature was "written out of office for my own personal amusement—(I don't play tennis or

7. The ABC in Lahore

whist or ride and my driving is no pleasure to me)." Robinson had already been struck with Kipling's literary talent and once in Lahore he was pleased to discover that Kipling did excellent "routine" work. The pair immediately set about changing the face of the newspaper, more in line with the London newspapers Robinson knew (undoubtedly to Wheeler's chagrin).

In a similar vein Kipling confided in Edith Macdonald in a letter from December 4:

> I've got a new editor — a *Globe* man — in place of my old chief who went home on five months leave. Between the two of us we've been making the *Civil and Military Gazette* hum. He is a young man an enthusiast and most delightful to work with.[2]

According to Kipling the public thought "the paper is immensely improved under the new direction" and he maintained, "we certainly have freshened things up all round." Kipling exuded a new-found confidence. His *Departmental Ditties* had appeared in print, and he had even received a complimentary letter about the publication from the viceroy.

Therefore, when the Afghan Boundary Commission once again set foot on British soil on October 31, Kipling as the "old hand" played a major role in the welcoming ceremonies. On the front page of the November 2 issue, a short notice announced that the Boundary Commission had been met by the Commissioner at Jamrood on October 31. This was followed by a second notice that "The Viceroy passed through Mooltan yesterday morning by special train, *en route* to Lahore, but did not halt." The Duke of Connaught planned to give his blessing to the formalities as well.

In preparation for this momentous occasion, the *Gazette* turned up the heat on its ABC coverage. On November 1 the newspaper published a long newsletter from Owen. Dated October 19, the report described the reception of the mission in Kabul. Owen remarked on the "many changes which have been carried out since our last occupation of this fertile valley." In addition to building palaces, roads, forts and gardens, the Amir had encouraged commerce and established a stable autocratic government. On October 20 the commission was received by the amir at a Durbar in the Baber garden. Abdur Rahman rode into the gathering under a huge black and gold state umbrella, accompanied by 30 bodyguards. After preliminary complements, the amir launched into a diatribe against his guests, because he had received reports that the English and Russian commissioners had been heard to be saying, "what was the use of fighting over the tail of the elephant, when the body has been settled."

Ridgeway countered, that the reported conversations had never taken place, so that the Durbar ended on a conciliatory note, especially after valuable presents from the British had been brought in and placed before his highness. From Owen's diary, we know these included "a very valuable necklace of precious stones, several handsome swords, a telescope, musical box, opera glasses and 4 valuable horses most richly caparisoned." No wonder "the Amir's tune changed," to quote Owen.[3]

A second Kabul newsletter published the next day described the reception for the ABC at the newly constructed palace, Harem Serai. The luxury and comfort of this palace impressed everyone and again the amir spoke for over two hours about the relations of his country with the British. He informed his guests that he had been made a general at the age of 12 and reassured Ridgeway that he would remain a staunch ally of the British Government, even if he had spent his years of exile in Samarkand and Russian Turkestan.

On November 3, Owen's final newsletter from Camp Rozabagh appeared. Owen covered the entertainment given by Perwana Khan, the deputy commander in chief on October 22, the durbar, private audience with the amir and parade on October 23, and their departure from Kabul on October 24. During the reception on October 22, the formalities were accompanied by a brass band, which "began to play Afghan airs so vigorously, that conversation could only be carried on under difficulties." This was followed by bagpipes. The guests "were surprised to find that the pipes were played as well as if they had been in the hands of *pucca* Scotchmen."

At the amir's private audience, all members of the mission were decorated with the Order of Bahad. Owen makes no mention of the packet given to Ridgeway for delivery to the Foreign Office, nor of his own letter from the amir thanking him for his medical services. By November 2 Owen was in Lahore.

Owen ended his diary on October 31, so his personal recollections for these hectic days are not recorded. In a diary entry for March 13, 1885, he wrote, "Heard from C&M saying they anxiously expected my letters and that two cheques were waiting for me at their office."[4]

Walker's presence in Lahore is attested by the list of participants at Government House on November 3. Upon arrival Owen would have received a copy of his article in *Journal of Indian Art*.

The ethnographical material collected by Owen and his colleagues gave both John Lockwood Kipling and his son a golden opportunity to "hunt and rummage" among the fierce Turkoman tribes of Central Asia. In a letter to Kay Robinson, Rudyard Kipling admitted, "For another thing I am deeply interested in the queer ways and works of the people of the land. I hunt and rummage among 'em."[5] The Kipling estate included one

Turkoman door rug.[6] It is not known if the Lahore museum or art school acquired any Turkoman rugs or jewelry at that time.[7] Enquiries to the Lahore museum were answered in the negative.

The Kiplings learned the truth about the "miserable Candie Stephen," who "ran away from us as soon as he could when he saw it was a dangerous game." In a letter to his wife from June 7, 1885, Owen said, "he is a devil who is bound to get on, don't yer know. I may explain 'don't yer know' is what he remarks to everything."[8] He later rose in the ranks to become in 1901 groom-in-waiting to King Edward VII.

Similarly Col. Stewart had been made a C.B. (Companion of the Most Honorable Order of the Bath) for services on the Afghan frontier. Owen's response:

> He was about 2 months here and did nothing. This is rather amusing to us. A d... shame that they don't care a cuss about us but when a fellow loafes home and sucks up to everybody he gets pretty much what he asks for.[9]

Even his colleague Edward Durand came in for his fair share of criticism: "He has not done a stroke of work since he came and yet expects from his position and interest to get all the plums stuffed down his throat."[10] Durand had departed for England and at that time was in London pulling all the strings necessary for obtaining his baronet.

Lahore had been spruced up for the visit of Viceroy Lord Dufferin, the Duke of Connaught, son of the Queen herself, a gaggle of turbaned Rajahs and the ABC to the city. The viceregal party arrived at Lahore Station on the evening of November 1. The following morning Lieutenant Governor Charles Aitchison was again at the station welcoming the Duke and Duchess of Connaught to the city. Of the equipment of the various visiting Rajahs, the *Gazette* reporter found that "His Highness of Kapurthalla's was the best turn-out and next probably that of the Rajah of Faridkote."

The arrival of these dignitaries marked a long litany of levees, receptions, parades, salutes, presentations, convocation processions at the university, speeches and formal expressions of loyalty. At a ceremony at the Punjab University "His Excellency the Right Hon'ble Sir Frederick Temple Hamilton-Temple, Earl of Dufferin, K.P., G.C.B., G.M.S.I., G.C.M.G., G.M.I.E., D.C.L. (Oxon.), F.R.S., Viceroy and Governor-General of India," received the degree of doctor of Oriental learning, *honoris causa*.

The focus then turned to the ABC. The viceroy planned a reception for the Afghan Boundary Commission at which Sir West Ridgeway would receive the K.C.S.I. and all the officers of the ABC were invited to a dinner in their honor at the Punjab Club "on Thursday, 4th instant."

In his capacity of big fish in a small pond, Kipling took it upon himself to honor the visitors with a long editorial on the "Return of the Boundary Commission" for the November 4 issue. He began with a flourish:

> It is not given to every man to represent his country against her traditional enemy, nor to every man so honoured does fate award success. Sir West Ridgeway, however, and his comrades, have the singular good fortune, having taken up a task full of difficulties in itself and rendered more doubtful by dubious sympathy from a Liberal Ministry at Home, to find their work accomplished in peace and honour.

Readers were offered a recapitulation of the accomplishments of Ridgeway in the wake of a "thinly, very thinly, veiled national humiliation." Although the empire was pledged to safeguard the amir's territories, the British had merely stood by watching, as the Russians pushed forward "beneath the eyes of our officers and men." The British had "allowed the Amir's soldiers to fight unaided and to be utterly defeated, without drawing the sword." The Anglo-Indian community had read with disbelief "of the narrow escape of our representatives from capture by the Russians on the one hand, and outrage from indignant Afghans on the Afghans on the other." The Afghans in retaliation had burnt the British camp. All this had taken place while Sir Peter Lumsden had commanded the Mission. Lumsden might have received his ovations from Gladstone's government at Charing Cross on his arrival in London, but the fact remained that Lumsden's "command of the Mission had been marked by nothing but failure and humiliation — who had left the Russians victorious and insolent, the Afghans defeated and distrustful."

On the other hand, "Sir West Ridgeway has no Panjdeh to boast of" but proved while establishing the border with Russia, that he could outmaneuver Colonel Kuhlberg "and even the great Lessar himself, whose diplomatic triumph over the English Cabinet in London was the most surprising feature of this queer chapter of Central Asian history — even M. Lessar has found himself matched in persistence and diplomacy by Sir West Ridgeway." The mission now found that it was received everywhere with respect, and the members had been "decorated by the Amir's own hand."

The Lahore reception carried in itself a certain weight in recognizing how "our honour" was upheld for two years in Afghanistan, because Afghanistan would be watching the proceedings. The fault of Eastern narrators is to exaggerate, "and in this instance exaggeration could do only

7. The ABC in Lahore

good." Ridgeway had succeeded where Lumsden failed. As if to make amends for the sour notes in the *Gazette* at the time when Ridgeway's appointment had been announced in the fall of 1884, the editorial admitted that he had left India "with no diplomatic trust" but in light of his accomplishments had proved himself to be "an excellent choice."

The mission distinguished itself not only diplomatically. The scientists with the commission had enriched Kew Gardens and the zoo, and the amir's letter of thanks to Dr. Owen for his medical services was proof of the great qualities of the members of the commission. The piece ended with a note on behalf of these members: "It is something to find that the uncern with which at one time it seemed that they were to be received in India, has been replaced at the last moment by meager military honors, and it is to be hoped that the more tangible rewards of pay, promotion or generous leave will not be forgotten."

Ridgeway lived his finest hour at Government House on Thursday, November 4, at 4:30 P.M., "when a Chapter of the Most Exalted Order of the Star of India was held to invest Sir West Ridgeway with the insignia of the 2nd class of the Order." The solemn and imposing ceremony took place in one of the upper rooms in Government House, which had been cleared and "arranged in a manner suitable to the occasion." The *Gazette* described the scene:

> At the head of the room was the throne for His Excellency the Grand Master and on either side of the centre passage were seated the Knights Grand Cross and Knight Commanders, and below them the Companions. Below the Companions, on either side were seated the officers and Native Attachés of the Boundary Commission. All heads of Departments were present and many distinguished visitors attended the Installation, who were provided with seats behind the members of the Order. The general appearance of the room was not unlike a chapel, as it is lit by a skylight from the top which only admitted a subdued light. His Honour the Lieutenant-Governor was present, welcoming the Maharajahs of Bahawulpur, Nabha, Jhind, and Nahun, and before the proceedings commenced he took his seat among the Knights of the 2nd class. The entrance to the Robing-room was guarded by non-commissioned officers of the XI Bengal Lancers and the archway leading into the drawing-room behind the throne was guarded by two non-commissioned officers of the 20th Punjab Infantry. About 4–20 P.M. all had been arranged, apparently to the satisfaction of the numerous arrangements in scarlet and gold, who had for some time been rushing about hither and thither, much to the satisfaction of themselves and the assembled company; and as the hour of the ceremony came near the face of the Under Secretary to Government in the Foreign Department assumed its usual diplomatic expression. At 4–25 P.M. His Royal Highness the Duke of Connaught arrived, all present rising

and the band outside playing the National Anthem. After a few minutes' interval the curtains leading to the Robing-room were drawn apart, and His Excellency the Grand Master appeared, preceded by the members of His Staff and followed the Secretary of the Order who wore his robes. All the assembly rose as His Excellency entered and remained standing until the Grand Master has taken his seat. His Excellency wore the ribbon of the Order and his breast was covered with the stars of the many orders of which he is a member. As soon as the Viceroy had taken his seat the Secretary of the Order advanced and informed the Grand Master of the business before the Chapter, *viz.*, that of the installation of Sir West Ridgeway as a Knight of the 2nd class. The two junior Knight Commanders, Sir Dinkur Rao and the Raja of Natore, accompanied by the Attaché in the Foreign Department, then proceeded to the Robing-room and led up Sir West Ridgeway to His Excellency. The Grand Master then rose, and in a clear and distinct voice said.—"In the name of the Queen-Empress of India, and by Her Majesty's command, I hereby invest you with the Honorable Insignia of the Star of India, of which the Most Exalted Order Her Majesty has been graciously pleased to make you a Knight Commander." Sir West Ridgeway then knelt before the Grand Master, who, after touching him on the shoulder with the sword of the Military Secretary, said, "Arise, Sir West Ridgeway." The new Knight, after making a profound reverence, then retired on one side and the Junior Knight Commander attached the Star of the Order to the left breast, the Attaché in the Foreign Department at the same time presenting the collar and badge of the Order as custodian to the Grand Master who invested the new Knight with the collar and badge. The newly-invested Knight, having made his reverence to the Grand Master, was led by the Secretary to his seat. The Secretary of the Order then reported that there was no other business.

All the members of the mission were then presented to his excellency, Ridgeway naming each officer as he approached the chair. At the conclusion of this exercise, the viceroy addressed the assembly of "Knights, Princes and Gentlemen," welcoming the members of the mission to India and praising their accomplishments.

Lord Dufferin and his royal highness then descended to the grounds of Government House to inspect the escort of the Boundary Commission. Even though the ceremony was sparsely attended, the *Gazette* accorded it full dues:

> Satiated with splendours during the last few days, Lahore and the Punjab gathered in less force than usual to view the inspection of the escort of the Boundary Commission. Yet they missed that which was the finest of all our recent spectacles. This was scarcely the fault of the absentees. A garden party at Government House was all that the majority had expected; and though the pleasure of enjoying His Honour's hospitality,

7. The ABC in Lahore

in common with a large concourse of native citizens, is great in any case, and on the present occasion was increased by the presence also of Royalty and Viceroyalty, yet nothing beyond a hint or two had gone abroad as to the method of the inspection of the Boundary commission. Something had been said about a tent behind the House; and indeed a tent of no very enormous dimensions would have contained all the European spectators present. This fact, however, was in due proportion with the ceremony whose dimensions were brought into the more striking contrast with the vastness of the interest it represented. On one small lawn, fringed on all sides with shrubs and trees, were drawn up certain soldiers in three sides of a square. They were few in number, but splendid in physique and bearing—just such a pocket-sample of our native army as an Englishman would like to send for our enemies' inspection. And the great significance of their peaceful presence among the rose-bushes of Government House, was that they had actually been so sent as a sample of our Indian army to look the Russians in the face; and had come back, proud to believe, and to say openly, that they—the native soldiers, foot and horse, of our Indian army—were better, man for man, and horse for horse, than these much-talked-of Cossacks; to say that under such officers as have led them back to India, they would cross again the man-slaying deserts and treacherous defiles of Afghanistan — willingly, fearlessly — to meet those Russians and hunt them, man for man, and horse for horse, back to their poverty-stricken Caspian. This is the message which each of those well-tried men, — who stood, cast in living bronze, motionless before the Viceroy, while he passed and smiled and spoke a word or two to each, — spreads abroad now in actual words among his untravelled comrades at home. This, too, was the message which their silent presence on Government House lawn gave to India and the Viceroy, and through them to England and the Queen.

A handful of men in three double lines; the ruler of the greatest dependency of any Empire on earth; the ruler of its most manly Province; and son of the Queen herself; groups of English ladies and crowds of Native Princes, Chiefs and Sirdars, —from the jeweled tiara of Bahawalpur to the zemindar of a few paternal villages— such a gathering to hear an unspoken message of such potent possibilities in the world's history, the sun has never shone upon. For once the ubiquitous photographer bobbing under his black sheet behind an unsightly tripod was welcome, and one wished that the light that glinted through the trees, here upon a Bahawalpur diamond, and there upon an Afridi bayonet, was favourable to the artist; and that the miniature display might be immortalized and enlarged hereafter on canvases at Home. No one present, from the new Knight of the Star of India and his officer comrades, who knew each of those men before him as trusted and trust-worthy followers, to the idlest of spectators, but felt that the Viceroy was splendidly finishing his duties in the capital of the Punjab by recognizing these faithful Indian servants of a distant Crown, who had confronted that Crown's traditional enemies on the heights above Herat, and in the valleys of the Oxus—the battle ground may be of the great Armageddon which shall settle between England and Russia, between light and darkness, the fate of the Old World.

No one that heard, and understood, the weird, yell of delight of our Afridi soldiers, the wildest, shiftiest, and yet staunchest of all the wild tribes of our rocky frontier, as soon as they had left the presence of the Viceroy and the Queen's son — the same fierce cry that has been the death-knell of many a brave Englishman foully done to death in Afghan Passes, but now wakening only the echoes of a garden-drive and startling ladies to inquire its meaning — but felt that a good day's work had been done that day. The Viceroy had spoken in the comparative privacy of a Grand Chapter of the Star of India, well and bravely, to the officers of the Mission. He had answered, through them the good and brave words of the Amir at Cabul. Through Sir West Ridgeway he had spoken to England's allies and to her enemies: and he spoke well. But in that few minutes' walk among those few native soldiers on the lawn he spoke to better purport still. Each cheery word and smile was a message to India, to her sons that fill our army, and her sons that till the ground. It told them that Viceroy and the Queen and the English nation beyond the sea were proud of them and trusted them; that while India sent such sons to serve the Colours as you, Afridi, — you, Punjabi, — you, Belooch, — India and England are safe. With the calm of statues the men heard him; saw him; felt him touch them as he passed. With the precision of machines, they turned and passed away. With the full-hearted pride and delight that makes schoolboys for the moment of the bravest and best drilled men, they yelled and scampered down the drive. The echoes of the shout will be heard again and again for ever, whenever England and India have need of stout Indian hearts to hold their own for the right, for kindly rulers and a grateful land.

The reference to the "ubiquitous photographer" presumably refers to John Burke, who advertised an album on *Photographs of the Lahore Durbar 1886* in a supplement to the *Civil and Military Gazette* for November 30.[11] Among the 24 photos illustrating the receptions and laying of the foundation stone of Aitchison College are five photos of the ABC: "19) BOUNDARY COMMISSION — Native Officers drawn up in front of Government House, 20) Ditto— THE ESCORT WAITING INSPECTION, 21) Ditto being inspected, showing VICEREGAL PARTY (Taken during H.E. the Viceroy's Speech), 22) Colonel SIR WEST RIDGEWAY and OFFICERS BOUNDARY COMMISSION, 23) INFANTRY ESCORT, BOUNDARY COMMISSION."

Kipling promoted the album with a review in the *Gazette* of Dec. 6, 1886.[12] In his description of native and English officers of the ABC, Kipling noted that "the tanned brown hands of the Englishmen show almost as darkly as the hands of the natives and in one case, specially, the demarcation between a bronzed face and a white turban-protected forehead is curiously distinct." As for photo number 21 he wrote:

> The Inspection of the Commission by the Viceroy is wonderfully good and Mr. Burke has availed himself of a chance not seldom offered to a photographer — that of photographing a rival. Now a man with his head inside the black velvet of a camera, and his legs much astraddle, is neither a comely nor dignified object, and his appearance just behind the lines of the Commission Escort is very funny.

The final act was the dinner for the 11 members of the ABC at the Punjab Club in the evening. Ridgeway dined with the viceroy and was absent, as was the twelfth officer with the mission, Edward Durand, who had deserted his colleagues in September.

> The dining room, whose length is, as a rule, preposterously disproportioned to the few round tales at which habitual Club-diners foregather daily, was occupied from end to end with a milky way of table-cloth and glass; and the seats from end to end were filled, with only one or two invisible exceptions. The speeches were few — only two in fact — and short, very short. Mr. R.T. Burney, Judge of the Chief Court, in proposing the health of the guests, adverted to the ceremonies of the afternoon, in which they had been the central figure; to the labours of the Mission in Afghanistan, when for two years our eyes had anxiously followed them across desert, rock and river. He compared the meal they had just honoured the Club by eating beneath their roof, with the probably extremely make-shift viands that must have tried their digestions at times on the Afghan frontier; but pointed out, what was obvious to all present, that the guests looked in the best of health and condition. His remarks were received with frequent applause, which was redoubled and prolonged when he said that the honour which had been shown to them that afternoon, was only a tithe of what they deserved. As a small but fairly representative gathering of the European community of the Punjab, the opinion of the gentlemen assembled there ought to carry some weight, and it was emphatically shown that not a man present but thought the returning Mission was not being treated well enough. "If they had all, instead of their leader only been made K.C.S.I's" said Mr. Burney amid cheers, "we should have been better pleased." That was doubtless a figure of speech; but a figure with meaning. Colonel Bax replied on behalf of the Mission, and thanked the club cordially for their hospitality.

Among the hosts and guests listed in the *Gazette*— E. Kay Robinson, Esq., R. Kipling, Esq., J.L. Kipling, Esq. In his autobiography Kipling says his life at the time revolved around the "Punjab Club, where bachelors, for the most part, gathered to eat meals of no merit among men whose merits they knew well."[13] Wheeler seldom came there as he was married, but Robinson must have become a regular guest. One can easily imagine who was behind the invitation to the officers of the ABC.

When Robinson took on the newspaper, the owners had instructed him to "put sparkle into it."[14] Kay and Rudyard had certainly achieved that goal with their coverage of the ABC's reception in Lahore. The report on the ABC festivities came out on Saturday, November 6. By Monday the *Gazette* was back in its role as a barb in the side of Government with a piece on the rumored appointment of the Duke of Connaught and Strathearn to the command of the Bombay army: "The present is hardly the time for entrusting the command of a Presidency into the hands of an amateur ... competing with officers of the Army for posts to which they by right of years and service have fairly established claim."

Owen had three months leave before he took up a posting as Civil Surgeon in the resort hill town Naini Tal. This was followed by duty as Officiating Agency Surgeon in Quetta. In April of 1889 Charles Owen at long last joined the staff of Sir Frederick Roberts as surgeon to the Commander-in-Chief India.[15]

Both Owen and Kipling moved to East Sussex in 1902.

Introduction to the Appendices

When Rudyard Kipling joined the *Civil and Military Gazette* in 1882, a major part of his duties consisted of translating into English articles from French in Russian newspapers dealing with Russian advances into Central Asia. The editor, Stephen Wheeler, did not expect any originality from this youngster foisted on him by James Walker, a co-owner of the newspaper.

After the fall of Merv in 1884, this topic assumed a more then passing interest. The British establishment in India grew increasingly obsessed with the idea that the ultimate goal of the Russian advances was India. Relationships with the amir of Afghanistan had to be quickly patched up. Surveying expeditions were sent into the Hindu Kush. Fearing that the Russians would attempt to stir up resentment against the Raj, a few hints at liberalization such as the Ilbert Bill found formulation. Ministers in India frantically endeavored to wake up a sleepy British Parliament to the dangers.

It was within this atmosphere that the Afghan Boundary Commission came to birth. Only a qualified group of military, political and scientific experts from Britain and India were to take part. The entourage was loaded with gifts for Afghan chieftains. The British hoped that they could make inroads among the warlike Turkomans and convince them to become faithful allies, duplicating thereby the British experience in India in a buffer zone between Central Asia and India. Walker, always on the top of things, engaged two members of the ABC as correspondents for his newspaper.

As a large part of its readership was among the military, the *Gazette* paid particular attention to the preparations of the Indian section of the commission. There were not only the usual cut-and-paste reports lifted from various newspapers, government blue books and travelogues, but the *Gazette* came up with editorials giving an insight into the confrontations between the Foreign Office and the military about the selection of the participants. Kipling's tedious translations of the memoirs of Alikhanoff, the victor at Merv, acquired a new importance when it was realized that Alikhanoff would be one of the Russian officers facing the British in the border region. His translations of the Russian newspapers provided vital bits of intelligence on the actual response to the commission in St. Petersburg and Moscow.

His first major piece on the commission appeared on January 7, 1885 (See Appendix I.1). The author gives a knowledgeable survey of the fragility of the Afghan dominion and touches on some themes (eg. Russian agents encouraging unrest, blundering British statesmen, Russophobia), which remained with him for life.

The articles written by Kipling during the conference at Rawal Pindi, although published anonymously, have been well known among Kipling scholars. Excerpts from them have been edited by Thomas Pinney in *Kipling's India*. A growing confidence in his own worth allowed Kipling to drop the façade of newspaper reporter and to produce some of his best early writing. New in this presentation is the reference to the maps, which accompanied the original articles. A unique complement to these articles is Kipling's diary for 1885, now at Harvard University. It remains one of the rare personal documents from India which Kipling was not able to destroy.

Writings on the commission have been grouped into four appendices. The first includes the articles and "scraps" which can be attributed to Rudyard Kipling, because they are mentioned in his diary, in his correspondence or in his scrapbooks collecting articles dated between 1884 and 1891.

Appendix II lists the writings on the commission, Afghanistan and Central Asia, which may be by either Kipling and/or Wheeler. Kipling's scrapbooks have been used by some scholars as the canon with which to determine the authenticity for Kipling's writings, but they only contain a fraction of Kipling's contributions. In a note at the beginning of his diary for 1885, Kipling recorded that he had supplied 230 columns matter for the newspaper in the course of 1884. A handful of these appear in the 1884 scrapbook. For 1885 he set his quota at two and a half columns of "scraps" and articles per issue.

Most of these items in Appendix II consist of only one or two paragraphs. They are not the sort of pieces for which the editor would call upon outside correspondents to write, when he had an assistant editor in his office, who was perfectly capable of supplying them. The only exceptions are the piece called "The Central Asian Question" (Dec. 24, 1884) and the long biography of "Abdul" Rahman. The latter seems to draw on several sources. Published on the eve of the amir's arrival in India, Wheeler would have laid particular weight on a good presentation.

Indications of Kipling's involvement can not only be drawn from references to his translations, but also by his consistent use of the spelling "Amir" for the ruler of Afghanistan, rather than "Ameer," Wheeler's preferred spelling. Wheeler could of course still come by Kipling's desk with his blue pencil, but he clearly could not check everything. One will see for instance "Ameer" in the title, but "Amir" in the text. Wheeler had his revenge during the Rawal Pindi conference, when every one of Kipling's headlines "To Meet the Amir" was converted into "To Meet the Ameer." It is worthy of note, that these "scraps" on the border conflict cease after March 17. Kipling left Lahore on the March 15.

Appendix III includes Kipling's translations, which were generally preceded by the expression "specially translated." Appendix IV lists the newsletters written by correspondents with the commission, which appeared in the *Civil and Military Gazette* up to the end of April 1885. Appendix V lists the members of the Afghan Boundary Commission.

Appendix I: Articles by Rudyard Kipling

Appendix I.1: The Central Asian Question (January 7, 1885, p. 2)
Appendix I.2: The Russians in Central Asia (January 28, 1885, pp. 1d, 3cd)
Appendix I.3: "Scrap"   (February 3, 1885, p. 1c)
Appendix I.4: "Scraps" (February 26, 1885, p. 1cd)
Appendix I.5: "Scraps" (March 5, 1885, pp. 1c, 3c)
Appendix I.6: The Rawal Pindi Camp (March 24, 1885, p. 3c)
Appendix I.7: To Meet the Ameer (March 26, 1885, p. 3bc)
Appendix I.8: To Meet the Ameer (March 28, 1885, p. 2bd)
Appendix I.9: To Meet the Ameer (March 31, 1885, p. 2cd–3a) with Kipling's map
Appendix I.10: The City of Evil Countenances (April 1, 1885, p. 4ab)
Appendix I.11: To Meet the Ameer (April 1, 1885, p. 2d–3ab)
Appendix I.12: To Meet the Ameer (April 2, 1885, p. 2cd–3ab)
Appendix I.13: [To Meet the Ameer] (April 2, 1885, p. 3b)
Appendix I.14: [The Rawul Pindi Durbar] (April 6, 1885, p. 5ab)
Appendix I.15: [The Rawul Pindi Durbar] (April 6, 1885, p. 5bc)
Appendix I.16: [The Rawul Pindi Durbar] (April 6, 1885, p. 5cd)
Appendix I.17: [The Rawul Pindi Durbar] (April 7, 1885, 3bd)
Appendix I.18: [The Rawul Pindi Durbar] (April 8, 1885, p. 3bd–4a)
Appendix I.19: [The Rawalpindi Durbar] (April 9, 1885, p. 3d–4a)
Appendix I.20: [The Rawalpindi Durbar] (April 10, 1885, p. 3bd)
Appendix I.21: "Scrap" (April 13, 1885, p. 1d)
Appendix I.22: The Rawulpindi Camp (April 14, 1885, p. 2cd–3a)
Appendix I.23: [The Rawulpindi Camp] (April 14, 1885, p. 3ac)
Appendix I.24: The Viceroy in Lahore (April 17, 1885, p. 2cd)
Appendix I.25: The Rumoured Trouble at Herat (May 17, 1888)

I.1: *The Central Asian Question*

by Rudyard Kipling[1]

Panjdeh, an important strategical position north of Herat, was only saved, the other day, from Russian occupation by timely reinforcements sent by the Afghan General at Bala Murghab. Although the *Journal de St. Petersbourg* may deprecate the misconstructions of the English Press with regard to Russian policy in Central Asia, we may safely assume that Russia will annex, more or less formally and completely, every inch of ground in Central Asia, not defended and safeguarded by England. Whether she will next attack India, must depend on the facilities which we leave open for such an attack. These facilities will be greater or less, in proportion to our foresight in laying down the line beyond which Russia may not advance without our declaring war, and to the strength of our measure for defending this line. Let us first take things as they are, and assume that the Delimitation Commission lays down a line of frontier following the course of the Oxus, from its "high mountain cradle in Pamere" to Khodja Saleh, and from Khodja Saleh to Serrakhs, or some point on the Tejend south of Serrakhs. Let us suppose again, that the British Government proclaims that this is to be the line beyond which Russian influence must not advance. What will happen when Russia conceives that the time has come for breaking through this barrier, with a view to embarrassing us, while she was playing her game in Asia Minor or European Turkey? We may be sure that some time would be chosen when we had troubles in hand elsewhere; say in the Soudan or in China. What would Russia's power of offence be then? To begin with, unless English officers were stationed in North-West Afghanistan, Russia could, under favourable circumstances, occupy Herat before we knew anything of the move, save perhaps for uncertain rumours. Merve and Serrakhs were occupied with the same secret celerity. For years past, English statesmen of both sides had accepted the view, that a Russian occupation of Merve would be adverse to British interests. On this point both political schools agreed, though there was a difference of opinion, as to whether such an event could, and ought to be prevented. But the news that it had come to pass, reached us only after the fact had been accomplished; and very much the same thing might happen in the case of Herat. From Serrakhs, the Russians could reach Herat, marching in force, within little over a fortnight. Simultaneous movements might be made on Balk [sic] and Chitral; both of which positions might, like Herat, be seized before a British force could even be placed in Kandahar. These movements are perfectly feasible. With Herat, Russia's communications could be quickly perfected, by pushing on the trans-Caspian Railway. From Balkh, an army could advance on Cabul; reaching the Ameer's capital in less than six weeks. From Chitral, Russia would intrigue with Kashmir and the tribes directly on our north-west frontier. Holding then, these positions, she would be able to insist on a rectification of the Afghan frontier; and England would have to recognize Herat, and probably Afghan Turkestan, as a Russian Province.

Without staying to suggest any measures that might be taken to prevent a Russian advance along the lines mentioned, we may go on to consider whether we should be right in regarding this advance as of no particular moment; even acquiescing beforehand, as some of our politicians would, in a Russian occupation of the country up to the Hindu Kush. Stated in other words, the question is, whether from her position, then, Russia could do us more harm than she can now. If she could, it behoves us to withstand, by every means in our power, any further advance of Russia from her present outposts; and if possible to induce her to evacuate some of the points, such as Sarrakhs [sic] and Pul-i-Khatun, already gained. To answer this question, it is necessary to compare the methods of defence [sic] needed, if Russia held Herat, with those which would have to be adopted, if we determined to prevent an advance to Herat. However much we might confide in the good will and fair promises of Holy Russia, it is obvious, that if Herat is allowed to become a Russian province, our defences [sic] must be made stronger than they are now. Would it be better to wait till our Russian friends get nearer to us? Competent authorities reckon, that if Russia gets Herat, the European army in Europe must be increased by one-fourth, and the native army strengthened proportionately. It would be found necessary to occupy Kandahar. There are some, no doubt, who deprecate the latter measure under any circumstances; but their number is rapidly diminishing, and even if we, inclined to agree with them, it is certain a more active policy would be followed. Even a Liberal Government, we firmly believe, would be driven to occupy Kandahar, were the Russians in Herat; if not Ghuzni and Cabul to boot. We should want 10,000 men, at least, to hold Kandahar; and a large force would have to be kept in readiness to meet a possible advance from Herat *via* Furrah. And while we were watching the Kandahar gate to India, we may be sure that Russia would be threatening us with more or less real purpose, from the direction of Cabul and Chitral. We should be expecting invasion from three separate points of attack. The perils of the situation would absorb all the energies of our Government. Little time would be left for the development of local autonomy, and other wise designs of our present rulers. The dangerous elements of native society could not fail to attain more dangerous dimensions. Paid agents of Russia — we seem even now, from time to time, to come across their track — would find a home in every native city, and at the court of every native chief. They would seek, and not in vain, to establish intimate relations with the various native societies, which, with more or less reputable objects, might soon become centers of disaffection. Everyone who felt dissatisfied with our rule, who was impelled by some real of fancied grievance into a feeling of disloyalty, would be tempted to hold communications with the agents of a Power which might be destined to upset our Raj. In many cases, such intrigues would be detected; and the discovery would only serve to aggravate the general uneasiness. The tribes on our frontier [sic] would grow more daring than ever. Even friendly chiefs, seeing the enemy at our gates, would begin to think the time had come for making overtures to the winning side. Within our own dominions, an increase of crime would be the inevitable accompaniment of the public insecurity. Colonel Ewart, of the Punjab Police, has proved beyond contradiction, that organised and systematic crime is far more widespread than was supposed; its ramifications extending wherever the Railway penetrates. The same dangerous spirit of lawlessness infects even some, if not several, of our native regiments. The absence of active loyalty, even among the better disposed classes of the native community — that passive indifference which we must expect in an Oriental country — would make the disloyalty and lawlessness of the disaffected class, much more dangerous than it would be otherwise. The disloyal and criminal may be few in numbers; but we can find no counterbalance in any warm loyalty or respect for the law — as the law of the land — in the remainder, though it may be and is, the large majority of the population. But if the picture is overdrawn, perhaps the Russophils and apostles of masterly inactivity will say, what they look forward to, when the Russians are in Herat. A friendly intercourse between the Russian Governor-General of Khorassan and the English Viceroy of India? A studious avoidance of every cause of offence on both sides? An Amir of Cabul, politely indifferent to his neighbours, the Russians, on one side; and gratefully effusive with ourselves, to whom he is beholden for the loss of third of his kingdom? And even supposing that these politicians may be right in expecting a millennium when the Russian and English frontiers will touch, can any guarantee be found for the permanence of their convictions as the guiding counsels of the Government of India? There are signs, indeed, that Government is awakening to the danger that threatens India; and already active measure are being taken to meet it.

That an active policy is needed, we fully believe. Every effort should be made to render it impossible for Russia to reach Herat; and to put a stop, once and for all, to her intrigues in Afghanistan. It should be generally recognised, that a Russian occupation of Herat and Balk [sic] and Chitral, would be a serious blow to our prestige and influence in the East; and it is high time, to state clearly and emphatically, England's determination that the states of Afghan Turkestan, Usbeg though they may be, ought never to be allowed to fall under the dominion of Russia.

I.2: *The Russians in Central Asia*
by Rudyard Kipling[2]

p. 1d: "Scrap"

ALTHOUGH THE RUSSIAN PAPERS HAVE SAID very little about affairs in Central Asia lately, we are able to publish in another column some interesting extracts bearing on such subjects. M. Lessar, the Russian engineer who has surveyed the country for a railway to Herat, has published an account of a rising that took place shortly after the conquest of the Akhal Tekke region. Amongst the leaders in this rising, of which we now hear for the first time, were two "Hindus"; Mahomedans, no doubt, from the Punjab. The *Nouveau Temps*, in which M. Lessar's communication appears, also states, apparently on his authority, that after the annexation of Merve, the Saryk Turcomans finally passed under Russian rule. "This is the very country," say the *Nouveau Temps*, "in which the Anglo-Russian Delimitation Commission will do their work." It may be pointed out that the English Government by no means admits that the Saryks, who occupy Panjdeh and Maruchak, are the subject of Russia.

p. 3 cd: THE RUSSIANS IN CENTRAL ASIA

The *Nouveau Temps* publishes a communication by M. Lessar relative to south-western Turkistan. It contains some important disclosures as to the Russian occupation of Merve. We read: —

"According to M. Lessar's own account, internal agitation sprang up shortly after our conquest of the Akhal Teppe. This was raised by a Turkoman called Siakh-Pouschem, and was seconded by a Afghan and two Hindus who resided in the country south of Merve. Their intrigues ended in the state of anarchy to which Turkistan was a prey throughout the summer of 1883. In order to support the numerous body of Russian sympathisers, a Russian detachment, commanded by General Komaroff, advanced into the oasis, and, on the 4th March 1884, occupied Kareschout-Khan-Kila. Siakh Pouschem organized some sort of resistance, which, however, resulted in nothing beyond an interchange of a few rifle shots, and occasioned no loss of life; but the expenses of the Russian expedition came to some tens of thousands of roubles."

"The consequence of the occupation of Merve, was the establishment of more regular relations with the tribes to the south of that spot, on the banks of the Murghab and Harirud. One of these tribes, the Saryks, finally passed under our rule. This is the very country in which the Anglo-Russian Delimitation Commission will do their work — a land which M. Lessar has just explored from one end to the other, from Yulatan in a journey extending over five hundred and twenty *verstes*."

We also find some further particulars concerning the new route which the Russians are opening up to Central Asia: —

"Colonel Beliavsky has explored the new route going from Mertvy-Koultuk to Taschkend — a route which has often been discussed in connection with Colonel Tchernaieff's journey. According to information published by the (Russian) *Gazette de St. Petersburgh* this is the same route which the Bekovitch-Tcherkaskey expedition followed in the time of Peter the Great. One knows that, at the present time the Mertvy Koultuk bears the name of Czarwitch Bay. From thence the road goes across the Oust-oust plateau towards Kungrad, then skirting the Oxus to Kheradj and finally eastward to Tashkend.

"According to observations made by Beliavsky, the minimum depth of the Mertvy-Koultuk is at no point less than four and a half feet — a depth which would render steam navigation perfectly practicable. The climate of the Oust-oust is only severe on the heights. In the low countries through which the route goes, the temperature varies between 26 (degrees) of heat and 20 (degrees) of cold: the mean winter temperature being — 8 (degrees). The land is moreover traversed by twenty-four thousand *Kibitkas* of nomads — a portion of whom stay there throughout the whole year. Beliavsky, like his predecessors, Alexandoff, Vanuschine and Tourbaieff, found drinkable water through the whole journey to Kungrad. The country is flat; and a road for wheeled vehicles could be easily driven through it.

"Nor is firewood wanting for much *saxeaul* and kindred vegetation are to be found. The route along the left bank of the Oxus is a very convenient one, inasmuch as, with the exception of some twenty verstes close to Kheradj, it connects Tashkend with that town. The drifting sand hills can be easily fixed by barriers of reeds — several of which contrivances already exist in the trans-Caspian country. It is possible to travel across the Oust-oust by four parallel roads — a most important matter from the strategical point of view. The road under discussion is the most direct of all, and the carrying company only charges r 1,c 77. per *pood* on the merchandise conveyed thereby; as compared with r 2. c 40 on all carried by the old line. The country has a population of three and half millions of inhabitants and close upon two million *poods* of merchandize circulate through it in the year. There are also a thousand of the ten-ton boats that navigate the Oxus. It is plain, therefore, that all conditions are favourable for the establishment of wheeled road through this country; but it will be necessary to establish a service of steamers through seven months in the year in the Caspian sea, to build a road stead and two lighthouses, several halting stations in the Oust-oust; grant a subvention of r 1000,000 to a steamer company for the navigation of the Oxus, and throw up the reed barriers before alluded to for the distance of some twenty *verstes*. The thing, it will be seen, is easy enough of accomplishment and according to Beliavsky's advice, we must abandon all notions of a railroad connecting Orenburg with Tashkend, Orenburg with the Aral sea and Merv and Askabad with Tashkend. As a matter of fact, two million *poods* of merchandise could not support so long a line.

Our next extract relates to recent examinations of the old bed of the Oxus: —

M. Kouschine, as he sets forth in an article in the *Messager Official* has verified Prince Gortschakoff's recent investigations as to the old bed of the Oxus, and has arrived at nearly the same conclusions as that traveller. According to him the basin of the Sarykamysch used to communicate at one time with the Aral sea, close to the gulf of Abonguine. In coming from the south-east, the Oxus used to flow into this basin, and by gradual siltings up the river was eventually divided into two streams and, when the Oxus turned its flow to the Aral sea, the Sarykamysch basin dried up. The southern portion was converted before long into a vast swamp, studded with numberless small lakes, while the northern part retained its original character of one big lake.

According to M. Kouschine the old bed of the Oxus terminated at the North-West extremity of the Sarykamysch: —

In such a manner, that the western Ouzboi from the Balla Ischem to the sea did not from a part of it. This agrees with the testimony of the old writers who referred to the Khurarezm lake into which the Oxus flowed. It appears further, from M. Konschine's researches, that the Sarakamysch [*sic*] basin must have been dried up at no very distant date, and at the same time as the peninsula of Dardja and the Caspian sea; that the waters of the western Ouzboi were pellucid and brackish with a very slow current, and that there were no traces of irrigation or habitations visible near it. Finally, the explorer's conviction is, that the western Ouzboi is not the bed of the river known to the ancients as the Oxus, but simply the overflow of the brackish waters from the Aral-Sarakamysch region into the Caspian sea.

Another paper gives us some insight into the internal affairs of Turkestan: —

Some curious information appears in the *Gazette de Moscow* as to judicial procedure in Turkestan previous to the Russian conquest. Judges it seems were of two kinds, *Kazis* and *Muftis*. These latter sat on the original side, and combined the functions of Judges, summoning officers, advocates and notaries. Both *Kazis* and *Muftis* were elevated to the rank of Judge by the *Bék*, after having undergone an examination as to their knowledge of the local code — the *schariat*. The number of Judges was unlimited; there being twenty in the large towns, and about half that number in the small. In default of district jurisdiction, each litigant could appeal to the particular Judge in whom he had the most confidence. Although bribery was severely punished by law, it was none the less practiced on a large scale. There were four grades of *Kazis*— one of which exercised police and the other military powers: marriages were solemnized by the leading *Kazi*. The powers of these Judges who closely resembled the ordinary *Judge de Paix* were, however, extremely limited. The greatest punishment which they could inflict was two hundred blows of the rod and confinement for six days in a filthy dungeon; but from these decisions it was possible to appeal to a general court of all the *Kazis* in the neighbourhood. The judgments were delivered with far more regard to precedent than the merits of the case, or any notion of justice and right. All manner of atrocities received the force of law had they once been put in force by it.

Great criminals were handed over to the judgment of the *Bek*. His punishments, which he dealt out at will, were as barbarous as possible. For a theft above the value of two hundred roubles, the right arm was cut off. Apostates to their religion were buried up to the waist and stoned to death; their bodies being thrown to the dogs. Unfaithful wives were punished in the same fashion. Murder, when brought home, was punished with death; but in a suspicious case a fine (*koun*) of two thousand roubles and a hundred camels was exacted. Anyone condemned to death was dragged through the town, and executed where the gathering of spectators happened to be thickest.

Since those days, however, and under the influence of Russian civilization, these barbarities have been much mitigated.

The following extract relates to the Russian Education Department in Central Asia.–

A Siberian paper publishes the scheme of the new schools founded near our consulates at Ourga and Kouldja. For a long time past, the want of men conversant with many languages spoken in the Celestial Empire had been felt; and it was to supply this want that these two consular schools were founded on the recommendation of the Minister for Foreign Affairs, the Minister of the Interior, and that of Public Construction. The schools were to open on the 1st of January. Manchu, Chinese, Mongol, written and spoken, will be taught at Ourga; and at Kuldja, Tartar, Kalmuck and some Central Asian dialects will be added to the curriculum. Young men of over sixteen years, who have passed through the district schools will be admitted and instructed for a term of five years. There will be two grades for outgoing pupils, that of interpreter and of dragoman. The first grade will elevated to the "fourteenth rank" at once; the latter, after two years' active service. Both grades are bound to serve the Government for a term of six years, in return for the gratuitous instruction which has been bestowed upon them. In order to secure admission into these schools, it is necessary to apply to the Governor-General; and the candidates will receive the expenses of their journey. One of the conditions of admission into the Kouldja school is a practical knowledge of Khirgiz.

I.3: "Scrap"

by Rudyard Kipling[3]

IN CONSIDERING THE PRESENT ASPECT OF THE Central Asian question, we may be apt to attach too much importance to the despatch of a Commission to delimit the boundary of Afghanistan. Although that may seem to the public the chief measure that has been taken, with a view to improving our position in Central Asia, it ought really to be subordinate to measures which, if less showy, are of far greater consequence. The danger is that, having arranged for the more striking portion of what should be our programme, we may neglect the rest; and this is specially probable when the British public is so taken up with a war in the Soudan, and with Fenian explosions in London. Among the most essential of those measures which ought to be carried on, *pari passu*, with the delimitation of the Afghan border, is the improvement of our diplomatic relations with Persia. At the time of the British occupation of Cabul, it was said that British influence was paramount at Teheran. No other foreign power came near us. Since then the situation is entirely changed. It is the Russian and not the English ambassador who enjoys the Shah's confidence; and besides Russian, we must now count also on German rivalry at the Shah's capital. One of the great drawbacks to the development of our influence in Persia, is the fact that British relations in that country are entirely under the control, not of the Indian Government, but of the English Foreign Office at home. Possibly in Lord Dufferin's time, we may see this arrangement changed. Speaking of Persian affairs, it may be noted that the Envoy Extraordinary and Minister Plenioptentiary from the Shah's court is still in St. Petersburg. We read in the Russian papers that Mirza Assidulla Khan, Vakil-ul-Mulk, had recently the honour of being presented to their Imperial Highnesses, the Grand Duchesses Elisabeth Feodorovna and Elisabeth Mavrikievna.

I.4: "Scrap"
Attributed to Rudyard Kipling

MR. CHARLES MARVIN IN HIS *Russians at Herat and Merve*, gives us some information about the available shipping on the Caspian. The Caucasus and Mercury Company have 19 steamers with an aggregate capacity of 20,000 tons. Messrs. Nobel Brothers have 12 large steel steamers, each big enough to transport 500 men. There are also a number of miscellaneous steamers; and it is reckoned that the shipping on the Caspian numbers over 1,500 vessels, of all classes. The passage from Baku to Krasnovodsk occupies 24 hours; so this section of the road to Herat would be easy enough. Say it would take three days to land 6,000 troops this side of the Caspian; which would be leaving an ample margin. From Krasnovodsk it is six easy marches to the railway; and it would take one day more to get to Kizil Arvat. Six trains could be run a day; and the first detachment would reach Kizil Arvat in about 8 days after embarking from Baku. The march from Kizil Arvat to Serrakhs would take three weeks; so in about a month's time the Russians could concentrate a formidable force at Serrakhs, from which place it is 13 marches to Herat. It was rumoured in London, at the end of last week, that Russian troops were being massed on the Afghan frontier; and it is easy to see, in the light of the facts we give above, that if orders were issued directly the news came of the fall of Khartoum, the end of the present month and the beginning of March would see the concentration of a force at Serrakhs quite large enough to meet any army the Afghans could put into the field.

THE RUSSIANS APPEAR TO HAVE QUITE THROWN off the mask. Mr. Cross, the Under Secretary of State for India, announced on Monday, that according to information received by Government, Russian troops have advanced as far as Pul-i-Khatun, and were reported to have also advanced to Sari Yari. We already knew that Pul-i-Khatun had been occupied; but had no certain intelligence regarding the simultaneous advance along the line of the Murghab. The immediate object of this latter move is to seize Panjdeh; whose governor, Yaluntush Khan, has already once succeeded in keeping the Russians out of this important fort, but may not be so lucky a second time. The Afghan garrison of Panjdeh is roughly estimated at 1,000 men with 2 guns. But it would be wrong to shut our eyes to the possibility that the present advance has for its ultimate object not only the occupation of Badgheis, but an attack on Herat itself. From Pul-i-Khatun it is six marches to Herat; and the distance from Sari Yari is, if anything, less. Even supposing Sir Peter Lumsden can throw himself into Herat, we are afraid the city could not hold out till the arrival of a force from India. Mr. Cross, indeed, says that Herat is garrisoned by a strong force of Afghans, and that any attempt on the part of Russia to occupy it would lead to serious consequences. But we may be pretty sure that Russian intrigues have been at work, and treachery is no more impossible in Herat, than it was in Khartoum.

[This report concludes with a map of the region between Herat and Merv].

IT IS NO USE DISGUSING THE FACT THAT unless the aspect of affairs on the north-west frontier of Afghanistan very quickly undergoes a change for the better, the Indian Government may be compelled, within the next few weeks, to once more occupy Kandahar, if not to march on Herat. The former measure would require a force of several thousand men. Merely to hold Kandahar would require three regiments of British Infantry, nine Native Infantry regiments, and six batteries of Artillery; besides a division to hold the line of communications. Possibly the question will have to be decided even before Lord Dufferin can meet the Ameer; for events of late have developed so rapidly, that the time seems imminent for action. We must not suppose that, if Russians really mean business, they will be content only to threaten us in the direction of Herat. We have noticed from time to time, signs of preparation for an advance on Balkh; and it is known too, that affairs seem very threatening towards Chitral. We may well look forward to what may happen in the next two month, with considerable uneasiness.

I.5: "Scraps"

by Rudyard Kipling

p. 1 c: "Scrap"

THE APPARENTLY ABSOLUTE POWER OF THE Russian authorities over their press is sufficiently shown by the fact that for two whole weeks, the *Novoe Vremya* has contained no mention of, or allusion whatever to the Central Asia question: while three weeks ago, every issue went more or less fully into the matter. The Dynamite explosions, the war in the Soudan, affairs in Lower Egypt, are all carefully followed by the journal which is silent on the — for Russia — all important topic of Afghanistan.

p. 1 c: "Scrap"

THE MAP WE PUBLISH IN ANOTHER COLUMN will enable the reader to clearly understand the meaning of Earl Granville's statement in the House of Commons. It will be seen that the Russians are pushing foward [sic] along two lines of advance. They have occupied Sari-Yari on the Murghab, and are within two miles of Panjdeh. They are also moving up the left or Persian bank of the Heri Rud; and have got as far as a place called Zulfikar, the position of which is plainly marked on our sketch map. The advance along the Murghab threatens to bring them in collision with the Afghan garrison of Panjdeh; which has been advised by Sir Peter Lumsden to resist any further encroachment. The British Government, moreover, who approve of Sir Peter Lumsden's action, have requested Russia to withdraw from Sari Yari. The advance from Serrakhs, though in Persian territory, is no less important. This route is fully described by M. Lessar. There are two roads between Pul-i-Khatun, which the Russians reached some weeks ago, and Zurabad. The shortest runs on the Persian side of the river over the mountains. The other crosses the river twice. Zurabad is described as a place of considerable importance, being occupied by some 2,000 kibitkas of the Salor Turcomans, who recently settled there with the permission of the Persian Government. From Zurabad to Dogarou, some 90 miles higher up the Heri Rud, there are three roads. The shortest is that *via* Zulfikar by which the Russians are advancing. It can scarcely be called a road, M. Lessar says; in some places there is not even a pathway or horse-track. Pack animals travel with great difficulty, and the construction of a road would involve great labour. There is plenty of water, however, and good pasturage for horses. The direct road from Serrakhs to Herat — which, *pace* the *Pioneer*, the Russians are *not* following — is on the east of the Heri Rud, and passes through Daukala and Adam Yolan. But geographically details, though essential to a correct comprehension of the telegrams, are scarcely so interesting as the political aspect of the situation. This may be summed up very shortly. If, in spite of the orders issued by the Russian Government to its officers, there is a collision with the Afghans, we are almost certain to be drawn into the quarrel; and a chance shot fired on the banks of the Murghab may entail the necessity of a British advance to Herat.

p. 3 c: "Scrap"

The *Moscow News* hears from the Caucasus that the new road into Central Asia from the Bay of Mertvi-Kultuck to Kungrad or, as it is called the "Tchernaieff route," for many reasons is acknowledged to be unsatisfactory, and all expenses incurred in its construction are thrown away. Last spring a party of recruits were dispatched from Astrakan by this road, and arrived at their destination without any hindrance. Beliavski a Colonel of the general staff, who led this party, on his return to St. Petersburg reported on this road to the Geographical Society, and the substance of his report tended to shew that the route presents essential advantages, in comparison, it is presumed, with the former roundabout way through Orengburg, which takes twice as long. As far as is known, on the strength of this first experience of the transport of recruits and reserves, it is proposed that a detachment of recruits detailed for the Central Asian army should this year also travel by this road. But the chief thing which speaks well for this route, is the traffic on it of Central Asian cotton going to European Russia. The Russian Transport Company concluded contracts for the carriage of a considerable portion of this cotton to Astrakan through Mertvi-Kultuk, but it has not once availed itself to the new road, yet is establishing its own flotilla specially for commercial transport from Astrakan to the Mertvi Kultuk Bay and back. The shallowness of the Bay which is noticed in the *Moscow News* is nothing new, and the authorities are now convinced that ships of light draught can traverse it without hindrance. As regards the new route from the port of Vaman, Airakhta on the Mertvi Kultuk Bay to Kungrad which is traversable by camels the construction of a cart road presents no difficulties, because there are no shifting sands, but the usual Steppe plain. Water is no less plentiful than on the other plains, but the chief advantage of the route is the possibility of junction with the Amu Darya, where steamers can ply freely.

We give below a sketch map of the proposed new route: —

[Here follows a map of the region between the Caspain and Aral Seas with an indication of the route from Vaman Airakhta to Kungrad. On page five of the same issue appears a detailed map of the region between Merv and Herat with inscriptions identifying the regions occupied by various tribes (Salors, Sarykhs, Alieli, Tekke and Jemsheds).]

I.6: The Rawal Pindi Camp
by Rudyard Kipling[4]

(*From our own Correspondent.*)
RAWAL PINDI, March 21

C'est magnifique mais ce n'est pas la guerre." The sterner elements of the programme are omitted; but Pindi is, none the less, fearfully and wonderfully martial. At present the Manchester Regiment, the 25th and the 19th Punjab Native Infantry, the Cheshire, the Seaforth Highlanders, the Royal Irish, the Carabiniers, the Highland Light Infantry, the 9th Lancers, the 4th Rifle Brigade, the Campbellpore elephant battery, P.3, L-A. R.H.A.: and several other are under canvass here; and the place literally swarms with wandering officers. Information, under these circumstances, paradoxical as it may appear, is hard to come by. Indeed, one Military authority (he was much overworked) has expressed an opinion that "no fellow on earth knew what regiments were or were not in the station." L.2. R.H.A., and the 1st Goorkhas come in tomorrow, Sunday; the 4th Goorkha's, the 14th B.L. and the 3rd B.C. on Monday; and the 19 B.L. and the L.3 R.A. on Tuesday. The quarters provided for their reception are not things to be desired after; for the mid-day sun is hot, and the Khannah plain, whence the crops have been but lately removed, parched and dusty. From the Viceroy's camp to the 2nd Infantry division is a cheerful trudge of some two miles or so, over roughly harrowed ground; and to the artillery camps a matter of half a mile further. From the Pindi Club, where men do most congregate, to the first mentioned camp is between four and five miles, for the most part over *kutcha* roads of exceeding roughness.

Three thousand carts of the Transport Department have been collected to minister to the wants of the vast assemblage that will find itself here a week hence; besides any number of camels, bullocks, mules and ponies. That the officers of the Transport Department are having a hard time of it goes without saying.

Traffic seems to have stagnated considerably about Jhelum, with the result that there are tents from sixteen districts still to come in, besides supplies and the like. A single line, such as our Indian Railways are most composed of, is utterly unequal to the strain of as much traffic as has been imposed upon it for the last few weeks. That the tents will eventually dribble in, there is no sort of doubt, but in the meantime the burden of each flying officer's song is, "Where are my (qualified) tents," with such variations as the most recent telegrams and chits may suggest. When you are under these indispensable articles, by the way, there is little comfort to be derived from their presence. "But for the honour of the thing (and thank Heaven

I'm a costing the Government a pretty penny) I'd as soon be in the open any day." These atrocious sentiments are quoted from the mouth of an exhausted gunner, who was mournfully riding his charger to water across Khanna plain. His words were the outcome of a thirsty and dispirited frame of mind, for the elephants of the Campbellpore battery were proceding [sic] him by a few hundred yards, and their shuffling feet pounded the hard clods to powder, and threw them up in dust, thick almost as the smoke of an engagement. If these things happen on an off day, what shall be done in the hour of review. Unless rain falls, I dare prophecy that the manoeuvres which are to impress Abdur Rahman Khan, and drive Thomas Atkins to despair a few days hence, will be eclipsed and blotted out from human gaze by the all pervading dust. But the dust is not allowed to interfere with "soldiering" in the barrack room sense of the word. A sultry journey through the artillery camp will prove this. All bright metal gun, gear as spotless as elbow grease can make them, limber and tackle symmetrically disposed by each gun and, once more, Thomas Atkins keeping watch and ward in the pitiless sun over these treasures.

As I write, 4–30, P.M., a trainful of A troop, 9th Lancers' horses has just arrived from Jhelum, and has been detrained. In something under ten minutes, about forty chargers and a ragged cohort of grasscutter's ponies have been conducted with "safety and dispatch,["] from horse box to platform and thence to their appointed lines. Properly speaking, the horse boxes are not horse boxes at all, but converted luggage vans; and one marvels what the tired and heated animals must have thought of their railway trip. One or two took no pains to conceal their displeasure; as a volley of resounding kicks on the iron skin of the vans abundantly testified. But the patience of officers and troopers never wearied: and above all the orders as to the loosening of certain ropes, and the adjustment of certain bars; could be heard the often repeated command "make much of 'em, men. Make much of 'em." And they were made much of, and soothed accordingly. The spectacle of half a dozen burly lancers, busily patting and caressing the noses of half a dozen big horses, is curious one, and somewhat touching withal. The troop have gone off to their station in the rear of the Viceroy's camp, where with the cavalry of the Guides, the L-A. Royal Horse Artillery and the Seaforth Highlanders, they will act as escort during His Excellency's stay here.

To-morrow morning it is expected that the Raja of Naba and his retinue arrive—no one seems to know exactly when. About thirty trucks of his luggage have already arrived, and to the intense joy of the Transport officials more are to come. Faridkhot came in last night and Pattiala's and Bahawulpore's troops are already in camp, though their owners do not arrive for some days. Visitors it seems are not encouraged to inspect the arrangements of the Viceroy's camp as they are not yet complete. Owners of carriages are laying themselves out to reap a rich harvest. As a favour it is possible to obtain a *ticca gharri*, for eight rupees *per diem*.

I.7: To Meet the Ameer
by Rudyard Kipling[5]

(*From our own Correspondent.*)
PESHAWAR, March 22

"We're making some of us, three hundred a month overtime. An' there's two hundred and eighty tracks still a waitin' in Jhelum yard." The overworked engine driver at Pindi last night, whose information I have just recorded, only spoke in truth; for the press of traffic between Jhelum and Pindi is heavy indeed. Seventeen long tailed trains, in addition to the ordinary ones, go up and down daily; and the tide is by no means at its full height. Commissariat siding, Viceroy's siding, main station siding, seemed to the eye, uneducated in railway matters, to be blocked and double blocked with goods waggons—and in this pleasing condition I left Pindi behind me. The Peshawar mail was only two and-a-half hours late—excellent timing under the circumstances. Peshawar's turn has not yet come, and compared with the bustle and excitement of the military camp to the south, the station is even torpid and sleepy. No one seems to know exactly when the Ameer will arrive; and the general opinion is, that he will be much later than was anticipated. So far as I can learn, he will be at Dhakka the day after to-morrow, the 25th; at Lundi Kotal on the 27th, and at Peshawur on the 28th. He will stay here, according to present arrangements, for two days—possibly more—possibly less; his own sweet will being, I believe, the sole guide. But never will an Asiatic ruler be received with more attention and care at Peshawur. A house has been taken for him opposite the Commissioner's, and this is now being fitted up, as trade catalogues say, "regardless of expense." Nine out of the ten rooms will be furnished with Bokhara carpets and divans *more Asiatico*—the tenth, as an English drawing room, in amber and gold. Furniture has been ordered for the purpose from Bombay; and the rooms are gorgeous with many hued chandeliers, five foot mirrors, and heavily framed oleographs. A French iron bedstead, with a wire woven mattress gilt knobs and unlimited silk counterpanes, will receive the royal limbs at night. (At Pindi, I fancy, they have provided him with mahogany hat racks and boot jacks. But this is a digression.) In the compound round the house are gathered a host of *durzies* busily stitching silk and satin hangings for the windows and divans; and house, compound and adjacent roads are thronged with labourers, *mallis*, and bullock carts full of carpets. Lest Abdur Rahman's eye should be offended by the barrenness of the land around his dwelling, several acres of cantonment land, leased out as kitchen gardens, have been levelled ploughed, turfed and planted with trees—so that in eight days the wilderness literally blossoms as the rose. What this may have cost, I am at present unable to say. Between one hundred and forty and one hundred and fifty ploughs were employed to level and break up the ground before a single sod of turf was laid; and three hundred and fifty labourers are now daily at work. The work of converting the ground was given over to Baboo Abdur Rahman, Muncipal [*sic*] overseer; and it may be mentioned here that the Peshawur Municipality has been most energetic in help of every kind.

From the Ameer's bungalow, the scene is a striking one. Here thirty or forty stalwart Afghans are hauling a stone roller up and down the paths with a magnificent disregard of the turf bordering; the same bordering is being slapped down, settled and watered at the rate of two yards in ten minutes by another gang. In the centre of the camp, a fountain, which is to throw a forty foot jet of water, is growing visibly beneath the builders' hands; while a police man lounges hard by, in case the brass nozzle and screw may prove too much for some *malli's* honesty. Everywhere the bhistis are watering the newly planted orange and rose bushes, or refreshing the sun dried turf sods: while through the screen of foliage round the Ameer's house, flash the amber purple and pale blue silks which the company of durzies are sewing together on the lawn. To descend, however, to more prosaic details. The Ameer's following must be fed and there has accordingly been provided for them the following bill of fare. Four thousand sheep; seven hundred and sixty maunds rice; two thousand seven hundred eggs; six hundred chickens (this may possibly account for the entire absence of "sudden-death" in the Peshawar dâk bungalow) twenty-five maunds of sugar; three hundred and thirty-three maunds of ghee; three hundred and seventy two maunds of *atta*, and lastly, for the proper disposal of this Homeric banquet, four thousand maunds of fire-wood and one hundred huge cooking pots. This last are now winking and shining in the sun, in the centre of the soldiers camp—on the principle presumably, that "coming events cast their shadows before." The Ameer brings with him no less than one hundred and fifty Sirdars from various portions of his territory; so that it will be seen, that the substantial list of food will not be at all too long. I subjoin the details of the Sirdars:—

From the Kizilbash tribe ..	25 Sirdars.
From the Logar tribe ..	25 Sirdars.
From the Kohistan tribe ..	25 Sirdars.
From the Gelzai tribe ..	25 Sirdars.
From the Warduk tribe ..	5 Sirdars.
From the Hazara tribe ..	5 Sirdars.
From the Guzni tribe ..	5 Sirdars.
From the Zurmat tribe ..	5 Sirdars.
From the Mungal tribe ..	5 Sirdars.
From the Hotuk tribe ..	5 Sirdars.
From the Toorkhee tribe ..	5 Sirdars.
From the Goorbund tribe ..	5 Sirdars.
From the Panjsheer tribe ..	5 Sirdars.
From the Nejrob tribe ..	5 Sirdars.

The full tale of the troops is still uncertain; as he will leave men behind at Dakka, and again at Peshawar to await his return from the Conference.

The Sirdars will be grouped in twenty six or thirty tents, close to the Ameer's house, over a space, two hundred yards long by two hundred and fifty broad. Beyond this space, again, will be the tents of the soldiery and followers; the area covered by both camps being close upon twenty acres. Kazi Abdul Kadir, who was for sixteen years in Shere Ali's service at Kabul, and for two years secret political agent to the British Government with Abdur Rahman, has, by virtue of his past experience, been deputed by the Commissioner to make such arrangements in the camp as would be likely to please an Afghan. The labour of arranging the decorations, superintending supplies and the like, rests with Messrs. Anderson and White-King, Assistant Commissioners. But unlike their bethren [sic] at Pindi, they will not be so desperately pushed for time and space; and the work here is proceeding quietly and without hurry. As I have said before, the Ameer's movements are as uncertain as could be expected, even from an oriental; and there will be ample time to set everything in order against his arrival.

I.8: To Meet the Ameer

by Rudyard Kipling[6]

(From our own Correspondent.)

PESHAWAR, March 25

The vagaries of a wayward child and an oriental potentate have one point in common, seeing the they are both difficult to describe and hard to bear with. Ameer Abdur Rahman Khan has certainly tried the patience of the officials here to the utmost. Yesterday we were assured that one hundred and fifty sirdars would accompany His Most Vacillating Highness to Peshawar. Last night's *dâk* brought in news that only fifty Khans, seventeen big guns and thirty three small bores—would come in. To-morrow these arrangements may be again upset, to the delight of all connected with the camp, and the confusion of all who wish to send accurate news therefrom. It has been announced, with some substratum of truth, that the Ameer had an objection to travelling by rail. To-day, at least, this objection has been overcome, and His Highness, if he remains in his present frame of mind, will be duly trained to Pindi, with all, or at least the greater part of his followers. The original intention, I believe, was to leave about one thousand of these at Peshawar to await his return northward.

He has announced his intention of staying here "a few days"—whether two or ten, nobody knows. It is not yet certain even when he will arrive in Peshawur; though the time has been narrowed to between Sunday and Monday next.

According to all Oriental notions of etiquette, the superior invariably arrives after the inferior; and the fact, that Abdur Rahman has kept the Viceroy of India cooling his heels for two or three days at Pindi, will redound considerably to the former's credit among his own people. Native public opinion in Peshawur, so far as it can be ascertained, sets strongly in this direction; and the situation has been tersely summarized by a refugee who has but little reason to bear the Ameer any good will. "He is a fool man—but he has made your Governor-General wait," and while the Governor-General and Peshawur waits, all the arrangements connected with the Ameer's arrival are being actively pushed on. Indeed, the camp is almost ready for his reception. I subjoin the following official programme which has just been issued:—

"His Highness Abdur-Rahman Khan, Ameer of Afghanistan and its Dependencies will reach Landi-Khana on the 29th instant, whence he will proceed to Rawalpindi to meet His Excellency the Viceroy.

2. The Commissioner of Peshawar, with a Military escort, will meet His Highness at Lundi-Khana [*sic*] and will conduct him through the Khyber Pass.

3. On arrival in British territory near Jamrud, His Highness will be met by General T. E. Gordon, C.B., C.S.I., Honorary Aid-de-Camp to the Viceroy, who has been deputed on the part of His Excellency the Viceroy to receive His Highness on the border. General Gordon will be accompanied by a further escort, and His Highness the Ameer will receive a salute of 21 guns.

4. On the approach of the Ameer to the Cantonment of Peshawar, the chief Civil and Military authorities, and such Native gentlemen as the Commissioner may invite, will proceed about two miles from the station boundary to meet His Highness. A troop of cavalry will be drawn up at the boundary of Cantonments, and a Guard of Honour, with band will receive him at his residence.

5. A salute of 21 guns will be fired on His Highness's arrival.

6. A Military and Police guard will, at the discretion of the Commissioner, be supplied for the protection of the Ameer's residence and camp.

7. A Ziafat of R. 21,000 will be presented to His Highness after his arrival at his residence.

8. A Native gentleman will be appointed by the Commissioner of Peshawar to act as Mehmandar to His Highness during his stay in Peshawar, and the District officer will take care that supplies &c., are liberally provided for His Highness and his retinue, who are all the guests of the British Government;

9. An escort and a Guard of Honour will be furnished on His Highness's departure for Rawalpindi, and a salute of 21 guns will again be fired.

10. The chief Civil and Military officers will be present at the station on His Highness's departure by rail.

11. At Nowshera and Attock, Guards of Honour will be present at the station, and receive His Highness as the train passes through.

12. If His Highness so desires, the train will stop for a convenient time, in order that the bridge may be inspected by the Ameer. In that case, suitable arrangements will be made by the Railway authorities, who will be duly informed of His Highness's wishes by the Commissioner of Peshawar."

General Gordon, with his escort — two squadrons of the 12th Bengal Cavalry — will meet the Ameer about three miles beyond Jumrud where 1-2 battery M-3, will fire a salute of 21 guns. The Ameer's carriage will be horsed by the Royal Artillery from Jumrud to Peshawur, where the other half battery will again salute him. The 2nd Dorsetshire Regiment will furnish a Guard of Honour of one hundred men and Band at the Ameer's residence during his stay here; and the 99th at Nowshera, where it is not likely that His Highness will stop long. This morning at 7-15 a grand brigade parade rehearsal took place. About four thousand troops were present — that is to say. M-3, Royal Artillery, the 12th Bengal Cavalry, the 4th King's Rifles, the 2nd Wilts, the 2nd Dorsets, the 8th and 9th Native Infantry, the 13th Native Infantry, the 30th Natvie [sic] Infantry and two companies of the Bengal Sappers and Miners. Those versed in such matters, and they are many in these parts, say that everything went off without a hitch.

But to revert to the preparations. Our worst enemies will admit that we are treating our visitor with open handed, not to say wildly lavish, hospitality. Here are a few instances. His Highness has a taste for sherbet, or to speak more accurately, sherbets. Accordingly — sherbets, orange, pine apple, sandal and one or two other sorts have been supplied by the hundred bottles—four hundred in all. To an Afghan, snuff is acceptable. Nine maunds of the pungent dust, in bottles, are stacked in the supply godown. His Highness is *exigeant* in the matter of tea; drinking only a particular sort compounded of two varieties. The civil authorities have telegraphed to Bombay for this, and from Bombay also will come daily, ten baskets of fruits— pummeloes, mangoes, bananas, &c. Moreover, twenty-five maunds of tobacco have been ordered for the collective Sidarial hookah; besides much spices and many condiments. The instructions in paragraph 8 of the official circular are being carried out sumptuously, as the thirty-eight *mohurrirs* and the cohort of check-takers and tallymen could testify, if they had time, for such matters. By the way, the haziness of the Ameer's arrangements leads to a hitch now and then. On the understanding that he would leave a thousand or so of his followers at Peshawur, instructions were sent to out-districts for sheep — many sheep, some thousands in fact.

But His Highness had decided to take horse and foot down with him; and the sheep will eventually be packed off to Pindi. The same want of *bundobust* must prevent any arrangements of the Sirdars in camp; and these gentlemen will, I fancy, be left to sort themselves as their own inclination directs. One hundred and one tents, including the durbar ones, have been erected for their accommodation, so that overcrowding will be impossible.

The Ameer's house is now almost completed, and, like the rest of the camp, has been arranged regardless of expense. The drawing room, as I have said, has been furnished in English style, with amber silk curtains, pale sage green and gold dado, many oleographs and some magnificent Persian carpets. All cup-boards and mihrabs are up-holstered in black and gold; the effect, if somewhat dazzling, being undeniably British, and much calculated to impress the occupant. The bed-room is bedizened with various coloured Chinese silks, Persian carpets and a superb purple velvet musnud, embroidered in gold, with *kinkab* cushions. On the French bedstead, lest His Highness should feel the cold, lie two *kinkob* quilts half an inch thick each, a Chinese silk rezai, and a foot thick purple velvet mattress, besides the proper furnishing of *kinkob* pillows, large and small. These last must be hideously uncomfortable to a thin-skinned sleeper —

but royalty has its obligations. A five foot plate glass mirror in the bedroom completes the list of furniture. The reception room, *duftar*, boudoir, it is called indifferently by all three names, is a blaze of rich carpets, silks and gold-embroidered *musnuds*, thick and board-like as so many elephant *jhools*. The verandah, whereof the pillars will be embedded in flowers, will be laid down with green baize; and a false ceiling of white frilled cloth has been fitted to every room. Outside the durbar tent in the camp, a tall flag

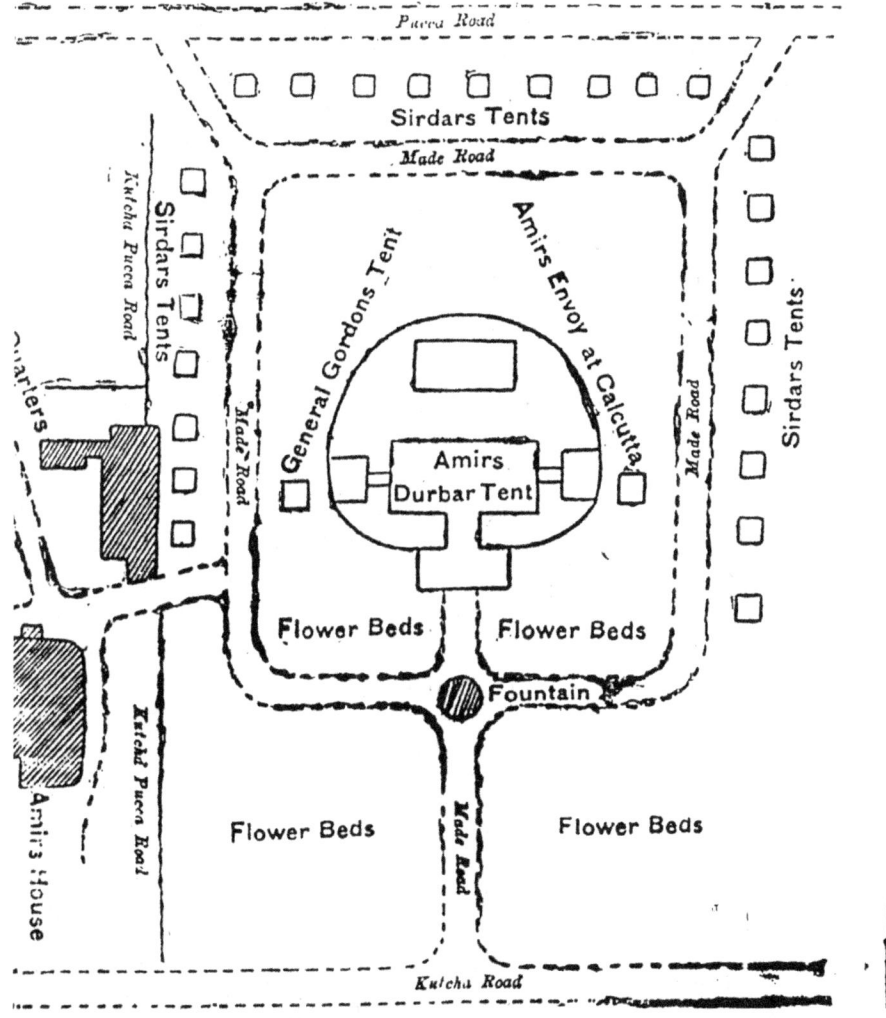

Ameer's Camp, Peshawur. Sketch by R. Kipling. *Civil and Military Gazette*, March 31, 1885.

staff has been erected; and this will carry the Ameer's flag when he arrives. The only difficulty is that His Highness has no distinctive flag, or for matter of that, sign, token or armourial bearings. The question will be solved, I believe, by hoisting yellow and red bunting, a non-committal policy, which no one will quarrel with. Twenty one *kinkob* bags have been prepared for the *ziafut*, which will be presented to him, in hard cash, on his arrival in Peshawur. Seven trays of three bags each, a bag holding one thousand rupees, will be borne in by liveried servitors, *Anglice* red chaprassis.

Later

As an instance of the utter futility of attempting to send accurate information, I may mention that fifteen hundred maunds of *bhusa* have just been sent to Ali Musjid, where it seems that the Ameer has resolved to stop for one day. If he should hold to his arrangements, this will land him in Peshawur about the 30th. Verily, the way of Easterns are strange and past finding out. Colonel Waterfield, with his escort, left Jumrood this morning at 9 o'clock for Lundi Kotal, where no one seems to know how long he may have to stay.

I.9: To Meet the Ameer

by Rudyard Kipling[7]

(From our Special Correspondent.)[8]

I send herewith a rough plan of the Ameer's camp as now arranged. To the north of the camp, and unrepresented in the sketch, lie the tents of the Ameer's army and their commissariat; while Colonel Waterfield's house is just across the road to the east. The tent to the left of the Ameer's Durbar tent, *may* be occupied by General Gordon; that to the right by the Ameer's envoy at Calcutta, who will meet the Ameer here. Round three sides of the squares run twenty-four tents for the Sirdars; the space to the west of the durbar tent being left free for followers *pals* and horses.

PESHAWUR, March 27.

At last the comedy seems to be approaching its end. Touched, doubtless, by the thought of Colonel Waterfield waiting in the rain at Lundi Kotal, our only Ameer has consented or condescended to put in an appearance at Peshawur on Monday next — the 30th instant. Add to this a couples of days' stay here, and our excellent Viceroy will only be detained for the better part of a week, amid the dust and confusion at Rawal Pindi. One of the Ameer's many intentions was to stop at Dhakka for a day, and to go on directly to Ali

Musjid. Accordingly, he halted for four and twenty hours at Gardi Sharkhani. He will spend the 28th, to-morrow, at Ali Musjid; the 29th at Jumrood; and arrives here the next day. This has endeared him to all concerned.

Two of his Sirdars arrived in camp this morning, and are at present enjoying their mid-day meal. Neither Kazi Kootb-ud-din nor Aga Hyder-Shah were pleasant to look upon, as they squatted on their charpoys and asked all manner of questions regarding the arrangements of the camp. The Aga was clad in a camel's hair garment adorned with gold stripes, and his lower limbs were encased in what looked remarkably like European trousers. He was short, thickset and of a florid countenance, laughing and talking a good deal. The Kazi, who lounged about picturesquely in a corduroy waistcoat with brass buttons and a pair of snowy white pyjamas, was meager, red-haired, and much lined and seamed with exposure. Both wore the Tartar cap of black Astrakhan fur, and both talked loudly and quickly. It is difficult to interview Kizilbashes satisfactorily, but, with the help of an interpreter, something — not much it is true — was extracted from Codlin and Short. A complimentary allusion to their silver mounted swords and belts — magnificent pieces of workmanship — was "cornered" promptly by the remark, that in *their* part of the world "arms were the ornament of a man. Nevertheless Peshawur was a great city." This somewhat inapposite codicil was thrown in, possibly to soothe the feelings of the degenerate white man who walks about with a cane. Did they know when the Ameer was coming? "The Amer was a *Badshah* and could come in when he liked." And with this significant answer, the conversation, as a novelist would put it, became general. Kazi and Aga plunged into the gulfs of their own strange speech, and the interview, if one may so style it, was at an end. The question as to the Ameer's arrival had been asked, I believe, previously by one of the officials in charge of the camp; and the answer then given had been almost identical with mine. Decidedly Abdur Rahman will come down imbued with a proper idea of his own importance.

The details of his Court, by the way, are rather interesting. I give below the list of his personal friends, councillors, attendants and the like, who will be most with him during his stay in Peshawur: — Mahomed Nahin; Nazar Safed Mahomed; Sirdar Nur Mahomed Khan; Mahomed Omar Khan; Mahomed Jan; Mir Mahomed Husein, ex–Mustafi; Jan Mahomed Khan, brother of the present Governor of Jellalabad; Kazi Shahb-ud-din, brother of Kazi Kootb-ud-din, at present in camp; Mahomed Khan, Chessplayer to His Highness, and a prophet of considerable honour in his own country; Dilawer Khan; Shere, Afghan Khan; Kurban Ali Khan, whose duty it is to attend to Ameer's Samorar [*sic*] among other things; Syed Ahmed Khan; Jamma Khan; Mahomed Akbar

Khan, water bearer (perhaps the only equivalent in the English language to this is the title of Groom of the Chamber[)], Mahomed Sirwa Khan, Chamberlain; Mahomed Alum Khan, door keeper; Golam Hyder, Commander-in-Chief; Mahomed Azim — the deaf and dumb painter of the Ameer's court; Ahmed Jan Khan, Councillor; Mirza Abdul Rashid, Doctor; Jan Mahomed Khan, Court tailor; Faizulla Khan, personal servant; and Mahomed Nubbi Khan, writer to the Ameer.

These the Ameer had with him at Dhakka; and unless he has made some sudden and unexpected change there, these will accompany him to this station. Everything, as I have already told you, is prepared for his reception, down to a cretonne bordered teapoy in the drawing room of the bungalow — and we can henceforward only possess our souls in patience, until the worthy gentleman actually arrives. Lieutenant Leigh, of the 60th Rifles, has gone on to Lundi Kotal with the Government carrier pigeons; but these useful birds have so far brought us no certain news about anything in particular. When Abdur Rahman has actually set foot within the limits of Peshawur, we may be certain of his arrival. Till then anything that may be written, rumoured or telegraphed, is of less than no value.

The unsettled state of the weather — among other things — is supposed to have delayed our illustrious visitor. For the past four days the sky has been gloomy and overcast, with heavy thunder and rain at night. At three this afternoon, a hailstorm broke, which would have stripped the trees of Peshawur had it lasted. Luckily it was all over in five minutes, after having whitened the ground with hailstones of from half an inch to one and a half inch in diameter. Some took more than ten minutes to melt.

I.10: The City of Evil Countenances
by Rudyard Kipling[9]

PESHAWAR, March, 28

Rolling thunder among the Khyber hills all day long; the day itself wasted in spiteful attempts to rain, varied by a shower of hail which clears the crowded streets as a mitrailleuse would do. Evening seems to have brought down the rain in earnest. A steady drizzling downpour blanketing the Fort, and the crops beyond, filling the roads with glutinous mire and the heart of man with despair. A downpour that shows little signs of ceasing throughout the night, neither the charms of an annotated Greek testament with strictly secular remarks written in the margin; or an odd number of the Calcutta Review with every other page torn out; or even

Eugene Sue's fantastic *Le Morne-au-Diable* (which must surely have crept into the dâk bungalow by mistake) can counteract the depressing effect of the evening. In the Amir's camp — swept and garnished for his reception — the *soorkee* of the paths has been converted into red gruel, and is discoloring the newly laid sods, the fountain basin overflowed a couple of hours ago and is now adding its share to the general slop. From the supply godown a puff of the evening breeze brings the scent of fruits and spices — or rotten pummeloes and curry powder, as romance or reality are uppermost in one's mind — and the mute eloquence of over-ripe bananas, tells us that the days are long and the life of Bombay fruit short. The last *mohurrir* has shaken the rain from his garments, and save for bottles of sherbet and certain gigantic *Samovars*, the godowns are deserted. The two Khans, fore-runners of the Ameer's army of temporary occupation, have gone to bed like wise men; their horses protesting outside against the vileness of the weather. Nor does the police sentry on guard appreciate it one whit more; but luckier than the horses, he has consolations denied to brute beats. As you watch him, standing shivering in the wet, the neck of his bayonet smokes furiously. Every now and then he takes the weapon between his teeth, and a few steps to leeward will tell you that native ingenuity has circumvented the *Sirkar's* ordinances against smoking on duty; and the regulation foot of cold steel is for the nonce acting as a *hookah*. The lower end of the socket has been deftly closed with a stone, above this has been jammed a pledget of fresh barley stalks, and over all the tobacco. The sentry applies his lips to the aperture by the locking ring. The cool stalks, in a manner, filter the smoke and the *hookah* is in full blast. Should an inconvenient officer arrive on the scene, the smoker stands to attention; covering his improvised pipe with the palm of one horny hand, and detection, unless the officer be blessed with a specially keen nose, is almost impossible. A smoke under these circumstances would scarcely be appreciated by a European; but the sentry appears to enjoy his stolen whiffs immensely, and is quite ready to explain how it's done.

Meanwhile, the City of Evil Countenances has become shrouded from sight by the incessant rain, and a journey to the Edwardes Gate means a mile-long struggle through soft oozy slim — to be undertaken only as a counter-irritant against the growing gloom of the evening. The road to the city is thronged with foot and horse passengers of all kinds; all utterly heedless of the downpour, and all, so it seems, shouting to a friend half a mile away. Strings of shaggy-haired camels, nearly as repulsive as their masters, jostle mule carts, ekkas and restive horses fretting under the punishment of their spiked bits. These ships of the desert can make but little headway through the ooze, blundering and swaying from side to side like rudderless galleons. Their long hair throws off the water as completely as a mackintosh, but the loads of bhoosa and green barley soak up a much as they can to the discomfort of the dripping driver atop. A camel's *esprit de corps* is an all-pervading essence which rain intensifies. His arrival is heralded on the wings of the wind, and his presence remembered long after he has passed away. Indeed, so powerful is the rank stench, that those who know least of him, maintain that it is the most offensive in the world. To this slander the unwashed camel driver gives the lie direct, and the Afghan no less. The healing rain that makes the onion to sprout and (six weeks later on) the white ant to suicide himself in the lamp flame, has no charms for these men, but rather acts on them as the sun on the rose. The evening city road is witness to the fact.

Under the shadow of the Edwardes Gate, the crowd thickens, and the continuous tide of humanity is broken up into eddies, bays and cross-currents. The waning light is darkened here by the houses, and though it is barely six o'clock they have begun to light the shop *chirags*. Then you shall see a scene worthy almost of a place in the *Inferno*, for the city is unlovely even beneath bright sunshine, and when set off with heavy slime under foot, dark skies and rolling thunder overhead, and driving scotch mist, everywhere repulsive to every sense.

Under the shop lights in front of the sweet-meat and *ghee* seller's booths, the press and din of words is thickest. Faces of dogs, swine, weazles [*sic*] and goats, all the more hideous for being set on human bodies, and lighted with human intelligence, gather in front of the ring of lamp-light, where they may be studied for half an hour at a stretch. Pathans, Afreedees, Logas, Kohistanis, Turkomans, and a hundred other varieties of the turbulent Afghan race, are gathered in the vast human menagerie between the Gate and the Ghor Khutri. As an Englishman passes, they will turn to scowl upon him, and in many cases to spit fluently on the ground after he has passed. One burly big-paunched ruffian, with shaven head and a neck creased and dimpled with rolls of fat, is specially zealous in this religious rite — contenting himself with no perfunctory performance, but with a wholesouled expectoration, that must be as refreshing to his comrades, as it is disgusting to the European, sir. As an unconscious compensation to the outraged Kafir, he poses himself magnificently on — degrading instance of civilization — a culvert, turning a very bull's head and throat to the light. Dirty *poshteen* melts into the back-ground of driving rain; neck, shoulders, and fiery red beard standing out in starting relief. But he is only one of twenty thousand. The main road teems with magnificent scoundrels and handsome ruffians; all giving the on-looker the impression of wild beasts held back from murder and violence, and chafing against the restraint. The impression *may* be wrong; and the Peshawari, the most innocent creature on earth, in spite of History's verdict against him; but not unless thin lips, scowling brows, deep set vulpine eyes and lineaments stamped with every brute passion known to man, go for nothing. Women of course are invisible in the streets, but here and there instead, some name-less and shameless boy in gril's [sic] clothes with long braided hair and jewellery — the center of a crowd of admirers. As night draws on, the throng of ignoble heads becomes denser and the reek of unwashed humanity steaming under the rain, ranker and more insupportable. A free fight takes place in a side gully and terminates, after a little turban pulling and hair snatching, in a gale of guttural abuse and the presence of a policeman, not as an arbitrator in the fight, but merely a dignified spectator of the *rixe*. What might have happened in other and happier lands across the border it is impossible to say. Here the wild beasts seem to obey their keepers to admiration; and after all they are well looked after; the Sirkar's benevolence permitting none to die by sword, bullet or epidemic disease, if it can possibly be avoided. The ever circulating night patrols, and the ubiquitous policemen — (Policemen are really ubiquitous in Peshawar) [–] bear witness to Government forethought in the first particular; the magnificent drain and water main which runs through the main streets of the city, are equally eloquent as regards the second. A lakh and a few odd thousands of rupees have been spent — much to the Secretary of State's disgust on economical grounds — in order that the city of evil countenances might, if it willed, wash and be clean; or at least refrain from drawing cholera from the roadside and typhus from the standing pool. Reservoired, watered, drained and policed in the face of all opposition, and for the benefit of a proverbially thankless race, Peshawur as it now stands, is a city that could only have grown up under English care and English rule. Holy Russia would have tamed the wild beats as effectually perhaps. They would have died largely under the process. France would have alternated barracks with cafes; lyceums of public instruction, and descents into the street of armed marauders. But it is easy to wax cheaply patriotic on this theme, as easy as it is to draw entirely erroneous conclusions from an evening stroll through one of the most wonderful cities on earth. The rancorous expectoration of our red-bearded friend — still on the culvert — as he performs his devoirs for the fourth time in the track of the on-going kafir may mean anything you please. A wanderer from the hills takes this opportunity of expressing his contempt for a whole nation — not even the long suffering missionary could credit him with influenza: or again neither security to life and goods, law, order, discipline, or the best blood of England wasted on their care, reconciles the calibans of the city of evil countenances to the white stranger within their gates. And to-morrow we do honour to the ruler of Afghanistan and its dependencies at Jumrood.

I.11: To Meet the Ameer
by Rudyard Kipling[10]

(*From our Special Correspondent.*)

JAMRUD, March 29th Day-break

Circumstances over which the local officials seem to have no control, prevent a journey to Ali Musjid. A modest *ticca gharri*, however, will convey you as far as the historic walls of Jamrud, and from thence, to the mouth of the Khyber is but two or three miles. His Highness the Ameer of Afghanistan is due this morning — no one seems to know at what hour. Meantime, the top of fort Jamrud is an elevated and decidedly airy point of vantage. The Four Winds of Heaven are fighting it out between them on the bastions, and each gust brings with it a douche of fine rain. The Khattak and Swat hills are swathed in mist. Only towards the north west and the Khyber, is the air comparatively clear. Along the undulating Khyber road runs a scattered line of the Ameer's camp followers, who have been dropping in all night and through a great portion of the previous day. Interminable files of camels, yaboos, coolies, and loud-voiced donkeys and flocks of sheep, stretch from the camp to the south of Jamrud, into the very jaws of the Pass and in the grey light of dawn, these resemble nothing so much as lines of black ants on a foraging expedition. Three hundred horses of the 12th B. C. are dozing in the enclosures below the walls of the fort.

Thursday's hail storm, by the way, was felt very severely at Jamrud, as long as it lasted; and, but for the fact of the beasts being picketed within brick walls, they would inevitably have stampeded over the face to the country. As it was, several of them broke loose under the stinging hail.

Half of the M.-3, R. H. A., lies under the northwest bastions, and as yet the only sign of life there, is the stamping of half awakened horses and an occasional squabble amid the drowsy syces. But it is impossible to slumber long in the teeth of the camp follower's [*sic*] chatter; and the babel of tongues that surges round the walls on every side.

7 o'clock. — The daylight has brought down the Scotch mist more densely than ever; and never did the Afghan hills look more rugged and forbidding than now. Jamrud has awakened the center of a little city, the population of which is increasing minute by minute, still no news of the Ameer. He has left Ali Musjid. He hasn't. The rain has delayed him. He will be here in the evening. He will be in in half an hour. Private Thomas Atkins, hard at work in the little pigeon box of a telegraph office, at the very top of the Fort, could probably tell us how much truth or fiction lies in these rumours, but his hands are fully occupied in the most literal sense of the word. There is only one decrepid "ticker" in the Fort, and this has to bear the burden of the day's telegraphic intelligence. Sister Anne's employment in the time of Blue Beard had at least one advantage over this morning's waiting and watching. There is no reason to believe that her toes were numbed and her teeth chattering in the keen morning air. Otherwise, her vigil was exactly the same. "Sister Anne, Sister Anne, do you see any one coming." Only a flock of sheep, a rush of obstreperous yaboos or a phalanx of slow-paced camels, working their way across the stony road. The troop horses below are hard at work on their morning's meal; "the wind is moaning in turret and tree," at least, it would if there were a tree available, and the thin rain penetrates to one's marrow. A descent into the maelstrom of camp followers near the police barracks, keeps the blood from stagnation, and reveals incidentally some curiosities of character. Undoubtedly, our friends beyond the border, though their *pals* are as filthy as themselves, and their horses, ungroomed since the day they were born, have a very good notion of camp pitching, and accomplish their work with not more than deafening clamour. Perhaps the rain has quenched them. A young Afreedee of thirteen is keeping watch and ward over a bunch of picketed yaboos. The lad's garments are filthy, but he smiles and swaggers affably; displaying at his belt a Colt's revolver. Subsequent investigation shows that it is loaded and as clean as oil and rag can make. It belonged to his father who departed this life a year ago, the embryo cateran does not say how, and the weapon was handed on to the son.

"Have you ever done anything with it?" The question is a somewhat brutal one, but the Afreedee regards it evidently in the light of a compliment. "Not *yet*, Sahib, but please God, I shall some day," he replies, with a cherubic smile, and swaggers over to his horses once more. A cheerful race these Afreedees.

8 o'clock.— Alarums and excursions. A dozen sowars and a European officer — all very wet — have come in from somewhere out of the mist and several bugles have sounded. The troop horses are being saddled, and the gloom is lifting a little. Tommy Atkins ticks away imperturbably in his dove cote; and the stream of camp followers thickens. More bugles; more camp followers and a gruelly streak of sunshine for an instant through the clouds. The hills riven into gorge and cavern, are chequered with light and shadow as though to do honour to the great man's arrival. But the great man makes no sign; and the clouds shut down gloomier than before. One by one the 12th Bengal Cavalry, prance out of the courtyard on to the maidan, and form in three Squadrons, bay, grey and chestnut, preparatory to moving out to meet the Ameer. All the men are shrouded in top coats and there is no colour visible. The artillery on the other side of the Fort, clatter out also into the open, and the advance begins. First the bay squadron; then the three guns, then the grey and chestnut horses. About 500 hundred yards from the fort, on the Khyber road, they pause. Then the artillery takes up its position on the right of the road, a few hundred yards away from it, and the cavalry lines the road on the same side, two deep; then they halt, and the temporarily interrupted stream of followers sweeps on. These latter are now moving by at their best pace. The Ameer must really be here before long. The three guns are unlimbered in readiness for the salute, and all Jumrood is a waiting. From the signalling tower — in spite of the life and babble below — the impression is one of intense loneliness and desolation. On every side the thriftless unfriendly land sweeps away to the foot of the hills as bare as the desert of Sahara. In the far distance, for the intervening veil of mist puts them miles and miles away, lies the belt of green crops that encircle Peshawar, and mark practically the limits of British rule. The stony ground runs up to the limit of the crops, and is doted [sic] here and there with the ominous heaps of stones, where a man has been done to death. Peshawur is invisible, and the frowning hills bound the view on three sides of the horizon. Only around Jumrood is there any sign of life, and the gathering of men here marks more strongly the silence of the hills and plains. The hour passes away, Tommy Atkins is drenched and doubtless grumbling as he waits by the guns; and once more the clouds lift. A solid column of men appears over the crest of a rise close to the mouth of the Pass. Without a doubt there are at last the Ameer's troops, and the Ameer with them.

10 o'clock. — The column has disappeared in a hollow, rises again and approaches rapidly. There is a stir among the gunners, and in a few moments a puff of white smoke tells the watchers on the signaling tower of the fort, that their watching is nearly at an end. One-two-three — twenty-one guns — the smoke hanging heavily at the mouth of the cannon; and by the time the last welcome is spoke, Abdur Rahman Khan, ruler of Afghanistan and its dependencies, has fairly set foot on British ground. For past ten minutes the field glass has shown him merely as a blot of blue on a small horse. A closer inspection is necessary, and this involves a rush through some two hundred Afghans, who are hastening forward to line the road. Colonel Waterfield and General Gordon are riding on the right of a handsome black-bearded man, in a blue *choga* embroidered with gold. The pace quickens as they near the camp, and the Ameer has passed. For those who are curious in such matters, it shall be recorded that he was smiling affably at the time, and looked about him on both sides of the way, with every appearance of interest. Behind him follow his cavalry, wild picturesque men on wild horses—to whose appearance it is impossible to do justice, while writing on the spot. No two sets of accoutrements are alike, *cela sa* [sic] *sans dire*, if I except the regiment of Usbeg Lancers. These resemble Cossacks in every particular, down to the high-set saddle and the shaggy circular cap of hair. One or two of the officers carry the short-handled double thronged Tailor whips, and all, without exception, ride splendidly. To the Usbegs, succeeds a nondescript following of horsemen, some with grey felt jockey caps and string bridles, some with fur trimmed smoking caps and muzzle-loading carbines. Their horses are all small fiery little rats, and under the circumstances keep line remarkably well. The riders represent every shade of Turanian and Mongolian blood, high cheek bones, oblique eyes, shaggy hair, flat noses, cavernous mouths.

Their speech, of course, is utterly unintelligible, and they are all talking and staring about them. One or two have calmly pulled up their horses to look at the Englishman by the wayside. They point like children, and their remarks would, no doubt, be immensely amusing to listen to. The men are all cantering, and it is difficult to give any idea of their *outre* and ferocious experience. Somehow, the back ground of dark hills, the sullen sky and the rain seems to set them off to perfection.

The Ameer's infantry preceded him. There were two regiments of these, I fancy. As I write, they are taking up their position on the encamping ground, and look as cut-throat a crew as one would wish to see. One regiment is dressed in white duck trousers, European boots, and a tunic of blue with red trimmings. They look in the distance like engine drivers out of employment. All are armed with Martini-Henry rifles, and march in two Indian files, each the width of the road apart from the other. The second regiment (both by the way are Duranis and are composed of picked men) wears black "understandings"; but in every other respect appears to be exactly like the first. Their notions of sentry-go are original and elastic; and many of them have their Martinis protected from the rain by dirty bits of cloth.

The screw—gun battery, six guns, which immediately preceded the Ameer, is the most workmanlike section of the force. It has already camped, set out the guns, quarter guard etc, *secundem artem*. The carriages are painted dull green, and the various parts of the limber and gear are carried by horses. Abdur Rahman, who limps slightly, now that he is off his horse, has just gone into his tent; a large blue and white *striped shamiana*, in the centre of the camp. Colonel Waterfield and General Gordon are doing the honours thereof, and Golam Hyder, Commander-in-Chief, is having his boots cleaned, preparatory to following them. Golam Hyder's uniform is a mass of gold braid — more gorgeous even than some Civilian uniforms — and he wears the Tartar cap of grey Astakhan fur. His saddle cloth is a blaze of gold and velvet, with monograms and devices, *ad lib*, on its surface. The Ameer, it seems, has been suffering severely from gout — hence the delay in his arrival — and is still very lame. Usbegs, Duranis, tag rag and bobtail, are settling themselves as comfortably as they can in camp. The Ameer has been left to himself, and the scene closes amid more rain, a wild confusion of horses, tent ropes, camels, guns, and a far-reaching tumult of strange tongues. The following must be close upon three thousand.

LATER — March 29th, 6 o'clock

No less than four contradictory telegrams from Jumrood, in the course of the afternoon. "First he would, and then he wouldn't: then he said he really couldn't"–and to this view of the case Abdur Rahman has finally stuck. If the spirit moves him, he may up-sticks and come into Peshawur in the middle of the night, but it is to be hoped that the blessed rain will keep him to some decent hour, and that he will arrive here to-morrow about seven. How long he will stay here is quite another matter.

I.12: To Meet the Ameer

by Rudyard Kipling[11]

(*From our Special Correspondent.*)

PESHAWUR, March 30.

As the Ameer's entry into British territory at Jamrud was marred by the rain, so to-day's spectacle in Peshawur has been utterly ruined from the same cause. It rained steadily throughout the night, and day broke once more in pouring rain, as chilling and depressing a day as could be imagined. Before day light, the regimental bands were hard at work, and by six o-clock the troops had lined the road from the head of the Jamrud road to the Camp and Ameer's bungalow — a distance of two miles, six hundred yards. Four thousand troops, in all, were turned out — the Wiltshire Regiment; two companies of the Bengal Sappers and Miners; the 8th, and 13th Native Infantry, the 60th rifles; the 9th and 30th Punjab Native Infantry and Dorsetshire Regiment. The British Regiments were mustered in review order, without protection of any kind; the native troops had wisely donned their over coats, and were thus, in some measure, kept dry.

Under foot the yellow mud was a couple of inches deep, and by the time that the men were in position, had been churned up to the consistency of water gruel. What the result of this happy day will be, Peshawur hospitals and the Doctors may soon ascertain. By seven o'clock all the Civil and Military officials were assembled under the partial shelter of a few trees at the head of the Jumrud road. General Dandridge, Commanding the Peshawur district, Major Dunnage, Commanding the Artillery in the District, Major Godwyn, Major Tidy, Officiating Deputy Quarter-Master General, Captain McCausland, Cantonment Magistrate, Lieutenant Bond, Executive Commissariat Officer; Mr. Tucker, Deputy Commissioner, Mr. Benton, Sessions Judge, Messrs. Walker, White-King and Anderson, Assistant Commissioners, Dr. Coates Civil Surgeon of Peshawur, Captain Nixon, D.S.P. Peshawur, Lieutenants Close and Palin A.D.S.P.'s and Mr. Hastings, in charge of police in the Hazara district. These and one or two others, mounted and unmounted, had to wile away the time as best they could, for two hours: from seven o'clock, that is to say till nine. If any thing expressive of warmth could be applied to the day's proceedings, I should say that they were merely a *rechauffee* of the weary vigil at Jumrud on Sunday morning. Nothing but the long wet road to look at, the string of dripping camp followers to criticize, and Private Thomas Atkins, turning from red to plum colour, to pity. He was the worst off of all, as he waited and — small blame to him — swore beneath his breath. The Ameer had made a move from Jumrood at 6–40, but was troubled by the gout, and was halting every half mile or so *en route*, partly on this account, and partly to allow the Camp followers to get well ahead of him. There was nothing for it but to wait and smoke. An officer, in full dress, with a cheroot between his lips is a fine sight, especially when he carries an open umbrella. No one, however, can be dignified under water, whatever his bearing, where fire is concerned. So, when Military, Politicals and Police clustered together like drenched barndoor fowl, beneath whatever shelter the road side trees afforded, the ridiculousness of the situation was lost in the sense of its keen discomfort. A well warmed spectator, in a balcony, could have made a jest of the proceedings from the beginning to end, excepting always the patience of the troops.

An hour and a half of desultory conversation, and the dreary splashing of restive horses, was brought to an end by the sight of the 12th Bengal Cavalry in the distance. Then the knot of officials moved about two hundred yards down the Jumrood road, and took position in the open. The 12th came by at a walk, splashed with mud from head to foot, shrouded in their cloaks, and looking, one and all, supremely uncomfortable. Then followed some twenty led horses, the Ameer's screw battery, infantry, cavalry, our artillery and finally the Ameer himself, with Colonel Waterfield and General Gordon, in a barouche drawn by Artillery horses.

His Highness wore a cap of grey Astrakhan fur, an orange coloured choga and side-toed Russian boots. His conveyance halted for a moment or so in front of the group of officers, civil and military, and compliments were duly interchanged. A rain-wept road, however, is not the best place for speeches and after a short detention only, the party moved on. Behind the Ameer's carriage were half-a-dozen other barouches filled with notables, and behind the barouches again, a regiment, horde or swarm of cavalry, horsemen, and a few camp followers.

The number of the Ameer's escort is variously reported at between six hundred and one thousand men. I fancy that the lower estimate is more probably the correct one. And while I am on this subject I feel that I owe some sort of reparation to these retainers whom I described yesterday, as "tag-rag and bobtail." Closer inspection shows, that they are by no means as bad as they look, and military opinion here is, that with European officering, they would make excellent soldiers. This refers more particularly to the Usbeg lancers, and the infantry regiments. The latter had all their Martinis carefully protected from the rain, in cloth covers, and nearly all the privates carried brown cane walking sticks in their right hands. A ribald bystander suggested, that they looked like a multitude of anglers, returned from an unsuccessful day's fishing. The high knee boots, and white trousers, added to this impression. Boots were worn as *articles de luxe*, and put on in curious styles. One or two had the foot at right angles to the calf; contenting themselves with pulling their feet half way down only, Others had wrenched the heels sideways: and the wonder was, how on earth they had struggled in from Cabul, in such outlandish gear.

Nearly every pony in the screw gun battery was as lame as a tree; the result, it is supposed, of severe marches. The lancers were by far the best mounted; their horses being fully equal, in many instances, to those of our own native Cavalry; but the distressing want of uniformity in saddle cloths, bridles and accoutrements generally, somewhat spoiled their appearance. There were 2000 baggage ponies. To return, however, to the Ameer: he was conducted slowly along the mall to his camp; and had ample opportunity to inspect the line of soldiers on either side. It is not recorded what he thought of them. The British regiments were throughout composed of small men of indifferent physique. This was specially noticeable in the case of the 60th rifles, perhaps their sombre uniform made them look smaller than they really were; but the contrast in point of age and stature, between this regiment and the two native ones, which succeeded it, was striking. On arrival at the camp, one half M.-3 battery fired the regulation salute from their own parade ground hard by. The Amir descended from his carriages, and accompanied by the Commissioner &c., went for a few moments into the Durbar tent in the centre of the ground.

An adjournment was next made to the bungalow, His Highness and the officials strolling leisurely through the rain. At the bungalow the *ziafut* of Rs. 21,000 was presented, besides several other valuable presents, and a sort of informal Durbar was held, lasting for a quarter of an hour or so. The Amir was wearied with his day's journey, and the gout in his left knee still troubled him. So the officials retired in all due form, and His Highness was left to himself. Besides gout he is afflicted with toothache, and Mr. T. Miller, the Surgeon dentist of Calcutta, has been summoned to supply him with new teeth, and whatever else may be necessary. Mr. Miller interviewed the Amir immediately on the departure of the other officials, and as there is a good deal to be done, and had another interview with him this afternoon. Thanks to the heavy rain, parades here will be utterly impracticable for the next two days at the least and all connected with him are doing their utmost to get him down to Rawalpindi to-night. As far as the matter can be settled, with so unsatisfactory a charge. Abdur Rahman will leave Peshawur by a special train at 11 o'clock to-night. Already seven hundred and fifty horses and ponies are being dispatched Pindi wards by two special trains; a third for "humans" starts at 6–10; and the ordinary mail at 9–20. Just now the scene at the station beggars description. Cabulis don't understand trains any more than their horses. Both men and beasts are slithering and scrambling about the platform in the mud and rain. They have been at it more or less, since one o'clock, and goodness only knows when they can get away. In the Ameer's camp the fountain is still hard at work, and the place generally is one vast swamp. Chaprassis are staggering through the quage with *dallis* of choleraic pummeloes, shaddocks and mixed fruits, besides bread and meats of many and varied kinds. Every tent seems to be bubbling over with Khans, Sirdars and their retainers, and the notice that the public are prohibited from entering that portion of the camp, set apart for the Ameer and his followers is scarcely necessary. Never were tents pitched and filled under more depressing circumstances. The rain has descended steadily throughout the whole day. As night approaches it falls the faster. The Ameer will be honked out of the comfortable divans, away from the pipe of contemplation, and worst of all, just after the evening meal, about nine o'clock. Then he will be compelled to discourse affably, until the special train is ready, and then, perhaps, we may let him go to sleep. (Fancy turning out into the wet, with twinges of gout in your left knee and an amiable smile on your countenance, at such an unearthly hour of the night.) He has kept Lord Dufferin waiting, it is true, but one is inclined to pity him none the less. Attendants have been shampooing the injured limb all this afternoon; and certain Khans, Nawabs and native big-guns have been calling on him. They were received affably, and it may be interesting to learn that some of them drank afternoon tea, standing up always in the presence of the Ameer, who was more plainly clad than any of his followers, and wore only a couple of small gold chains and a few rings as ornament. His walking stick had jewels set in at the top, and on this stick he leant himself whenever he moved. His laugh is a open and hearty one, and he is easily moved to mirth, for an oriental that is. His is destinctly [sic] of a full habit, and possesses a pair of keen dark eyes, which enliven an otherwise flaccid and expressionless visage.

N.B.— The decorative fountains pouted vehemently in the face of the downpour.

PESHAWAR, March 30.

Monday night, half past eight; pitch dark and the platform of the Peshawar station, covered with the Ameer's horses, which are at the present moment entraining for Pindi. Unless you are actually on the platform, in serious danger of your life from flying heels and panic stricken horses, you will not appreciate the beauty of the situation. His Highness really starts to-night at eleven o'clock, more or less exactly, and before that hour strikes, seven hundred and fifty horses are to be cleared away somehow. Four detachments have already gone off. This is the fifth and, I fancy, the last. The Assistant Commissioner is, apparently, the only man who can interpret the *Pushtu* of the yelling crowd, to the natives around. Neither Cabulies nor horses have seen a train before; but the former are adapting themselves wonderfully to circumstances. In the first place they are absolutely fearless; plunging head first, into the squealing, kicking truckloads of yaboos, without a moment's hesitation. Hyder Ali, Commander in Chief of the Ameer's army, has recognized the gravity of the situation and — think of Cs. in C. all over creation — is working like a navy [sic] in the midst of his men. Three horses are down in a wagon of eight, and from the appalling noise inside, seem to be kicking each other to pieces. Hyder Ali, guided by a single lantern, dives into the tumult, directs, superintends, harangues and — from the tone of his voice — swears till the wretched beasts are set right. If one restive grey stallion could speak, he might even tell us how the Commander-in-Chief backed him, protesting and snorting, up the slippery gangway and into his fellows once more. What Mr. Anderson's work through this dripping afternoon and evening have been, that unfortunate officer only knows. It is admitted, of course, that the

Punjab Commission understand "a little bit of everything"; but to turn one of that distinguished body, for the nonce, into a Trooper-cum-Traffic Superintendent-guard-cum-syce civilian, *does* seem rather hard. However, the horses *must* be got away, and the 9–20 mail train to Pindi, starts as near her proper time as may be.

In the centre of the platform stands a huge baggage cart drawn by two bullocks; and round this the tumult rages unceasingly.

"Duserah gorah lao." "Kubberdar!" "What the deuce is this 'ere man a saying of sir?" seems to be the keynotes of the cats' concert; Pushtu gutturals, and a running accompaniment of kicks, all down the wagons, completing the chorus. The horses are all entrained, with their packs on; consequently when one falls down, the work of picking him up is rendered doubly difficult. Each Cabuli, too, carries a heavy load on his back and is as difficult to move as the horses themselves. Ammunition cases, in red wood, home-made Martini-Henri rifles; tent poles, furs, food, samovars, hookahs, saddles two feet high, and every other sort of odds and ends, lie about in wild confusion. Everything is wet and clammy to the touch, and in the black darkness one stumbles across men and horses at every step. If the scene could be reproduced on canvas, it would be ridiculed as wildly impossible. Usbeg lancers and locomotives cheek by jowl; tartars and telegraphs, jostling each other; western civilization and eastern savagery, blended in the maddest fashion, and on the just and unjust alike, the ceaseless pitiless rain. No words in my power could do justice to the tableau. After an hour and a half of hard work, the Commander-in-Chief retires; the Assistant Commissioner, soaked from head to foot, follows his example, in order to snatch a little rest before the Ameer's "special" is taken in hand, and the wagons of horses and men steam off into the darkness; the thump, thump, thump, of their four-footed occupants, ringing in our ears as long as the tail lights of the train can be seen. It may be remarked here, that the ingenuous "Yaboo" only showed his astonishment at the iron horse. The Cabulis *may* have been surprised, but they took snuff and concealed their feelings.

The whole business — admirably as it was dispatched — the mail train was not more than an hour or so behind time — was a huge mistake. Seeing that Abdur Rahman had been already so late in keeping his appointment, and that the mischief of this delay was beyond repair — a day extra would not have mattered. This would have given time for entraining the horses quietly, and possibly another four and twenty hours will mend the weather at Rawal Pindi, where, like Peshawur, it has been raining heavily.

I.13: [To Meet the Ameer]
by Rudyard Kipling[12]

RAWAL PINDI, 31st March, 5–30 A.M.

That last sentence was a mistake altogether. The weather has not mended, and Rawal Pindi in the grey dawn is only Peshawur turned up side down. Here are the Yaboos and Cabulis coming out of the train instead of entering it. Here too are the sodden, rain-soaked followers; the gruelly mud under foot, and the heavy clouds overhead. Abdur Rahman left Peshawar last night at eleven for a wonder. I am unable to record the departure. It must have been a depressing function at the best, but he will be here in two hours and a half. Meantime, some drenched coolies are decorating the station, with mournful bunting and depressed laurel boughs, and sight seers, even at this unholy hour, are beginning to drop in. The red cloth is weighted with an unromantic brick, lest it should take unto itself wings.

Later.—The Guard of Honour—Royal Irish Fusiliers—has arrived and are being rained upon. Several big wigs, with plumed hats and restive horses, are being treated in the same manner. Also the K. D. G's in blue cloaks, and the 14th Bengal Lancers and the 15th Bengal Cavalry and a battery of horse artillery. Lots of prancing and curvetting in the mud; more rain, gouts of mud everywhere—and a bevy of umbrellas on the station roof. The umbrellas are agitated, and a rush is made to the business side of the station. Up to the present we umbrellas, have been watching the troops below—and commenting on the appearance of the Punjab Volunteers. One company has yellow gaiters. Every one of the umbrellas is consumed with envy. The other companies have no gaiters. "Aren't the fellows getting wet" say the umbrellas, and forthwith dismiss the volunteers from their minds. The Ameer has arrived, the Guard of Honour presents arms; the Band strikes up, and our respected Lieutenant Governor, Sir M. Biddulph, Mr. Perkins, Commissioner, Colonel Henderson, and another cocked hat or two, emerge warily from the shelter of the waiting room verandah, and prepare to receive His Highness. His Highness is not in a hurry to come out, but finally descends—very lame—clad in a black surtout with gold trappings, and the invariable Tartar cap—and shakes hands all round. Desultory conversation in the rain, which the cocked hats appear to enjoy immensely, and then a rush for certain barouches, four in hands, landaus, &c., which have been waiting outside. Where were the elephants and the Judges of the Chief Court, the Commissioners, the Durbaies, who were to mount them? Forty two animals, swathed as to *Jhool* and *Howdah* with canvas and looking for all the world like huge dbobies' [*sic*] donkeys with the week's wash on their backs, have been swaying pensively in the mist for an hour past. These are now shuffled homeward riderless, and with the glories of gold embroidery and silk trappings hidden from view. Thus ended the elephant procession which was to be the greatest sight that Asia had ever seen. Man durbars but Jupiter Pluvius downpours, and the game is a losing one for thin-skinned mankind. The barouches are trotting away, and the K.D.G.'S, the 14th B.L., the 18th B.C. and the guns form the escort in front and behind them. Neither rain, nor mud can destroy the beauty of British Cavalry or prevent their presence from impressing the bystander. In spite of mired horses, and soaked cloaks, the escort was an impressive sight and it is to be hoped that the Ameer looked at them as he passed. They have all gone away to the Commissioner's house — pro tem the Ameer's bungalow, the Guard of Honour playing "for he might have been a Roosian" &c. Ribald, is it not? At the bungalow the third *ziafut* of Rs. 21,000 will be presented. As the umbrellas descend from the roof of the Station, the welcome news goes round that to-day is a *dies non*. There will be no durbar, and the review is postponed till Saturday. "So home" as Mr. Pepys said "which pleased me mightily to change my filthy raiment, and thank heaven that the king comes not thus everie daye."

I.14: [The Rawul Pindi Durbar]

by Rudyard Kipling

(From our Special Correspondent.)
RAWALPINDI, April 1

Alas for the glories of the Rawal Pindi con-conference [*sic*]; the glitter and the pageantry that were to strike Abdul Rahman Khan with amaze! The pitiless rain has put an end to it all; and unless the conference is prolonged for another fortnight or so, there is small chance of reviews or open air spectacles of any kind. Of course, the Amir has visited the Viceroy, and equally of course, the Viceroy has returned the visit. Both functions took place under the most unfavourable circumstances. About four o'clock yesterday evening a barouche and an escort of sowars splashed through the mud and rain, past the knots of spectators at the Club, down the mall, and to the Viceroy's camp. This was the Ameer. About 10–30 this morning the sowars and the barouche went from the camp to the Ameer's house, while thirty-one guns informed us of the interesting fact. This was the Viceroy and the Duke of Connaught, returning the Ameer's visit. Of the results of the two interviews little is known. This much at least may be taken for truth, the Ameer professed himself wholly on our side, with regard to the coming inevitable struggle; hinted delicately at arms, munitions and assistance generally and was vastly courteous throughout. The imminent danger of losing Turkistan has forced him to show his hand pretty clearly. Our Viceroy, so far as can be learnt, was also courteous, affable, conciliatory, but contented himself with merely opening negotiations; and nothing defenite [sic] has been settled. This, of course, is only natural. For the results of the interviews and our dispositions will not be made public till after the end of the Durbar and the conference. Until this happy day arrives, those "who know, you know" are reticent and cloaked in mystery. Those who do not, of course, are ever most full of information, and one single day's rumours here would stock your paper for a week, with something to spare. As one wearied official put it — when asked for the twentieth time, whether India was going to annex Cashmere, and Scindiah, fight the Mahdi single handed as a proof of his loyalty and devotion: — "A lot of youngsters with nothing else to do spend their whole time manufacturing these squibs; and I've got something else to do than to waste my time contradicting them."

A propos of loyalty and devotion, the Punjab Chiefs and many others — who, by the way, have this forenoon been visiting the Duke of Connaught, were most profuse in their offers of help and assistance in every way; and should the worst come to the worst, it may be taken for granted that Russia will have to deal with a united India, instead of, as she hoped, a land divided against itself, and scarcely kept from bursting in revolt by the bayonets of its rulers. But a little sunshine — a few hours light — would have made these facts infinitely more pleasant. As princelet after princelet — Pattiala, Nabha, Jhind, Bahawalpur and the rest — trotted up the Viceroy's camp this morning, each with his escort of cloaked and dripped sowars, one felt how sadly the effect of the display had been lost. Comparatively speaking the Viceroy's camp is clean and dry. A double drive, well sanded, embracing a plot of grass, ornamented with keosques, gilt headed posts and green chains, leads up to the main tent. The Duke of Connaughts habitation — the most effusive loyalty shall not induce me to call the sombre *shamiana* a palace — lies on the left of this; and the Foreign Office, Government of India satellitites [sic], cocked hats, political uniforms and ivory handled swords, live in two parallel lines of tents, stretching from the Viceroy's stationwards. Words cannot paint the envy with which a dweller in the Civil Slough regards the double flies, well sanded drives, and rain drinking soil. The race course runs, all round them, and the dwellers within that charmed circle "live like gods together careless of mankind." One may continue the quotation as follows: — "For they sit beside their simpkin, and the thunder bolts are hurled to the leftward and the rightward, on the drenching and dripping world. Where the uniforms lose polish and the plumes become uncurled."

The Civil camp is a swamp — mud lying from six to eight inches deep in front of the messtent. Brick paths and straw pugdundies have been laid down in the main thoroughfares. These serve only to accentuate the general wretchedness, and the worst of it all is, that Pindi was blazingly hot ten days ago, and the world and his wife came up in khaki, white ducks, muslin dresses and all manner of hot weather frivolities. Now the world and his wife would sell all they possessed for thick blankets and a waterproof. Some have not umbrellas, some no greatcoats, all are disgusting and wet. This afternoon there was some sign of the weather lifting; that is to say, the rain ceased and there appeared in the sky two distinct patches of blue. Then the world took heart; and his wife a new bonnet, and ordered round the domestic cart. At four, however, the Murree hills gave up a long-brewed thunderstorm. The lightning flashed; the welcome — because dry — wind dropped; and the rain beat upon those tents, and because they were founded on a maidan, and indifferently well banked; they became exceedingly damp and the puddles grew and increased. The Foreign Office were sent to bed — officially — because there was nothing else to do, and so the situation remains at present. Ceaseless gentle rain, now rising to a *crescendo* of shilling big drops; and now sinking to a subdued murmur on *kannat* and *shuldari*. None the less incessant, insinuating, and to all appearance, resolved on the making a night of it.

Below our own particular circle of this moist inferno lies a third and more terrible one. The Volunteers near the icepits, and the cavalry, artillery and infantry bivouacked on Khanna plain, share it between them. The former, either intentionally or by accident, omitted to ask for cots and are lying on straw. Their ground is more or less firm, and beyond a stray river or two by night, and acute discomfort by day, they have but little to complain of. Khanna plain — as I told you ten days ago — is naturally a ploughed field. When I last rode over it, the dust was more than ancle [sic] deep, and the heat abominable. When a ploughed field is rained upon heavily for three days, it becomes moist; not to say clammy. When some ten thousand men live on it, it becomes impossible. At least so I found it to-day. The mire on the *kutcha* roads is in places over eighteen inches deep, and on the plain itself well over a pony's knees. How the men get on there is a wonder. The horses are dying, by ones twos, of colic, and there were eight or nine cases under teatment [sic] in the Artillery and Cavalry divisions this morning. The nearest end of Khanna plain is three miles from anywhere, and the furthest nearer six. Young England — in the shape of the joyous subaltern — takes life cheerfully. "Lay on my charpoy last night" says one "and felt it sinking under me, foot by foot." The playful exaggeration is received with a shout of laughter, and each contributes his quota of strange stories—moving accidents by field (deep plough) and flood, winding up with a hearty "anathema maranatha" against the weather. When the Durbar will come off, no one knows. It has been suggested that this should take place in the market place, and that our troops should be defiled on front of the Ameer. At present, the Durbar tent only wants a few brace of snipe to make it a minature [sic] *jheel*. Parades are impossible, and will be so for at least another five days, even if the rain should stop at once. This, it shows no signs of doing. The Ameer has been dozing this afternoon, and his followers have been driving about to see the sights. They don't exactly understand European carriages. For instance, four Sirdars occupy one carriage and take with them one servant. As all five are profoundly indifferent to wet, they have no objection to sitting beside the driver. A Sirdar accordingly mounts the box seat, and the servant gets inside. One of our native chaprasis, acquainted with the ways of the *sahib log*, suggests that this is somewhat *infra dig*. The servant scorning to descend *via* the steps, makes a plunge for the box from the back seat, and is hauled down again by his coat-tails, and makes his exit decently, and in order. This was all that was of interest to be seen in the Ameer's quarter today. What to-morrow may bring us, no body knows. More rain for a certainty and an indefinite postponement of all *tamashas*, is the general verdict. Meantime, the tents are leaking, the rain is falling and the world waits for the Rawalpindi conference to move on. If it had *only* been in Lahore!

I.15: [The Rawul Pindi Durbar]

by Rudyard Kipling[13]

[*From our Special Correspondent.*]
RAWUL PINDI, April 2

"Now is the winter of our discontent made glorious summer by the sun of March, or at least early April." The weather broke last night and Pindi awoke this morning in a flood of brilliant sunlight, to dry itself and see the world at large. A high dry wind followed the sun, and the roads in cantonments are drying marvelously. The mall is spotless, and the Viceroy's and Commander-in-Chief's camps delightful to walk though. The Civil Camp, the Lieutenant-Governor's mire pit, and the native Chiefs' tents, are, of course, still very bad: and Khanna plain as much a slough as ever it was. Still, if the rain only holds off, a couple of days more will see us all clothed as befits the occasion; warm, dry and comfortable.

Meanwhile we wait. There will be no public *tamasha* till Saturday, when, weather permitting, the Grand Durbar will be held. Nothing particular is being done, and it would be affectation therefore, to say that there is anything to tell.

This morning it was announced that the Duke of Connaught would return the visits of the native princes and princelets. Then came word that the road to their camp was still unpracticable, and His Royal Highness contented himself with miscellaneously perusing about Pindi. It is not said whether he enjoyed himself; though one of the latest fictions is, that Lord and Lady Dufferin are so smitten with the beauties (natural) of the place, that they contemplate a lengthened sojourn, as the *Court Circular* would say: —

His Excellency — to be strictly accurate — promenaded up and down the camp this morning in company with his Private Secretary, and — like humbler humanity — dried himself, for the Viceregal canvas, it is reported, has been untrustworthy here and there. This filled up the day till tiffin time: and, as was only natural, the innocent constitutional gave rise to the wildest rumours.

After tiffin — at three o'clock that is to say — two-fours in hand, a couple of barouches and an escort of lancers, conveyed Abdur Rahman Khan and his principal followers to the entrance of the Viceregal *shamiana*. The visit, it was announced, was an informal and private one, not bearing directly on the negotiations. It lasted about three-quarters of an hour, and the scene was a curiously impressive one. Whatever may be said, every visit that is interchanged between Viceroy and Ameer, is to a certain extent, a move in the great political chessboard, and as such, interesting. This afternoon, they may merely have complimented and counter-complimented each other; or proceeded to the regular cut and parry, parry and cut business. This will be made public later on. At any rate, as I have already said, the visit was worth recording, and, above all, worth witnessing as far as might be. The sanded paths of the camps had been swept bone-clean by the rain, and the tents bleached snow white by the same agency. A cloudless sky and powerful sunlight, brought out sowars, motionless troop horses, speck and span barouches, and red coated postillions, in one magnificent sun photograph. A few booted and spurred by standers, waited for the Ameer's outgoing; but, beyond this most meagre attendance, there was nothing to show any interest in the great game that was being played through its first and most crucial stages, behind the canvas walls in front.

In about twenty minutes, a ragged, in the sense of straggling — cohort of Usbeg lancers clattered up the main drives to take their lord and master home again. As one contrasted their unkempt horses, irregular accoutrements and general *neglige*, with the immobility of the Native Cavalry escort, the order and symmetry of the camp, the Highlanders on sentry duty, and the heavy field guns that studded the drive — with all the outward and visible signs of our rule and dominance in the land — one was tempted to think: — "Surely there is no power like our power, and no nation like our nation." A glance at the grey changeless countenance of the Murree hills, that looked down upon us all from the background, changed the bombast to something very like humiliation. Men, horses, guns, tents were dwarfed and dwindled in the face of the hills, to the play, things on a child's nursery table. All of which gave rise to many excellent moralities which it is needless to inflict upon you here. Let us reckon ourselves on the Imperial scale, and see how all feudal India has risen up to help her Suzerain against the hour of need, if it comes. Imprimis— Kasmir places all the resources of his State at the service of the Government. The Rajputana Chiefs— Oodeypore, Jeypore, Jodhpore, Ulwar, Dholepore Kotah and Bikaneer; the Central Indian feudatories Scindia, Holkar, Bhopal, Rewah, Dhar, Ooreha, Punna, Rutlam and Jowrah; the Punjab — of course Patialia, Bahawalpore, Nabha and Jhind — all these twenty have made similar offers. Hyderabad, so long as there is fighting somewhere, does not care where, he sends his men. The Mahdi or the Muscovite, is all one to him; and in the event of the Soudan trouble being tided over, will heerfully [sic] despatch [sic] his Army to the Afghan Frontier. The list is still an incomplete one, for many persons of wealth and influence in the native community, have come forward with offers of money and personal influence. These things will tell their own tale to strangers, and foreigners. A propos to foreigners, there exists— as your own correspondent has already hinted — a mystery in the Ameer's Camp. He looks more like a wild Irishman than anything else, commands troops and gives rise to innumerable vain tales concerning his nationality. The irresponsible subaltern starts the tale, and as it wags, it grows longer. In this respect it resembles the accounts of the second attempt to derail a train on the Pindi Line. All conclusions point to this being a "put up" case, and the investigation should reveal some interesting little facts of a personal, but not of an alarmist nature. This is disgracefully ambiguous, I admit; but the contagion of official coquetry with news is catching — and besides this is all that can yet be ascertained of the incident. A horse of the Viceroy's escort died from Loodiana fever last night. If the disease spreads, it will assuredly deprive the conference of one of its greatest ornaments, the presence of Cavalry. However, energetic measures are in hand, and it is to be hoped that the case will be a solitary one, aggravated by cold and exposure. On Khanna plain, the horses still suffer a good deal, though no further deaths are reported. The plain will certainly not be fit for the racing that is advertised for the day after to-morrow.

I.16: [The Rawul Pindi Durbar]
by Rudyard Kipling[14]

RAWALPINDI, April 3

One does not settle the affairs of nations on Good Friday but goes to Church instead. So to-day has been utterly eventless. Pindi Church was crowded with all sorts and conditions of men and women in the morning. In the evening, every one took horse and rode to witness the polo match between the 15th Bengal Cavalry and 18th B. Cavalry; which the 18th won. There were on [sic = no] salutes to disturb our peace of mind, and no more than the ordinary allowance of bugles, to break our rest. Several of the Punjab Chiefs—Nabha, Jhind, Pattiala and other have been visiting the Secretaries and big guns in the Viceroy's camp. To visit in style, two fours in hand, a barouche and twenty sowars are necessary, in addition to liberal quantity of red cloth, gold lace and pink turbans. These things are so frequent and recurring, that Pindi, at large, has begun to lose interest in them. "Only another Raja" we cry, as the gay cavalcade sweeps past, and do not trouble ourselves to lift the chick, or step out into the verandah. Goorkha emissaries, resplendent in diamond tiaras, wealthy nawabs, sirdars, parsees, and baboos—any man in fact with avant courier and an afterguard, is a Raja to our unsophisticated minds. As Wordsworth touchingly observed: — A Raja with his regal fuss: — a simple Raja is to us, and He is nothing more. If they didn't all dress so gorgeously, identification would be easier. For example yesterday the Hyderabad representatives collectively, and Salar Jung's brother in particular, went abroad to be photographed. Eyes dazzled with gold and plumes, cockhatry and jeweled sword slings, could not believe that an ordinary youth, in a uniform closely resembling that of an Austrian Hussar, could be anything much in particular. Altogether, there were not more than two square feet of gold braiding on the front of the jacket; and the interesting fact, above mentioned, remained unrecorded till to-day. As regards more serious matters, let it be laid down once and for all, that nothing can be known of the negotiations in progress, between the Viceroy and Ameer until the end of the conference. And for this very good and sufficient reason, that at every interview the Viceroy limits the attendance to the Foreign Secretary, the

Ameer, whom it would be inconvenient to dispense with, and the Ameer's Minister, Mirza Mohommed Nubbia Khan, Dubbur-i-Mulk. Between these four men the secret rests, and, so far, has been religiously preserved. Reduced to its elements, the situation stands thus. Negotiations by letter between India and Afghanistan, were found to be impracticable, and the appearance of the Ameer was required to confer with our ruler. At the present time the Ameer and Viceroy are doing nothing more than talk the business over, and out of this palaver, may or may not, spring a definite and binding treaty between the two countries. What Abdur Rahman wants is pretty generally known: what His Excellency will give, do, or pledge himself to, is a different matter. Of course, there was no interview between the high contracting parties to-day, but — alas that I should be compelled to be so unprofitably vague — much was done on both sides, and the Foreign Secretary went over this forenoon to interview the Ameer.

The day of rest has been spent by those who have the management of the conference, in up-setting all the previously arranged programme, and in preparing and printing a new and correct card. Here is the amended result.

In the first place, the grand Durbar is not be come off on Saturday, but on Wednesday next. To-morrow, at 1 P.M., the Viceroy will receive the Punjab Durbaris, and in the afternoon there will be racing.

On Monday, at 10 A.M., there will be the grand parade on Khanna plain; and an inspection of the P.V.R's., by the Viceroy at 4–30 P.M. The honour is a great one, but it will be difficult to keep all the men over Sunday. Half an hour later, on the same day, the Viceroy will drive over to the Ameer's camp, and there inspect His Highness's troops. In the evening, there will be a banquet to the Ameer, followed by an evening party, at which every one in camp, more or less will attend.

On Tuesday, there will be "manoeuvres" at 10 A.M. This is distressingly vague; but those who can, must wait till Tuesday, and see what happens. On Tuesday afternoon, Lady Dufferin will give a garden party in camp, and all the world and his wife, will appear therefor the second time. On Wednesday at noon, the grand Durbar will be held, as originally arranged, in the big Durbar tent — and after that one must again wait and see what happens. In all probability this will not be the end of the conference. No information of any kind has been received regarding His Highness's departure. There will at least, be no hurry under the head. The troops who have to march back to their stations in the heat of April, will appreciate the delay.

It must be admitted, that if it sometimes rains in Pindi, it dries up marvelously fast. Twelve hours after our three days soaking, there were flying dust clouds along the mall, and an army of bhisties were energetically watering the Viceroy's camp. All the main roads are now perfectly clean, and except in the civil camp, and in one or two other places, the bogs have disappeared. To-day has been cloudy, sultry and over cast. The weatherwise, when they hear of the new programme, answer grimly "Don't they wish they may get a half of it"; and, indeed, there is every chance of a second downpour to-night. If this should happen — but the notion is too awful, and we refuse to believe it.

The camp is nothing less than a huge city covering some dozen or so square miles of ground, with many suburbs; and excepting frontier shaves, news travels slowly from one quarter to the other. Those who have friends and acquaintances among the 5th Goorkhas, may be interested to learn that, yesterday, a swarm of bees attempted to rest themselves in the camp, and, so the story goes, succeeded remarkable well. It is not stated how the 5th repulsed the enemy, or contented themselves with evacuating the camp.

I.17: [The Rawul Pindi Durbar]
by Rudyard Kipling[15]

(*From our Special Correspondent.*)
RAWUL PINDI, April 5

The Viceroy visited the Ameer yesterday evening and held a conference with him for some two hours and a half. To-day things are at a standstill, and unless a special interposition of Providence is made in our favour, this wretched fiasco may hang on indefinitely for a week or ten days more; of course, the rain is responsible for this sweet state of things. It started afresh yesterday forenoon, at the beginning of the preliminary rehearsal — I beg its pardon, the reception of the Punjab Durbaris, and has been showering on and off ever since. Every appearance in the sky points to a regular water bath to-night, and in that case, farewell to to-morrow's review which is to take place on the King's Dragoon Guards' parade ground close to the walls of Pindi Fort; the second downpour having thrown back Khanna plain into its original filthiness. The rapidly drying roads are once more coated with greasy mud; and the oldest inhabitants of Rawal Pindi pervade the place murmuring: "Oh it may go on like this for another week or ten days yet." However, the weather may comport itself to-morrow, and the succeeding days. The Rawal Pindi conference has collapsed in wet and mud; has dragged lost point and become an utterly wearisome and distasteful thing. Many of our visitors, who came to stop, remain to do anything but pray: and many more have shaken off the mire of the place against us, and are returning to their homes with all possible speed. The clerk of the weather has never made "April fools" of one or two thousand Englishmen so successfully before. But to revert to the history of the ceremonies — such pitiful remnants at least as may be snatched from the wet. The Punjab Durbaries were received in State by the Viceroy at one o'clock yesterday. Your own correspondent describes the internal arrangements elsewhere; but he may have omitted to state, that the Durbaries were popularly supposed to be so deathly tired driving about in gorgeous vehicles and getting their turbans wet, that, with one accord, they entreated to be either Durbared and let go, or kept on and drowned. Also that the small durbar was a preliminary canter to ascertain that all the officials understood where to put who, and how to get him out of it again, without hurting his feelings, or causing him to be jammed and huddled with his fellows more than was good for his health. Total absence of sunshine and a weak-minded drizzle took all the gilt off the external display which ought to have been rather imposing.

As the battery to the left of the entrance to the Viceroy's camp saluted, the smoke from the guns drifted up the street, and for the time being blurred all the colours and shapes there. The roads were lined sparsely with native spectators; but the interest taken in the procession of carriages, prancing horses and gay coats, seemed to be very, very small indeed. This lack of interest is observable — except among the contractors throughout Pindi. In the forefront of the whole show, where guns did most bang, and gold lace was the gaudiest, stood half naked and wholly unashamed — two brown grinning *mehters*, basket and broom in hand — as unseemly reminders of the foundation whereon India rests. So much for the externals of the Durbar. The internals must be left to other hands than mine. As an instance of the scarcity of conveyances just now, I may mention that many officials had to put up with the most extraordinary vehicles to take them to the Durbar. One gentleman, not a hundred grades removed from that of a Commissioner, being accomodated [*sic*] with a Murree tonga on whose hood were printed in letters a foot high: — "The Phoenix Carrying Company, Limited."

After the Durbaris had been duly *attared* and *panned* out, men's minds turned to the afternoon racing — and the rain began to fall viciously. In the course of an hour or so, the ground was overlaid with a coating as of fine glue, and the tent ropes began to drip with that monotonous babble which we, who have lived for a week in swamp, know so well. Then everyone decided that nothing could happen, and sat down to abuse every thing and everybody within reach. However, since lotteries had been held the previous night, and that a horse — if also held — could struggle round the course without setting down, those interested in racing matters saw the card through and grew unpleasantly moist in the process. A few ladies attended, but the first day of the long talked of Durbar races was flat — distinctly flat — and I doubt if any one enjoyed themselves.

Certainly His Excellency had no particular reason to enjoy himself, even though he was spared the delights of the race meeting. He had to inspect both the Volunteers and the Ameer's troops — operations which he wisely undertook in a closed gharri, and did not linger over. Then followed his Conference with the Ameer, and the usual [crop] of "Shaves" concerning it at the Club in the evening.

All conclusions that may be drawn are based, of course on the idlest supposition, but it is curious to notice how public opinion, directed by one or two master minds, runs in one direction, *sidelicet* [sic] that the Ameer has asked for one crore of rupees, &c.; and has been courteously refused. Also that his request for European officers for the Afghan Army is under consideration by the authorities, and that certain well known military men will, in the fullness of time, be sent up to Kabul.

The appearance, on paper, of the Second Army Corps, has for a military metropolis, as Pindi is at present, excited wonderfully little interest. An impression is abroad that any movement of troops will be delayed for months — perhaps even to the end of the year; and that when the movement takes place, it will be nothing more than a demonstration. Now, if there is one thing which the British officer loathes more than another, it is the prospect of a "demonstration" — especially in the Peshin valley and in the hot weather. The chances of active work or as they elegantly term it — "a regular row," would put every lad who now devoutly prays, that his "hill leave mayn't be stopped for this blessed nonsense" on the qui-vive at once, and eager to go forward. I believe I am interpreting public opinion correctly when I say, that the general idea here is, that the two Army Corps will be required to do nothing when they *do* move, and that under these circumstances they are both nuisances pure and simple.

Sunday has been devoted to discussing the chances of war, and since the one invariably entails the other, unlimited abuse of Mr Gladstone and all his works. Besides this there is nothing else to do. The weather, as a matter of interest, has been played out long ago, and we view it now with the calm despair born of quagmire tents and soaked garments. In the Viceroy's camp there reigns a holy peace, and as with us — melancholy resignation. Things are at a dead stop all round, and if Monday brings us rain once more — as from the appearance of the sky it most certainly will — we shall have to halt this funeral procession for another four and twenty hours at least. Tuesday's manoeuvres on Khanna plain have been eliminated from the programme, and the parade ground on which the review takes place to-morrow, will permit of very little room for extended movements. By the way, the programme has not yet been officially made public, and a good many people are still in the dark as to what takes place when and where it will be necessary to go. But the blackest ignorance of all reigns among those who ought to know better. Not a soul is posted up on the one absorbing question of the day: — "When o when, shall we get out of this?" "It may be for years and it may be for ever." Love, I know not when or how" is the burden of our daily song.

"There is always something in the pleasures of our friends which profoundly disgusts." Every account received from the Ameer's part of the station tells us that both Abdur Rahman and his following are having a delightful time, and are not in the least hurry to move on. Of the Ameer, I am unable to speak authoritatively: for the ruler of Afghanistan is as zealously guarded as a *pardahneshin*. A Sabbath day's journey to his camp, however, has convinced me that his troops at least are in clover. Their tents are pitched about a hundred yards to the right of the Commissioner's house, looking towards the station on a slight eminence with good drainage. This qualification of camping ground is exceedingly necessary; for without any aspersion on their valour, I may say that the Ameer's troops must be about the dullest that ever hammered tent peg into the ground. They are picturesque — immensely so. The Usbeg lancers, in their mustard-hued coats, shaggy caps and strange accoutrements, would make an artist's fortune. So would some of the interiors of the tents, where rich carpets, quaint Persian aftabas, turquoise-studded brow and breast bands, Russian Samovars, orange peel and slices of red raw mutton lie about in picturesque profusion; everything being toned down by dirt and use from its original brightness and purity.

The occupants of these tents are as frank and inquisitive as children; and air their few words of broken Hindustanee, or in rare cases, English, with a pride delightful to witnesses. What they want they ask for. For instance the apparition of an English visitor in a tent brought round him half a score of Usbegs chattering like daws. His boots seemed to excite the greatest admiration; then the texture of his clothes and finally his cheroot. One lancer watched this last article of attire–indispensable in *that* camp, and finally suggested that the Sahib should give it to him for a few minutes to smoke. The Sahib's caste prejudices against mutton fat and grime stood in his way here, whereupon the lancer promptly replied, "Have you any more about you" and lest the questioner should be led into a lie, passed his hand rapidly over and into the sahib's breast pocket. Another worthy suggested an exchange of foot gear, and was considerably astonished on being refused. In their own country they must be beau ideals of ruffianly caterans. On their best behaviour in British territory they are simply amusing boisterous Fridays, and a Robinson Crusoe sort of tour through their tents is a novel and very amusing experience. In their manners towards each other they are loud, not to say impolite. Firewood lies stacked about the camp in large quantities and a heated argument concludes sometimes with an interchange of small logs and several screams. At least this happened twice in half an hour while I was there. Their horses are much cleaner than themselves, and are mostly short-legged, iron-grey Cabulis of demonstrative habits. The saddles, apparently, are but seldom taken off, and the horses are nobbled as well as heel roped. The officers mix freely with the men, and hold little levees of their own outside their tents; a group of from five to ten men lolling on the ground in front of each officer.

The lancers apparently do "stables" in full review order, and whenever the spirit moves them. These things make the mustard-coloured coats dirty and the horses unkempt. The mutton carcases for the day's consumption are placed, tenderly, on a charpoy. Sometimes the charpoy is occupied by a man, more generally by a dog. One further peculiarity of these interesting savages is worth recording. They blush like girls; the blood showing plainly under the fair skin. Those anxious for a novel sensation, I would recommend to compliment an Usbeg on his martial appearance, and to stand by while the burly giant looks down on the ground; plays with his lance sling and becomes tricked into confusion.

I.18: [The Rawul Pindi Durbar]
by Rudyard Kipling[16]

(From our Special Correspondent.)
RAWALPINDI, April 6

At last we seem to have started work in earnest and the gloomy forecasts of yesterday have been but partially fulfilled. To be sure the sky is as black as ink all round the horizon, but the clear patch of blue in the centre, and the restless winds, promise April showers at the utmost, and not the steady wet to which we dwellers in tents have become so painfully accustomed. In an hour or so, the grand Review of troops in camp will begin. Meantime, carriages and riders are already beginning to assemble by the three huge sheep pens which mark the spots whence the Viceroy, the Punjab Chiefs and the common folk, are to view the ceremony. Of decoration, beyond the naked pole to the saluting base, there is no sign — the army here gathered together is to march by with no scenic accessories, beyond those of gloomy skies, wind-shaken woods in the back ground and the shrill whistle of the iron horse in front. The King's Dragoon Guards' parade ground, lies to the right of the Jhelum road and to the left of the Rawal Pindi Fort, but looking in the same direction. It is situated, in the language of the guide books, on a slight eminence, overlooking a fold of low hills below the fort. The Jhelum road and Punjab Northern Railway, bounds it on the left, and the fort on the right. As nearly as I can judge, the wooden sheep pens face due south, commanding a most un-Indian landscape. But for the white turbans and *puggris* studding the railway bridge, it might be a view at the foot of the Sussex Downs, anywhere a dozen miles inland from Lewes. The Review is to be merely a March Past, without manoeuverings of any kind, and Abdur Rahman is to sit still by the Viceroy's side, and watch the living tide roll by. He should be weary of watching before the work is over. Pindi Fort is the better part of a mile away from here, and already the slope below the bastions is sown with little red specks, which shuffle and agglomerate themselves, until they finally assume the shape of two red bars, and moving on, are lost to view behind the trees on the Jhelum road. This is the first regiment getting ready for the March Past, and at least half a score of field glasses proclaim that it was the 33rd. The company, in every sort of vehicle, from the lordly "fitton" to rattling ticca gharri, is assembling as fast as may be; and whenever there is a lull in the rolling of wheels, the air becomes alive with the music of unseen bands of regiments moving into position along Jhelum road. Already half a dozen worthy gentlemen of mature years, mounted on fiery untamed steeds, and thickly covered with gold lace and red cloth, are caracoling from one end of the ground to another, and shouting multitudinous directions, apparently about nothing at all. Certainly the Police who have been told to keep the crowd in order, pay not the least attention to their blandishments; certainly the regimental bands, which have taken up their position in front of the saluting base, are beyond their jurisdiction, and as yet no regiments have appeared. But their exercise appears to afford the wandering knights errant considerable satisfaction, and they are riding as if for life. First a hasty gallop from left to right of the parade ground, and a peremptory mandate, so it seems, to the rolling clouds in that direction. Then a tug at the curb, a flourish of horse tail and human spurs, and a fourteen-anna burst in the opposite direction. And so *de capo ad lib.* and with as much martial expression thrown into the business as a pulling horse and an insecure helmet will allow. These vagaries always foretell a good review — as much as the flight of the returning swallows, herald spring in England. Carriages and horses are arriving in shoals as I write, and the somber skies greet, with a sharp shower of rain, an assemblage which includes half the best known men in India and a fair sprinkling of the great ones of the earth. But the Viceroy and Ameer have not yet put in an appearance, and we have yet the excitement of the Viceregal salute to undergo. When three or four hundred vehicles are all jammed together in a space a few hundred yards long, the consequences of thirty-one guns just behind the horses are likely to be interesting.

11 o'clock or there abouts. The guns have fired, the horses have protested, and His Excellency, Earl Dufferin, Viceroy and Governor-General of India, and His Highness, Abdur Rahman Khan, ruler of Afghanistan and its dependencies, are riding side by side to the saluting point. The Viceroy is in plain clothes, with a star on his breast. The Ameer, like Alice Fell, is clad in duffel grey, with a gold embroidered black belt, long boots, and the tartar cap of grey Astrakhan fur. He is riding a small bay pony, and looks burlier and more thick set, than ever. With these two, ride a miscellaneous escort of English and Afghan officers, all well-mounted, and ablaze with gold and silver trappings. They take up position to the right and left of the saluting point, and the show begins.

First the Commander-in-Chief and his staff, and Sir Michael Biddulph and his Staff, ride past to their post, opposite the Viceroy's, and draw up in line with the bands. Then, without a word of warning, the railway bridge to the left becomes alive with the glitter of steel, and the bevey of red coats, as the 33rd, the head of the first division, debouches into the open, at the double. And here I may point out the one disadvantage of the ground chosen. To get down from the Jhelum road to the open ground below, the troops have to walk down an embankment — which naturally threw them out of their step — dress and close up as best they can, and go straight on past the Viceroy. They have about three hundred yards wherein to recover themselves, and except to some ultra military eye, seem to go past perfectly. After, the 33rd, come the Royal Irish — a strong regiment in every respect, and now we are fairly settled down to business. The bands in front of the saluting point, play the men through as they go. The unattached officers have ceased from galloping, and there is a great quiet over us all.

The 14th Sikhs, the 31st Punjab Native Infantry, the Rifle Brigade, the 4th and 5th Goorkhas, little men taking long strides, the Royal Irish, the 21st Punjab Native Infantry, the 1st Goorkhas and the Volunteers, have passed by. Red, khaki, green, buff, maroon, coats and facings, — an infinity of booted feet coming down and taking up, with the exactness of a machine — thousands of pipe-clayed pouches swinging all in the same direction, and all with the same impetus, dazzle the eyes, and produce on the mind, the impression of some interminable night mare. Finally. one loses all idea that the living waves in front are composed of men. It has no will, no individuality—nothing it seems, save the power of moving forward in a mathematically straight line to the end of time. It was a positive relief to cast one's eyes to the end of the parade ground, and watch the columns, ragged and extended, in their scramble down the side of the road. The procession still continues, and the Scotch regiments are appearing on the scene. The Highland Light Infantry, the 78th, followed by the Guides, the 19th Punjab Native Infantry, the Cheshire, with their riddled colours and the wreath atop, the 1st Punjab Native Infantry, the 3rd Sikhs, the 2nd Manchester, the 24th and 25th Punjab Native Infantry, and then, thank goodness, a pause for the Cavalry. The Jhelum road, as far as the horizon, is covered with returning troops, outlining the curves of the road, in red and dun colour. Abdur Rahman Khan is not to be lightly spoken to, so that it is impossible to say for certain, what he thinks: but his hands are dropped on his ponies withers, and with head slightly bent forward, he is watching the incoming and outgoing line. Even an Englishman, accustomed as he is to talk of the degeneracy of our armed forces in these days, has, for once, to let such idle cavilling be, and content himself with wonder, pure and simple, at the harvest of the dragon's teeth, which we garner within our borders. Dublin and the Deccan, Paisley and Punjab, Nepal and Lancashire, one might continue the antitheses indefinitely, have all contributed to the crop of armed men ready for war, and it may be that the grey clad figure in the fur cap, is reading, marking and inwardly digesting the lesson. But no muscle on his face shows any signs of emotion, and the arrival of the Cavalry bands forces me to relinquish gush, in order to gaze on the next scene of the pageant. This has at least more life and movement than the former, seeing that no regulations on earth will keep horses' heads from nodding up and down in irregular time, and there was something terrible in the utter immobility of the foot soldiers. The 9th Lancers open the ball, and of these it can only be said, as of all the others, that they are fine men on fine horses—albeit the latter look a trifle drawn and tuckered up, from marching and exposure to the rain. After the 9th come the 14th and 19th Bengal Lacners [sic], the King's Dragoon guards, the 3rd Bengal Cavalry, the 15th Bengal Cavalry, the Carabiniers, the Guides and the 15th Bengal Cavalry, in Squadrons, shaking the earth as they pass. Are there any words to describe adequately, the appearance of well-mounted well-drilled cavalry? The military world here contents itself with saying, that such and such a regiment went by better than such another; that one squadron kept its distance, whereas another did not, and so on; but the absolute symmetry of the whole; the wonder of it all, are taken as matters of course, grown familiar by long usage.

Abdur Rahman Khan made no sign through out this last revelation — for this it must be to him. But when the artillery makes its appearance there is certainly something very like surprise visible on his countenance. Three batteries of Royal Horse Artillery, four field batteries the European screw gun batteries, and three native mountain, batteries file by, all as neat as new pins. The Field and Horse batteries, go past as one gun. A little thickened and blurred in the outlines, as if seen through a mist, but nevertheless one gun. How it's done, the civilian's mind cannot tell. To all appearance, the driver of the near wheeler lays the stock of his whip lightly on the withers of the off wheeler — and there you are, with about six inches between axle and axle, as level as though all six guns had been planed across the muzzles, jammed into a gauge and left there. This too, after guns and limber had to plunge down the embankment, recover themselves, and reform in about three hundred yards. It may be said: — "But this is only what we pay for, and all you have described, are but the incidents of an ordinary march past." When twenty thousand men march past in a straight line for two hours, in the presence of the men who will have to make the history of the next four years, the occasion is of anything but ordinary importance; and it is only fair, therefore, to record how superbly the whole function went off. The one touch of the ludicrous, to relieve the almost oppressive gravity of the proceedings, comes in appropriately enough at the end, in the shape of the elephant battery. Left to himself, my Lord, the elephant, is an imposing beast; but there is something very comic in his appearance when he is harnessed, "random" fashion, to a siege gun. The weighty piece of ordnance bundles after him like a child's toy, and all the ropes and chains and pads, wherewith his massive form is begirt, look like so many pieces of pack-thread. The Campbellpore behemoths bring up the rear of the Indian Army, at a sober and dignified pace; while behind them again come the battery bullocks, and our old friend the Punjabi *bylawalla*, thinly disguised in a uniform, prodding them with a stick. So we drop from all the pomp and circumstance of glorious war, from patriotic enthusiasm and much gush, to the things of everyday life again. But for a little while only. The Ameer has yet to see what manner of troops our feudatories could bring into the field, should occasion arise. Pattialla, Nabha, Jhind, Faridkot, Kapurthalla Bahawalpore, have all contingents to show — and the sight must shock the Ameer exceedingly. When he was driving from the station on his arrival in Pindi, he asked several question[s] regarding the native contingents, and expressed the utmost surprise that the British Government dared to allow the dragon's teeth to be sown anywhere but in her own borders. But they took part in the last Afghan war, said the officer with him. "Ah ! and were killed off that way," was the Ameer's reply.

"No they kept our lines of communication open in the Karrum Valley." "Did they? I should have sent them where they might be thinned a little." Evidently His Highness does not approve of armies within armies, and the close of the review must shock him exceedingly. Here are contingents of well-drilled, well-armed men in a conquered country, playing their bands, giving their words of command, and above all dragging their artillery, the deadly guns of the English, under the very noses of their rulers. And truly the native contigents [*sic*] are magnificent troops to look at. A little ragged in their dressing here and there, and below comparison with English batteries, as regards their artillery, but still magnificent men. I am unable to say which are which, for field glasses are of no avail here; a catholic taste in buttons preventing accuracy of observation.

They were all good, and would have been better as regards the cavalry, if so many of the horses had not been the pink nosed, mottled squealers that one is accustomed to associate with circuses, all the world over. About three thousand in all have gone by, and the guns are making ready to salute. Viceroy, Ameer and escort have swept round to the road, and are making haste to begone, as a sharp thunderstorm is doing its worst among us just now. But the abominable weather of the past week seems to have broken for good, and this is merely an April shower. The road to Khanna plain is still full of troops, and the elephant battery is shuffling home hastily to tiffin. The great review of the Pindi Conference is over; and could scarcely have taken place under more favourable circumstances. There was no sun, which in April is distinctly a blessing; there was no dust, and the turf holds no mud, so the troops have gone by speckles; and so far as can be, after having been in review order for some four hours or so, untired. From beginning to end of the performance, there has not been one single hitch of any kind. Abdur Rahman has seen for himself the harvest of the dragon's teeth as we grow it in this country, and doubtless has drawn his own conclusions. The sword is mightier than the pen by far to an Afghan: and each bayonet and field piece will carry more weight with our guest, than the courteous preambles of the Conference proper.

I.19: [The Rawalpindi Durbar]
by Rudyard Kipling

(*From our Special Correspondent.*)
RAWALPINDI, April 7

We are getting on. Last night at the banquet given in his honour at the Viceregal camp, Abdur Rahman rose, for all the world like one used to after dinner spouting, and delivered a speech in reply to the toast of his health, proposed by Lord Dufferin. His Highness spoke in Persian, and confined himself to amiable generalities. He trusted that Afghanistan would continue to prosper as England, in the future, and that the English arms would be victorious wherever they went — with *more* of the same sort, of course. As an Oriental statesman, he committed himself to nothing definite, and succeeded in pleasing every one about him.

In the end, three cheers were given for the Ameer, and responded to by the guests with a good deal of enthusiasm. The banquet was attended by about sixty persons. After the banquet came a reception and evening party combined, at which every one in Pindi was expected to attend. As a matter of fact, the threatening weather kept many away; but there was a mighty gathering, native and European, nevertheless. It lasted till about eleven o'clock, and was throughout a most picturesque spectable. Diamonds and kincobs, gold lace, medals by the hundred, swords, jewels, clanking spurs and the civilian's magpie garb, all lit up in the brilliantly illuminated shamiana; and outside the pitchy blackness of night, rent from time to time by vivid violet flashes of lightning, beyond the Murree hills. Lightning that paled the lamps of the Durbar tent, and for a brief moment eclipsed both gold and jewelry. The thunderstorm broke in rain, just as the guests were taking their departure; and every one went to bed lulled by the falling rain, with the comfortable conviction that there would be no parade on Khanna plain to-morrow.

This last was written overnight, and like so many of my weatherwise predictions heretofore, is wrong, entirely wrong. The sun is shining brightly, a high wind is doing its best to dry Khanna plain, and at this hour (8–30) of Tuesday morning, the troops in Cantonments are already beginning to get under arms. Pindi is the maddest station in India. The pukka roads are already as clean as if they had been swept and this too in spite of last nights' shower. Khanna plain, over which the file of carriages pitch and toss like ships at sea, is still fairly sticky, but not enough so to impede the movements of troops. The grand stand, three steps of masonry shaded by thin calico, an edifice much too low and slightly protected, shows from some distance off, between a couple of rifle butts.

In whichever direction one looks, the undulating brown soil seems to be alive with moving troops, and beyond the troops is spread a snowy back ground of tents, the Murree hills looking calmly down on us all. What is the actual extent of the plain I cannot say. Pindi Fort is at one end and a veil of tender blue haze at the other. The kutcha roads are vile, although a huge iron roller has been travelling over them since dawn, and every now and again a carriage in front becomes stuck in the mire; necessitating a halt all along the line. The sunshine has hardened the mud to the consistency of freshly poured toffee, so that the same rut which causes your horse to pitch forward on his nose, is tenacious enough to hold back the wheel. A large company of visitors are riding, and the entire procession bears a curious resemblance to an Indianized Derby day. The exhilarating breeze, and the rolling landscape both help out the delusion. Decidedly it is an ideal day for a review, if it will only stay as it is. The troops have marched on to the ground and, as yesterday, there is the usual percentage of hoarse-voiced gallopers, scuttling about in all directions. At the present moment, Infantry, Cavalry and Artillery, are drawn up in line of quarter columns, about five hundred yards from the spectators in the grand stand; that is to say, they lie like a solid bar of humanity one mile long. The infantry face is eight hundred odd yards, the cavalry six hundred yards or so; the balance being made up by the Artillery. There is to be no display of native contingents, to-day, our own modest twenty thousand being quite good enough to "astonish the Browns." Seventeen hundred and sixty yards of man horse and gun, in battle array, is worth travelling some distance to see; even from Cabul to Rawal Pindi — and he is dull indeed whose blood does not course the quicker at the sight. Yesterday we saw the same men file by, and knew them to be strong, because they took a couple of hours to pass. To-day we have them full in front standing still, and the effect is infinitely great; inasmuch as we secure the full effect of every regiment and every gun. Except with the strongest of field glasses, it is impossible to tell the less well known regiments. So after a hasty skirmish from one end of the grand stand to the other, in search of points of vantage, we content ourselves with patriotic sentiments and speculations, as to the arrival of the Viceroy and the Ameer. The other dignitaries have already arrived, and are grouped — some on horses, some in hearses — that is to say, the Lieutenant-Governor's Camel carriage, and five or six on a State elephant, gay with red and gold trappings. A timely notice in the Club advised intending visitors to the plain, to ride, as the state of the roads was not particularly good. This accounts for the quantity of riding habits, and the complete absence of what ladies call "pretty frocks." Indeed, the scores of uniformed officers who throng the enclosure, have it all their own way; and are as gorgeous as poppies in the more sober corn.

N.B. His Excellency and his Highness have arrived, both on horse back and are now riding to the right of the line to inspect it. With them ride all yesterday's cohort, and it must be confessed, that the knot of moving horsemen, look much more imposing out in the open and in the sunlight, than they did grouped round the saluting post on Monday. His Highness has an excellent opportunity of inspecting the troops at close range. He is making the most of it, and riding slowly from the extreme right to the extreme left, and back again to the saluting base. This occupies nearly half an hour, and meantime the sun reminds us that April is April in India, and his rays, after his long exclusion, as powerful as ever they were. No one however thinks of retiring to the shelter of the much misnamed grand stand: the rush being all for the railings nearest to which the troops are to pass by. This is done in columns of brigades, a shorter method than the columns of companies adapted yesterday. And at this point I find that all description ends. As far as the excellence and appearance of the regiments go, there is nothing to add to what was recorded yesterday. We have the same regiments paraded before us in different formation, and pacing by with the same awe striking steadiness, to the music of the various bands. All these I have done my best to depict; but as the army goes by, and a review, finer than that of the Delhi Assemblage — the most superb some say that has ever been held in India — is taking place, one feels the utter powerlessness of words to describe the picture. Brigade after brigade forms up in the distance, comes nearer, springs to the rhythm of the band, salutes, passes on, and returns to take up its original position in front of the Viceroy. After the Infantry come the Cavalry. Field, horse, mule and elephant batteries; Then the cavalry by squadrons, trotting past while their band played "The keel row." Then a halt of a few minutes, and artillery and cavalry tear back at a gallop. The guns wheeling sharply to the right after they have passed the saluting post, to let the squadrons go by. This is the crowning success of the whole ceremony, and as is always the case, is rapturously applauded by the ladies. "Aren't they *darlings*" murmurs a pink umbrella "to a white one" as the heavy guns, bound and plunge and thunder across the open: and the air is full of the music of flying hoofs in their wake. "Aren't they *sweet*?" cries another, as a fresh torrent of men and horses gathers way and shoots past. Why the sight of military spectacles should be always so "sweet" to feminine eyes, it is hard to say. This last grand finale is sobering to watch, and saddening as well. What would the end of it all be? Where would the superb army be dispersed before the year's close? And of the thousands that were gathered to-day for one man's pleasure, how many should we have fighting with, for or against him in the same time?

  The troops have once more assembled in review order, and advance in a mile long wall, straight for the grand stand, with their officers in position in front. Then His Excellency rides forward to meet them, talks for a few minutes to Sir Michael Biddulph, wheels and canters back, the guns salute, and this review, too, is at end. Those who have seen it, only can be able to think of it as it actually was. No words of mine could help those who did not.

I.20: [The Rawalpindi Durbar]
by Rudyard Kipling[17]

(*From our Special Correspondent.*)
RAWALPINDI, April 8

The last act of the great drama has closed, and it only remains for us now to speed the parting guest to his home in the hills; and take stock of the results of the great Rawal Pindi Conference, that draggle-tailed function, which has been so long and so often delayed by unfavourable weather, that, to the onlookers, it has lost much of its interest. "Whatever happens," we said this morning, "the Durbar has hung fire too long to impress us as it ought." So we hailed the music of bands early this morning, and the tramp of the First Division, lining the roads from the Ameer's camp to the Viceroy's, as the overture to our emancipation from Rawal Pindi and all its qualified pleasures; put on our uniforms and dress coats, as we happened to be officers or civilians, and went Darbar-wards. One word on the subject of dress coats for Durbars. Could no other garment be found more suitable for the occasion? Court clothes and knee breeches, if necessary, would serve our turn; but it is unfair to drag the decent companion of a hundred suppers and "swarrys" into the cruel crude light of a blazing April sun. By lamplight, he is black, glossy and speckles. By day we perceive that he is none of these things, and with this knowledge, sink at once to the level of so many disreputable waiters of night Clubs, who, with the advent of day, have nowhere to lay their aching heads. Lord Dufferin's role is not that of a red-hot reformer; but he would confer a public benefit by altering some of the sumptuary regulations for daylight assemblies and durbars. This however is a digression, and, after all, the plain magpie was distinctly in the minority. Seventy five per cent of us blossomed into uniforms — red and gold; black and silver; Khakee, brown, mustard colour; every shade almost under heaven. With the out-crop of uniforms, of course, came the medals and decorations, sown, it seemed, broad cast among the assembly — Crimea, a few; Mutiny, fewer still; Bhutan, Jowaki, Umbeyla clasps; Egyptian and Afghan medals and stars literally by the score, interspersed with C.S.I.'s., C.I.E.'s., and, of course, the hideous Delhi plaque, with its broad cattle show red riband — decorations that would have driven a foreigner wild with self-appreciation shall we say — glistened everywhere. Their owners bore their burden meekly, and after the manner of Britains, deprecated any reference to them; considering the whole business a "bore" from beginning to end. Certainly the preliminary waiting was somewhat tedious, but there was much to notice, and, if one was not *blasè* in the matter of durbars, to admire. The huge shamiana itself formed a T; the upright being upholstered in pale gold coloured cloth, and the cross piece sea green, with a roof of green and white stripes, sadly washed out and be-draggled by rain.

The official notification of the proceedings informed us, that Civil and Military Officers of Government, and gentlemen on the Darbar list in the Punjab, were requested to be in their places by 11 A.M., after which admittance would not be allowed. As a matter of fact, nearly everyone was in his place by 10-30, and the labours of the officers in charge of the proceedings must have been considerably lightened hereby. The First Division had been told off to line the roads from the Ameer's camp to the Viceregal one; the main street of the camp being lined by cavalry, and behind the horses State elephants in State trapping. These were the most effective portion of the external display. A Guard of Honour of the Seaforth Highlanders was drawn up before the Durbar tent; the artillery, for the salutes, occupying a position to the left front of the camp. The sun, that made everything so pleasant for those inside, could hardly have been appreciated by helmeted Thomas Atkins, who was forced to face its rays without stirring for some two or three hours, exclusive of the time that he had taken tramping from Khanna. The general effect, however, was superb, and like so many other spectacular effect, quite beyond reproduction on paper. The same may be said of the inside of the tent, which was one blaze of colour, where the Durbaris sat; and of jewels where the ruling, Chiefs of the Punjab were ranged. These gentlemen dropped in at five minute intervals, from a quarter to eleven till half past: their arrival being signaled by the saluting guns outside. First Chamba, and then Faridkhot, Kapurthala with a gorgeous tiara of diamonds and the plumpest face ever vouchsafed to mortal boy; then Nabba and Jhind, both elderly men, with their attendants. Bahawalpore with his long locks, arranged over his shoulders like some cavalier of Charles II, in a brocade coat, and a huge white turban, covered with tastelessly arranged jewels, and a diamond tiara. Pattiala, who came last and had the seat of honour in the assemblage, was the most modestly attired of all; and was followed by his younger brother and the members of the Council of Regency. These Chiefs were ranged on the left of the red cloth lane, to the Viceregal dais — with the exception of Pattiala, who was seated immediately below the dais to the left of the Viceroy, — their attendants, almost as gorgeously clad as their masters, being seated behind them. To the right of this lane, sat the Durbaris of this province, arranged in the order of their rank and labeled like rare exotics—one cluster bore the legend "Punjab official block" in large printed letters: and led to much unholy laugher and many esoteric jokes, before we had fairly settled down to the gravity of the function. The Viceregal dais was in the centre of the cross-piece of the T, and was guarded by eight of the Body Guard, and the usual cohort of resplendent mace bearers and *ch bdars*. Three silver chairs, one for the Viceroy, one for the Ameer on the right, and one for the Duke of Connaught on the left, were disposed on the dais; seats for Brigadier General Gordon, on special duty with the Ameer, our Lieutenant-Governor, the Lieutenant-Governor of the North West Provinces, the Commander-in-Chief in India, and the Maharaja of Pattiala being reserved below. Everybody who has attended a durbar—and in India who has not—will understand what an imposing array it all presented—would realize how the intense sunlight lit up velvet and brocades like jewels; and jewels like stars—how the air was thick with perfumes of attar and sandal wood—how the huge pierced emeralds and rubies clanked and tinkled as our Punjab pincelets turned their heads—how the great guns boomed and thundered outside: and how, ever and anon, a wearied elephant would trumpet in response to the artillery; and lastly, would know far better than I could tell him of the sea of impassive British faces turned doorwards to the glare without; and can hear the undercurrent of whispered comments and questions, as one by one the planets of our firmament wheeled into position in the shawl covered chairs arrayed for them. The order of their coming was somewhat altered from that given in the official programme, but eventually the Commander-in-Chief of India, the Commanders-in-Chief of Madras and Bombay, Sir Charles Aitchison, Sir Alfred Lyall, and the members of the Executive Council, gorgeous in black and gold uniforms, the sun-flowers of the Political Departments—were all received, made much of and ushered into their seats in the left of the line, or close to the Viceroy, as the case might be. Then we waited long and anxiously for the return of the deputation that had gone to fetch the Ameer; for the Viceroy and the Duke, who was to honour the Durbar with his presence. Once the band outside led off with "God save the Queen," and the assembly rose to their feet as one man. But this was a false start, and our loyalty was proffered in vain. We reseated ourselves, and stared round at our fellows, and commented upon the appearance of ladies in Durbar. To allow them at all is a mistake for many reason; and though it may seem a brutal and ungallant remark, they seriously impair the effect of a public ceremony in oriental eyes. There is—it has been said over and over again—but one way in which an Asiatic regards a woman, and that way is the reverse of complimentary. Wherever men meet together, her presence is an intrusion and an impertinence to his mind; and when men meet in solemn conclave, something a good deal worse. Until he comes to see things with our eyes, he will be of this way of thinking, and it is useless to look at the fact in any other light. At the Umballa Conference of 1869, the same mistake was made and commented upon by the writers of those days. To-day, at a far more important Durbar, we have repeated the mistake. But this is another digression.

The Viceroy, the Ameer and the Duke of Connaught arrived together; Royalty and Viceroyalty, with all their honours thick on their breasts; the Ameer in a plain grey suit, huge black leather boots and the inevitable black fur cap. His only ornament was a diamond star in the head-dress; and his followers were as severely plain as himself. As the burly thickset figure limped towards the dais, it produced somewhat the same impression as might be the apparition of a bear in a ball-room. Never was there a more striking contrast. Was it just the least little touch of pique that drove the ruler of Afghanistan to such studied simplicity in the midst of so gorgeous an assembly — the last protest of the savage against the civilization that could not let him rest where he was, but must needs drag him southward to confer for his kingdom's safety with the Kafir? Or was it merely the jewelry and brocade have no charms for him, and oiled Turkoman boots are preferable to the varnish of patent leather? He mounted the dais with evident difficulty and dropped into his chair with as evident relief. From that point of vantage, he proceeded to take stock of the assembly and then turned to begin the conversation, as advertised, with Lord Dufferin. What was said, what was translated and what was the reply, was utterly inaudible at two paces distance; and for twenty minutes the Durbar watched in silence a most edifying piece of dumb-show. Then entered the blood red chuprassi by scores, with trays in his hand, bearing gifts for the Ameer — silver claret coolers, desks, instands, guns, swords, walking sticks, a portrait of Lord Differin [sic] and the Queen a huge silver hookah and unnumbered kincobs, cushions, silks, and satins. While this was going on Abdur Rahman stared above the level of the presents at the assembly around, and appeared supremely unconscious that this could in any way have to do with him. Bangles for his wives, garments for his sons and attendants, mechanical toys, of these more hereafter, and any number of other trifles. His Highness's heart must have been with the twelve elephants, two hundred bullocks and heavy guns outside, for to all outward appearance, this display did not move him in the least. We could only tell by the consequences how deeply he was stirred, and the consequences came suddenly and, I fancy, unexpectedly Abdur Rahman was moved to make a speech.

It was not so nominated in the bond, for the notification said that, after the presents had been set out and taken away, His Highness would retire. Captain Talbot translated, and this was what the Ameer said:—

"I am greatly obliged by the kindness shown me by His Excellency, the Viceroy, and the favour shown me by the Queen. In return for his kindness very possible service will be rendered by me, both as regards my army and my people. As England has declared his intention of assisting in beating off my external enemy from Afghanistan, so the Afghan nation will join in the firmest manner, and stand side by side with the British Government"

Whether there is any official report of the speech I am unable to say. I should fancy not, but this is as nearly as possible a verbatim report of the speech. I say as nearly as possible advisedly, inasmuch as the speech was interrupted shamelessly by a mechanical singing bird—one of the presents to the Ameer's sons—placed on a tray in the centre of the Darbar. Perhaps the wretched creature had been wound up previously, or perhaps there was a little left in it from its last performance. At all events, as if prompted by human malignity, it went off spasmodically in full Durbar, while Captain Talbot was translating. His voice was soft and low—"an excellent thing in *woman*" but hardly necessary when a important speech is in question, and the mechanical warbler had rather the best of it. The speech if fully reported, would read something after this style. "His Highness the (*"whit whit whit"*) desires me to (*chic a see ki see— whit"*) that (*"whit"*) he is &c. Every one smiled even on the Vicergal dais; so strangely did the irrepressible little warbler intrude itself on the manufacture of history, and one of the grandest Durbars that has been held in the land.

At the conclusion of the speech there was loud applause—an undignified proceeding to say the least. The applause was repeated when Lord Dufferin presented the Ameer with a magnificent sword of State, softly murmuring something to which the Ameer replied that "he hoped, with this sword, to strike down any enemies of the British Government." This last performance brought the proceedings to a close, and the Viceroy, Ameer and Duke passed out together, succeeded by all the Commanders-in-Chief and Lieutenant-Governor's, the ruling princes and finally the English visitors. More than two hundred guns had to be fired, so that the scene afterwards was sufficiently exciting. In all there were something like five hundred guns fired at the entry and exit of the various great men, and all native Pindi, gathered ten deep along the roads, declared that such a tamasha never was. And for once Native and European opinion is in accord.

I.21: "Scrap"

Attributed to Rudyard Kipling[18]

WE HAVE STILL TO HEAR THE LAST OF the Durbar at Rawulpindi. A correspondent writes to us: — "The experiment of admitting a number of lady spectators to the Rawul Pindi Durbar was not an unqualified success. In the first place, they were somewhat unfortunately placed opposite the native officers, and the native officials of the Punjab; and at the far end of the tent, where the natural levity of their dispositions could not be effectually controlled by the compelling eye of the Viceroy. In consequence of the latter part of the arrangement, they behaved indifferently throughout. To begin with, they indulged in a small demonstration of disfavour when the Hon'ble Mr. Ilbert entered the Durbar tent. Then they refused to conduct themselves with the church-like seriousness which becomes a Durbar; and talked and laughed persistently throughout the ceremony: particularly while the presents of the Ameer were being brought in. Indeed, the sounds from the ladies' block were audible all over the tent; and seriously interfered with hearing the words which the Ameer addressed to the Viceroy and those that Captain Talbot addressed to the Ameer. Finally, not a few ladies got up on chairs, and gazed long and deliberately at the Ameer and the Viceroy through field glasses. No doubt the ladies' block was badly placed for seeing, and should have been arranged at the far end of the left side of the Durbar tent. As it was, however, the ladies should have accepted the situation, and contented themselves with such view as it was possible to get from their seats. Many native gentlemen of the old school must have been horrified on Wednesday, at seeing English ladies behave in Durbar, with what, according to their ideas, was a utter disregard of decorum."

I.22: The Rawulpindi Camp

by Rudyard Kipling

(*From our Special Correspondent.*)
RAWALPINDI, April 10

The beginning of the beginning has come. Our canvas city is vanishing, tent by tent, like a city of smoke, leaving only acres of straw sprinkled ground to show where it once stood. The Commander-in-Chief, General Hardinge, Sir Frederick Roberts, Sir Charles Aitchison, Sir Alfred Lyall and their various satellites, are all gone and the coolie and the packing case ravage the land. Every one who can get away, has taken train and departed, and we are only waiting now until it shall please the Ameer to return to Peshawar in the saloon carriage which our Lieutenant-Governor has so generously lent him. Just now His Highness sits like a child, surrounded by his presents and is apparently in no hurry to leave Pindi behind him. After all, why should he be? His return to the north can but bring down on his head, in redoubled volume, State cares and anxieties that he has left behind him. From one tented field, where peace is assured, and good things of this earth abundant, to another where he may have to battle, as best he can, for the integrity of his borders, the step is not a pleasant one to contemplate; and Abdul Rahman Khan may be forgiven, if with oriental fatalism, he should resign himself to a "little sleep, a little slumber and a little folding of the hands to sleep," before seeking his own troubled territories once more. For that there will be war, and war to the bitter end between the Lion and the Bear, is everywhere held to be beyond doubt. The Russian attack on Panjdeh leaves no room for negotiations, satisfactory or unsatisfactory. In consequence, those whose trade is war, are of a light heart, and as behoves every Englishman in time of struggle, confident of success. They are not to be called upon to demonstrate, but to do battle when the time comes, so the subaltern sells off his *polo ponies* at ruinous reductions, learns from his seniors certain novel and starling facts, as to the heat in the Peshin valley in July, and waits prepared for either fortune. At the Club, on the Mall, at the races, ever the one absorbing topic of conversation, is the impending strife, and everywhere among military men, the conviction that the hour cannot be much longer delayed. But to be faithful in my chronicling. I must record, that in the face of this current of opinion, there exists an "under tow," as it were, of men who proclaim that the chances of active service are as remote as a year ago. Their authority for this opinion is not given, but inasmuch as they are, presumably, well-informed officials of standing and experience, their words are bound to carry a certain amount of weight. Nor do the "latest telegrams," full of outrage and breathing war in every line, shake their confidence one whit. Panjdeh is annexed, and explanations are called for by our long-suffering Government. Still the chances of war are remote. The Commission, to all appearances have been mixed up in the fray, and at the present moment are within some five miles of the Persian boundaries at Kirpal [sic], ready to move across, should occasion arise. War with Russia is extremely improbable we are told, and we may believe as much or as little of the statement as we please. These things are an enigma, and their solution is hidden from us. Had the propounders of the conundrum been merely "men on the mall," the matter might have been dismissed in a few words. As it

The Rawulpindi Camp

is, they are persons having authority, and speaking, we may suppose from data unknown to the world at large. And the world at large, from Khanna plain to Club, will have it, that war is intended and inevitable — the sooner the better that the present state of suspense and uncertainty may come to an end. Until the hour strikes however we amuse ourselves with racing, dances, smoking concerts and polo. In the press of other matters, the first and second day's racing took up but little of public attention. Besides the weather on the first day, at least, was abominably wet, and the attendance of spectators small.

Sir Frederick Roberts and a few ladies were present. I give below a brief summary of the result.

First Day, April 4.

1st Race.— Pindi Plate. For Ponies 13 hands and under. ½ mile. Rs. 500 added.

Lahore Confedy's b c-b m *Nina*, 11–6, Mr. Little	... 1
Mr. DeGex's b c-b p *Boxer*. 10–7, Mr. Bruce	... 2
F. Johnson's b a p *Czar*, late *Auchinleck*, 9–9, Owner	... 3

Czar and *Nina* were favourites. *Nina* won in a canter.

2nd Race.— Arabs and C.-B.'s. 1½ miles. Rs. 1,000

Maj. Chisholme's ch a h *Hassarac*, 8–7, Blackburn	... 1
Maj. Willoughby's g a h *Kushdill*, 8–13, Capt. Alexander	... 2
Mr. Thuillier's ch a h *Ariel*, 8–3, Robinson, Jun	... 3

Four false starts. A close race. *Hassarac*, well ridden, won from *Kushdill* by a short head. Owing to the state of the ground, *Zigzag* slipped and fell with Kendal. No harm done.

3rd Race.— Great Northern Stakes. 1 mile. Added money Rs. 1,000.

Maj. Cook's ch c-b m *Gazelle*, 8–5, Mr. Little	... 1
Kishore Singh's g a p *Strathmore*, 10–3, Native	... 2
Lahore Confedy's ch a p *Pioneer*, 10–3, Tingey	... 3

Gazelle won easily by about three lengths.–Time, 2m. 7s. Eight started.

4th Race.— All horse race. 1½ miles. Rs. 1,000 added.

Mr. F. G. Johnson's b au h *Sylvanus*, 9–13, walked over

5th Race.— Selling Race. 3/4 mile. Rs. 500 added

Mr. Milton's b w g *Puritan*. 9–7, Robinson	... 1
Kishore Singh's b w g *Kesmick*, 10–7, Capt. Alexander	... 2
Mr. Oliver's b w m *Ballet Girl*, 9–0, Native	... 3

Puritan won easily by three or four lengths.

6th Race.— Punjab Stakes. ½ mile. Rs. 500 added.

Lahore Confedy's b c-b m *Nina*, 9–1, Taylor	... 1

Capt. Carandini's ch c-b m *Ercilie*, 9–7, Tingey ... 2
" Alexander's r c-b g *Souvenir*, 9–4, Owner ... 3

    Five started. *Nina* favourite. Won in a canter.–Time, 62 sec.

    The racing course runs round the Viceroy's camp, and interfered with a clear view of the starting and much of the race. Consequently no time was taken in many of the races.

Second Day, April 8.

    The racing succeeded the Durbar on Wednesday, and the weather was then all that could be wished. Nearly everyone in Pindi attended.

    1st Race.—Galloway Handicap. 1 mile

Lord W. Beresford's b a g *Dynamite*, 8–13, Tingey ... 1
Major Cookes ch c-b p *Heliotrope*, 8–6, Robinson, Jr ... 2
Mr. F. G. Johnson's ch a p *Firefly*. 8–11. Kendall ... 3

    Four started in the race which *Dynamite* won easily.

    2nd Race.— Pony Handicap. 13 hands. 3 furlongs.

Lahore Confedy's b c-b m *Nina*, 11–10, Captain Little ... 1
Mr. Beddy's g c-b p *Robin Grey*. 9–7, Capt. Alexander ... 2
Captain Beresford's g c-b p *Potboy*, 9- ... 3

    A good race, won by about half a length.

    3rd Race.— All Pony Handicap. 5 furlongs.

Captain Neeld's g a p *Dilpasand*, 8–10, Kendall ... 1
Kishore Singh's g a p *Shelbourne*, 9–3, Robinson, Junr ... 2
Lahore Confedy's ch a p *Pioneer*, 9–10 Capt. Little, ... 3

    A very close race, won by a head.

    4th Race.— All Horse Handicap. 1 1/4 mile.

Kishore Singh's b w h *Keswick*, 8–4, Robinson ... 1
Lord W. Beresford's b w h *Tim Whiffler*, 8–10, Tingey ... 2
Mr. Oliver's blk w m *Ballet Girl*, 7 — 7 ... 3

    5th Race.— Arabs and Country Breds. Handicap. 1 3/4 miles. Five started for this race, *Hassarac* being the favorite.

Mr. F. G. Johnson's b a h *Zig-Zag*, 8–10, Kendal ... 1
Major Willoughby's g a h *Khushdil*, 9–7, Blackburn ... 2
Major Scott Chisholme's *Hassarac*, 9–5, Tingey ... 3

    Good race, won by a length.

    6th Race.— All Pony Handicap. Round Course

Captain Neeld's g a p *Dilpasand*, Kendal ... 1
Maharaja Kishore Singh's g a p *Strathmore*, Robinson, Jr. ... 2

    Won easily. Bad third.

    7th Race.— Maiden C.-B. Ponies. 3/4 mile. Rs. 200 added.

The Rawulpindi Camp

Mr. R. A's r c-b g *Souvenir*, (13–2,) Capt. Alexander	... 1
Captain Beresford's b c-b p *Potboy*, (12–3½) Native	... 2
Mr. Broughton's b c-b p *Parah*, (13–2,) Mr. Little	... 3

Won by about 1 length

Third Day, Saturday, April 11.

1st Race. Selling race. All horses. 1½ miles. Rs. 400 added.

Major Scott Chisholmes b c h *Edendery*, 9–9, Capt. Alexander	... 1
Mr. Milton's b w g *Puritan*. 9–0, Robinson	... 2
Kishore Singh's b w g *Keswich*, 11–0, Khadim	... 3

A good start. *Puritan* led nearly from the start to the finish, when *Edendery*, well ridden by Captain Alexander, passed him on the post and won by a length.

2nd Race.—All Chargers. ½ mile. Rs. 200 added.

Lord W. Beresford's b w g *Prospero*. 13–0, Owner	... 1
Maj. Scott-Chisholmes b c b g *Whalebone*, 10–8, Mr. Little	... 2
Mr. Oliver's Bck w m *Ballet Girl*, 12–4 Capt. Tipping	... 3

Whalebone and *Prospero* were the only horses who made any show in this race. About sixty yards from home *Prospero* was let go, and won as he liked.

3rd Race.—Selling race for Ponies. R. C. Rs. 300 added.

Mr. Macpherson's b a p *Telephone*, Robinson, Junior	... 1
Mr. Oliver's g w m *Greyhen*, 10–7, Capt. Tipping	... 2
Kishore Singh's c a p *Vile*, 10–0, Khadim	... 3

Bismillah led off *Greyhen*, *Vile*, *Telephone*, and the others close up. At the turn into the straight *Telephone* was seen to have the race at his mercy, and won as he liked.

4th Race. Selling Race. 13–2 C. B's. 3/4 mile. Rs. 200 added.

Mr. R. A.'s r c-b g *Souvenir*, 8–07, Ivemy	... 1
Capt. Alexander's dun c-b p *Miranda*, 9–0, Owner	... 2
Mr. Thuillier's g c-b m *Miss Puff*, 10–7, Mr. Bruce	... 3

This race lay actually between *Souvenir*, and *Miranda*. The latter was completely beaten at the distance, and *Souvenir* won in the commonest of canters.

5th Race. Selling Race. All Ponies 13 hands. 5 Furlongs.

Mr. Beddy's g c-b g *Robin Grey*, 9 0, Captin Alexander	... 1
Mr. DeGex's b c-b m *Boxer*, 11–0 Mr. Bruce	... 2
Mr. Willet's ch c-b m *Josephine*, 8–7, Native	... 3

Boxer got off with the lead, *Robin Grey* close up and about one length separating the rest. Down the straight, where they were next seen, *Robin*

Grey, Boxer and *Josephine* were all riding. The rest well behind; *Miss Chic and Leila* having practically pulled up. Close to home, *Robin Grey* shot ahead and won by a neck; about the same distance dividing *Boxer* and *Josephine*.

6th Race.— Arab and C.B's. Sweepstakes. 1 mile Sweepstakes Rs. 69.
T. B. Confederacy's ch c-b p *Endbrook*, 8–10, Tingey ... 1
Mr. Waller's ch a h *Ariel*, 8–0, Ivemy ... 2
Major Chisholme's c a h *Hassarac*, Mr. Little ... 3

This requires hardly any description. *Endbrook* went ahead and won as he liked; the favourite, *Nelly Bly*, not being even placed.

7th Race.— Match . Rs. 200
Mr. Thuillier's b c-b m *Leila v.* Mr. Hamilton's b c-b m *Miss Chic*.
A good race won by *Miss Chic* after a close finish.

Since an Englishman, even under our Indian sun, cannot be happy without his national recreation, a cricket match was arranged between the Combatants and non–Combatants of the assembly. This was played off on the 9th and 10th instant on the Club cricket ground. The Combatants, as might have been expected mustered a very strong team, including three or four of the best bats in Upper India. The non-Combatants, on the other hand, were scarcely able to get a team but, as events turned out, did not make so very bad a display after all. The Combatants won the toss, went in and put together 111—a lower score than had been anticipated. The non-Combatants fell to pieces at once, and were all put out for 56. In their second innings, the Combatants made 160, leaving the other team to struggle up as near to 215 runs as they could. This the non-Combatants failed to do by thirty-four runs: making in their second innings 181—a vast improvement on their first efforts. For the Combatants, Manners-Smith of the 3rd Sikhs made 55. For the non-Combatants, Mr. Belmont's 51 was the best score. This team was specially good in fielding, and the bowling analysis showed that the bowling of Meredith, Beatty, Lauson, Smith and B. C. C., were above average.

I.23: [The Rawulpindi Camp]
by Rudyard Kipling[19]

RAWAL PINDI, March 11 [*sic*]

Decidedly, public interest has shifted from the Ameer to Russia. His Highness has been for some weeks before our eyes, and we suggest that it is time that he returned to take his place on the great chess board, ere the game begins. At 9-30 this morning he left in the L.G's., saloon carriages for Peshawur, accompanied by Colonel Waterfield and various other officials. But his last day's stay in Rawal Pindi seems to have interested him more than any one — more than Monday and Tuesday, when he watched the harvest of the dragon's teeth near Fort Rawul Pindi and on the Khanna Plain.

Yesterday His Highness and the Commander-in-Chiefs, under the guidance of Major Kinsman, the officer in charge, went over the Rawal Pindi Arsenal, and inasmuch as the Oriental has no notion of blasêness as we understand it, Abdul Rahman took some three hours over his visit, in spite of the fact that his gout was very troublesome and compelled him frequently to sit down. Arms and ammunition are things that the ruler of Afghanistan thoroughly understands and appreciates, and if all accounts may be believed, he passed a most enjoyable forenoon, investigating arms and accoutrements, asking questions, and emphatically expressing his admiration of everything he saw.

He had been in Russian arsenals he said, but had never seen anything like to this one for size and symmetry. What was the bore of the guns? How and where were they made? What did they cost? How many were in stock? were the questions with which he plied the officer in charge, Golam Hyder, Commander-in-Chief, meanwhile counting the stands of rifles with a loving eye. Finally, the Ameer suggested that he would like to visit the Powder Magazine and to the Magazine accordingly he was conducted, spurless, swordless, and bootless — or at least with his huge black leather knee boots encased in Magazine slippers. The descent to the Magazine is a steep and dark one, but neither the gout nor the steepness of the way prevented the Ameer from making a minute inspection of the piled barrels and cases. He lost all his reserve and chatted as freely as any sight-seeing T.G on his way through the world, but all the time as one who thoroughly understood what he was talking about. As a finale to the visit, he ascended one of the bastions of the Fort, and from thence surveyed the country below. His autograph in Persian is in the visitors' book at Fort Pindi — a second by the way exists in the Duchess of Connaught's birthday book — and he has been eloquent to all around him, in describing the wonders that he has seen. As a memento he takes away some photos of the big guns at Woolwich.

But to return to His Highness's departure this morning. Day dawned much as it did on his arrival, and there was every prospect of a drenching rain till night. However, nature compromised the matter with a sharp shower before the escort and carriages came in sight, so that the spectators — there were not many of them — could rest in peace on the station step. The Irish Fusiliers, with band and colours, furnished the Guard of Honour on the platform, and K battery R. H. A., outside the station, fired the salute. The roads from the Ameer's camp to the station were lined with troops, and the Ameer's escort was composed of the K. D. G.'s and the Viceroy's Body Guard. Abdul Rahman, accompanied by Lord William Beresford, Mr. Mackenzie Wallace, Colonel Henderson, Mr. Perkins, and other Civil and Military Officers, reached the station about twenty minutes past nine. As he came on to the platform, it could be seen that he was decorated with the order of the G. C. S. I. Also that he smiled affably at everyone around. Owing to some delay in the home telegram I believe, the decoration was only bestowed on him just before he left his house, when a deputation, on behalf of the Viceroy, performed that solemn function. Wednesday's Durbar would have been by far the better occasion for such a gift, but this of course was impossible. Once on the platform, His Highness did not keep us waiting long. He shook hands briskly with the assembled officials, and with his train full of followers and attendants, steamed slowly Peshawur-wards. From the top of one of the station towers, it is possible to obtain a magnificent view of Rawul Pindi and its environs—from the orderly lines of the Viceroy's camp on the north, to the faint white streak, across the trees, which shows where the Khanna camp is situated. Even with so many regiments departed, and with three large camps—the Commander-in-Chief's, the Lieutenant-Governor's and the Civil Camp, swept off the scene, the long lines of tents were sufficiently imposing, and it was here that the best view of the panorama could be obtained; only the figure of the men below were dwarfed in the face of surrounding nature. That Abdur Rahman Khan's reception in British India was not without its due effect on him, may be judged from the few words—it would hardly be fair to call it a speech—which he delivered at the platform. "The reception accorded to him by the Viceroy had exceeded all his expectations; he had regarded the troops at Rawul Pindi with pleasure and satisfaction, and finally trusted that the friendship at present established between England and Afghanistan would subsist to the end of time." So the train bore away Abdur Rahman to work out his destines in the north, while India waits on the march of events, reflecting on her engagements to Afghanistan. And what those engagements exactly are is not easy to ascertain. Lord Dufferin—moved surely by the spirit of bitterest sarcasm—is said to have complained that affairs of State, political and military movements and the like, are too hastily made public and bruited abroad—a state of things which he is determined to put a stop to. It may be permissible, however, to make one statement in the face of this determination—a statement which may or may not be right, but which, to use the hackneyed phrase, once more comes on the best authority. In the course of his interviews with the Viceroy, Abdur Rahman stated, that if India were prepared to stand by his distressful country, he should not require an increased subsidy, but arms and munitions of war only. That as the Afghans found it hard to forget and forgive a war, barely four years concluded, he would much prefer that no British troops were moved into Afghanistan for the present at least. In reply, he was informed that there was no intention of any such movement until the Afghan nation actually demanded the presence of troops to assist them.

I.24: The Viceroy in Lahore
by Rudyard Kipling[20]

(*From our Special Correspondent.*)
LAHORE, April 15

The City of Destruction could not have been more swiftly abandoned than were the various camps at Pindi two days ago. Thanks to the indiscriminating generosity which packed the Ameer's followers, from the highest to the lowest, in first and second-class carriages, accommodation for the flying Englishmen was limited; and there were those who, in despair of aught better, were fain to roost on the floor of a second-class compartment, already crowded to overflowing with half a dozen natives and their bundles. For the last week, six or eight troop trains have been running daily, in addition to the ordinary traffic, on the Punjab Northern State Railway; and the officials have their hands full. Private Thomas Atkins, and Nubbee Buksh, on their way, as they fondly imagine, to immediate death or glory, are, though somewhat obstreperously inclined, perfectly amenable to discipline. Still, his very numbers give trouble. There is so much of him and his accoutrements; he is so helpless and required such an immensity of looking after. Nubee Buksh indeed will sit patiently all night within the shadow of the platform pillars, smoking the hubble-bubble among his friends. Thomas Atkins, too smokes and the spirit (animal) moves him to stentorian song from time to time, as he waits the arrival of his train. His conversation is of war, and the nature of canteen beer — especially the former topic. He believes, and states his belief with much unction, that the time has come, and that—"if this 'ere bloomin' bayonet don't crinkle up like brown paper"— he is the man to drive the Russian into the Caspian. Nor does he stop here. His mind is athirst for information bearing on the coming struggle. He rises, *experto crede*, from the midst of his meals by the platform side, and his affable "I say, Mister" is a prelude to a whole host of questions, anent matters military and military-political. Carlyle says somewhere, that the soldier who, with a tangible weapon, is prepared at a definite word of command to undoubtedly run you through, is the only reality in a world of shams and make-beliefs. Thomas Atkins, eager to know when "this row's a comin' off," is a restful fact, after a Conference which has left us the outlines of as invertebrate a policy as the mind of man ever framed. The nature of Abdul Rahman's rule among his subjects is fairly well understood. His power extends just so far as a Cabul-made Martini-Henri will carry, or as a messenger may travel with a bribe. Knowing this, as he has good reason to do, he asserts that he is able to meet any force that Russia can at present put in the field, if a just and generous Government will only provide him with arms and ammunition and, when need arises, money. In return, the Indian Government promises that he shall, for the present at least, have the game to himself; that supplies shall be forthcoming and that, if the worst comes to the worst, our own troops shall step in to put matters straight. Holy Russia, on the other hand, has all the loot of all India to offer the wild tribes that she "civilizes." When a river rises in spate, the dam breaks, not so much from the power of the water, as the impact of the uprooted trees, which the flood brings down with the force of battering rams against the barrier. The men of the hills recognize that conflict with the mysterious octopus-like Power that has her agents everywhere, leads to little beyond death and defeat. By going forward with the tide, they may find plunder, fair women, horses, nose-rings and coined money in plenty; their lot being, in any case, better than fruitless struggle against a puissant and penniless power. If Abdul Rahman can guarantee that no one of the tribes under his government will be of this way of thinking; that the contagion of one secession will not spread like wildfire; or that, if it does spread, he has an army, willing and able enough to suppress both the internal rising, and repulse the external attack, our agreement with him has been well made. If not — Well, we have but the "only reality" to fall back upon — an expensive unacclimatized, but hard-fighting article. And he has taken me far enough away, indeed, from the subject matter of my letter, which was the Viceroy's arrival in Lahore station this morning.

In the first place, our station was never built as a place of reception for the dignitaries of the land. Very few stations are. In this part of the world the red cloth lane is, by custom, laid down directly in front of the ticket office and the bridge that connects the up and down platforms, and the Guard of Honour forms up in front of the waiting rooms. Perhaps the only advantage of an Indian station, considered as a Divan of Audience, lies in the fact, that the arched roof of corrugated iron is a magnificent sounding board; and the loyal strains of "God save the Queen" reverberate as though each bandsman had laid his instrument to the bystander's ear. In spite of this fact, neither receivers or received ever appear to enjoy themselves much under the station roof, and are always glad to adjourn as quickly as possible to the carriages in waiting outside. His Excellency to-day was doomed to linger long. He arrived punctually at 1–45; the train being, for some reason or other, three quarters of an hour late from Rawul Pindi. During that time, the two Guards of Honour, the 24th Punjab Native Infantry and the 1st and 3rd Punjab Volunteers, had time to get into position, and the spectators to argue whether a gold braided uniform or thick "black diagonal" morning coats were the warmer articles of wear on a sultry April day. The balance of opinion ran in favour of military and political uniforms — owners agreeing. (Since one reception is so absolutely like another, it is necessary to dwell on these frivolous details.) His Excellency's train eventually ran in, made a shot for the red cloth, missed it, tried back, moved forward, and eventually pulled up a little to the left. Lord Dufferin appeared, hesitated for a moment, was received by Sir Charles Aitchison, and then and there — disappeared from view. Without in the faintest degree intending to be disrespectful, I may say that our Viceroy's descent into the irrepressible crowd that awaited him, resembled nothing so much as the effacement of a kite amid a swarm of mannerless crows. Natives and Europeans closed around him and stared; while Sir Charles Aitchison, sorely hampered for want of elbow room, was introducing various notabilities. Had the Queen's representative arrived alone, and unaccompanied by his family, this would not have mattered quite so much, but when Lady Dufferin and her daughter had to stand back from the press, close to the door of the railway carriage, one felt that the Guard of Honour was a superfluous matter — every one knows our loyalty — and that, if the Police were absolutely unavailable, the volunteers would have been better employed in checking our exuberant manifestations of it. At this point, Lord Dufferin with a space of at least two clear feet around him, was confronted by the Lahore Municipality and addressed. The Address was a long one, and here again Lady Dufferin had to stand and wait till it was all over, amid the heat, the crush, and the plague of flies, that our station breeds throughout the year. Neither the President's elocution, the illuminated borders of the Address, the tasteful casket and the kincob bag wherein it was enclosed, and the sentiments of loyalty and devotions with which it teemed, were sufficient to overcome these little drawbacks. To the Address, Lord Dufferin replied on the spot, in the words which have already appeared in your paper; and it could be seen, that, as he lifted his head to speak, our new ruler had that nameless something called "presence" — a matter entirely distinct from the prosaic limitations of feet and inches, which even the surroundings could not lessen. It is unkindly perhaps, to go out of one's way to draw comparisons, but there have been occasions when neither three feet of red velvet dais, gold chairs of State or mace-bearing *chobdars*, could give dignity to the Common-place exalted. Lord Dufferin's reply was naturally inaudible three feet from his lips. Indeed he would have had to have shouted aloud, to make it otherwise, in the din throughout the station. After it had been delivered, a road was cleared with some difficulty, and His Excellency proceeded to inspect the Punjab Volunteer's Guard of Honour. Here, too, his remarks, if he made any, passed unheard. Immediately after this, he returned to the red cloth, and accompanied by Sir Charles Aitchison, went out to his carriage, and so on to Government House. The 14th Bengal Lancers formed the escort, and disappeared in a cloud of dust after they had trotted a few paces. Then, after a decent interval, and the departure of the Staff &c., the mob departed — Coolie jostling Colonel; and Babu, Barrister. Decidedly His Excellency could not have enjoyed his experience, and it is devoutly to be hoped that, in the spring and summer months at least, the experiment of Railway Station receptions may never be repeated. At eight o'clock on a January morning, a stumbling, jostling crowd of natives, elbowing their way amid an assemblage of Europeans, is not wholly objectionable. Toes and tempers are alike warmed. In April, the performance is unpleasant, and if unpleasant for men, doubly so for any ladies that may be in the throng.

  At five o'clock this afternoon, Lord and Lady Dufferin and party, and the indispensable escort, drove out to Jehangeer's tomb amid the rose burdened gardens of Shahdera. There are times in the spring evenings, when the broad reaches of the Ravi, golden and opal in the dying sunlight; the tender greens and greys of the woods along its banks; the smoke from the burning-ghats by the wheat fields and the forlorn grandeur of the gardens themselves, are best seen alone. When the inlaid chamber where Jehangir rests in peace, and the roses above his tomb wither from week's end to week's end, is good to visit on foot and unaccompanied. But these things may be viewed possibly quite as well amid a crowd, and with a cicerone to explain how successive marauding rulers, more than the lapse of years, have played havoc with the glories of minar and marble cupola and how, untended and out of sight in the jungle beyond the garden walls, are the graves of twenty or thirty British soldiers who died while hutted round Lahore City forty odd years ago. When Lord Dufferin puts India into a book as he did his American experiences we may learn how these things impressed him. To-day's visit was a private one, and Shadera has been spared the indignity of addresses reserved for even lovelier Shalimar to-morrow night. A Levée in this part of the world has furnished an overwhelming amount of comic writing; and has been described and re-described *ad lib*. The one held at Government House to-night differed from none of its fellows, except in point of time. It was a short function. Every one, of course, was levied *en masse*, but Lahore is empty just now, and there could not have been more than two hundred and fifty men present. If twenty thousand men, fifty abreast, took something under an hour to march by, two hundred and fifty, walking briskly in single file, take about twenty minutes.

I.25: *The Rumoured Trouble at Herat*

In a letter to Edmonia Hill dated May 15, 1888, Rudyard Kipling expressed his annoyance that newspaper editors were again soliciting his opinion on the possibilities of a war with Russia. By 1888 Kipling had begun to make a name for himself with his published works and he dreaded the thought of returning to the drudgery of newspaper work. He wrote:[21]

> The Jamshidis of Herat have expressed a desire to become Russian subjects and that stormy Petrel Alikhanoff is on the wing again. I s'pose I shall have to grind out something about it later on. What in the name of commonsense have I to do with Jamshidis and complications across the border? I was hundreds of miles away when that pestilent Reuter turned up and he is trying to pull me back again, into the slough.

With his translations of the diaries of Alikhanoff and the reports on the Afghan Boundary Commission, Kipling had built up quite a reputation for himself as an expert on Central Asia. He finally came around and completed one of his last articles for the *Civil and Military Gazette* on May 17, 1888. It is titled "The Rumoured Trouble at Herat."

The telegram from Simla published in our issue of yesterday, stating that the Government of India had heard nothing of the alleged disturbances near Herat ought to go far to ally the feelings of anxiety raised by the *Standard's* account of the complications there.

It is next to impossible that an event of such importance as a rising among the Jamshidis against the Afghans should have occurred without the knowledge of our agent at Meshed, General Maclean. But the incident is, in a way, important, as it shows the public the manner in which Russia, *when she really means business*, will make use of her enterprising and unscrupulous frontier officials, of whom Colonel Alikhanoff is by far the ablest and most daring. That the Jamshidis have risen against the Afghans is most improbable. They are essentially a peace loving people, now only too anxious to enjoy the period of rest from Turkoman raiding, which has resulted from the Russian subjugation of the Tekkes and Salors, and the demarcation of the frontier. Open resistance to Afghan authority, even though backed by Russians, would help them but little, as their only town of any importance — Kushk — could easily be laid waste and ruined by the Amir's soldiery before assistance could arrive. It is however, not improbable that the Jamshidis are a little discontented at the present time. The failure of last year's crops, with no remission of taxes, and the location of Zamindawaris and Ghilzais on their lands between Kushk and Kara Tapa, added to their Governor Kazi Saud-ud-din's somewhat high-handed mode of administration, are all reasons for causing dislike to the Afghan rule: and, no doubt, when everything is ripe for Russia's pounce on Herat, the oppressed Jamshidi will be a useful tool in the hands of the astute Alikhanoff. However, the Jamshidis are good Muhamedans, and it is difficult to believe that they will ever *ask* for Russian rule of their own free-will.

Appendix II: Articles on Central Asia and Afghanistan Attributed to Kipling or Wheeler

Appendix II.1: "Scrap" (September 16, 1884, 1c)
Appendix II.2: The Delimitation Commission (October 8, 1884, 5b)
Appendix II.3: The Afghan Boundary Commission (October 28, 1884, 2d–3a)
Appendix II.4: "Scrap" (December 16, 1884, 1c)
Appendix II.5: The Central Asian Question (December 24, 1884, 2a)
Appendix II.6: "Scrap" (January 6, 1885, 1c)
Appendix II.7: "Scrap" (January 16, 1885, 1b)
Appendix II.8: "Scrap" (January 21, 1885, 1c)
Appendix II.9: "Scrap" (February 4, 1885, 1c)
Appendix II.10: "Scrap" (February 5, 1885, 1c)
Appendix II.11: "Scrap" (February 11, 1885, 1c)
Appendix II.12: "Scrap" (February 19, 1885, 1b)
Appendix II.13: "Scrap" (February 24, 1885, 1b)
Appendix II.14: "Scrap" (February 27, 1885,1b)
Appendix II.15: The Russians in Central Asia (March 2, 1885, 1a)
Appendix II.16: "Scrap" (March 9, 1885, 1c)
Appendix II.17: "Scrap" (March 11, 1885, 1d)
Appendix II.18: The Ameer Abdul Rahman (March 11, 1885, 3c)
Appendix II.19: "Scrap" (March 12, 1885, 1d)
Appendix II.20: "Scrap" (March 13, 1885, 1b)
Appendix II.21: Russia and Herat (March 14, 1885, 1,4)
Appendix II.22: "Scraps" (March 16, 1885, 1c)
Appendix II.23: "Scrap" (March 17, 1885, 1b)

Appendix III: Translations by Rudyard Kipling

(Pertaining to Central Asia and Afghanistan in the *Civil and Military Gazette* between October 21, 1884, and April 3, 1885)

1. "The Central Asian Question" (October 21, 1884, p. 3)
2. "The Russians in Central Asia" (January 28, 1885, p. 3)
3. "The Russian Press" (January 31, 1885, p. 3)
4. "Scrap" (February 11, 1885, p. 1)
5. "The Russian Press" (March 16, 1885, p. 5)
6. "The Russian Press" (March 20, 1885, p. 5)
7. "The Russian Press" (March 27, 1885, p. 3)
8. "The Russian Press" (Apr. 3, 1885, p. 5)

III.1: The Central Asian Question

[SPECIALLY TRANSLATED]

The writer in the St. Petersburg *Nouveau Temps* asserts a Delimitation Commission of the Afghan frontiers in which England is concerned will react detrimentally on Russian *prestige* in Central Asia. According to his arguments the Boundary question should have been settled between Russian and Afghanistan directly.

Another writer who signs himself EX-DIPLOMATIST contradicts this; basing his arguments on the fact that the two articles which he has published have been the subject of diplomatic correspondence between the two countries. He says that although the idea of conquest may not have been an integral portion of the Russian policy in Central Asia, still the configuration of the Russian possessions there fifteen years ago could not but be considered as definitely settled. On the Bokhara side matters were quiet enough, but, says the EX-DIPLOMATIST, this was not the case with other points on our Asiatic frontier. Khiva especially, which by reason of its position was held to be inaccessible caused us grave embarrassment, and consequently military operations in this direction seemed unavoidable. "The rivalry of England where Russian interest was concerned (a rivalry which was well known by all the Central Asian potentates) rendered this task a very ticklish one. As far as material interests were concerned the situation of England in Asia was a far better one than our own. Her possessions in India, defended along the north-west Frontier were a source of much wealth to her. Nevertheless the success of Russia in Central Asia disquieted her. She looked then for a barrier against this advance beyond her own frontiers, and found it in Afghanistan, a country which in the year 1857, had entered into a treaty of alliance with the Viceroys of India.

Under these circumstances than it was material that the two powers of England and Russia should have been at some pains to arrive at a material understanding and *pourparlers* were consequently entered upon eventually both realized that the question could not be satisfactorily settled without establishing a zone of influence for either country. At first though there was some idea of defining a "neutral zone," but this was abandoned in the face of the many difficulties which would attend on its establishment. It was resolved to lay down in Central Asia a line of demarcation which should be respected not only by the two Powers, but also by the Khans which came within the range of their respective influences. The line of demarcation, as was laid down at the commencement of the year 1873, was to coincide with the northern limits of Afghanistan. By virtue of this arrangement Russia would have as little to do with the affairs of Afghanistan as England with those of the Central Asian Khanates.

"Particular importance had been attached to the eastern portion of the line of demarcation — that is to say, the line running from the Soree-Kul lake in the Panier district to the Afghan outpost of Khodga Salekh, on the left bank of the Oxus, as it served as a boundary between the possessions of the Khan of Bokhara and those of the Amir of Afghanistan.

"Our recent conquests of the Turcoman steppes necessitated in a fresh demarcation of the western portion of the line of limitation. The conclusion of the Russo-Persian Convention of the 9th of December 1881, was made an excuse by England for offering to mediate in the question of extending the boundary of the trans-Caspian province eastwards from the Babadour was, its north-east extremity. The St. Petersburgh cabinet considered all mediation superfluous as Persia was a friendly power, declined England's offer and added, that it would be unquestionably necessary to resume negotiations in order to set the portion of the Afghan frontier which had only been very vaguely defined in 1873. Matters remained thus up till the time that Merve was annexed and the Ootolan Turcomans passed under our protection. The negotiations which were resumed this year resulted in the formation of the Anglo-Russian Commission."

In accordance with the facts which have been stated above the delimitation of the Afghan Boundary could only be settled with the concurrence of England. Moreover, Abdur Rahman, the present Amir of Afghanistan, who has been raised to the throne by the English, could not hold his obligations towards her so cheap as to enter into negotiations with us. It behoves us too to hold to our engagements in this respect. What would the Russian press say if England, for stance, were to interfere in the administration of Bokhara?

Notwithstanding this, however, objectors to the Anglo-Russian Commission insist that under existing circumstances it would have been better to have no delimitation of frontier whatever. "EX-DIPLOMATIST" is of another opinion. According to him, Russia's refusal to the plan would be unfavourably interpreted in England, and besides, every one knows the evils which arise from a badly defined frontier. This fact is so incontestable that there are no less than four delimitation commissions at work this year on the Russian frontiers in Central Asia, between the Caspian and the Pacific.

The assertion that the hidden motive of the Commission is to assure the Amir of Afghanistan the possession of central points of strategic importance in the north, need not be considered seriously. The mixed Commission is composed of a Russian representative as well as an English one, the former will know how to safeguard our interest."

III.2: The Russians in Central Asia

See **Appendix I.2** with writings by Kipling. Kipling mentions working on this piece several times in his diary for 1885. On January 24 he wrote: "worked at long translation from the *Journal de Saint Petersburg* which took home to finish." On the 25th he wrote: "Three hours hard work in the morning finished translation, proofs, papers and all the rest — Did nothing else all day." On January 26 he wrote: "Translation (as I had expected not wanted)." Then on January 27 he wrote: "Russian translation went in today."

III.3: The Russian Press

[SPECIALLY TRANSLATED]

The *Novoe Vremya* of December 30th, gives the following information regarding the improvements of the Poli Harbour. Poti is a port on the eastern shore of the Black Sea, and is a very important link between Russian proper and her Caucasian Army. It and Baku, a little south, form the Black Sea termini of the Railway through Tiflis to the Caspian Sea at Baku:-

The works connected with the construction of the Poti harbour are being rapidly pushed forward: the northern and southern jetties are already completed, and the deepening of the harbour by dredging has been commenced. If, as is promised, 120 cubic sajens (844 cub. feet,) are daily dredged out, two years almost will be required for the completion of the work. This period could be reduced by half, if another dredging machine were added, like the one now in use, the cost of which is not more than 40 or 50 thousand roubles (about £ 7,500). In this case, not only would the Treasury not lose, but would gain; as the yearly interest can be deducted from the expenditure, as also the maintenance of overseers and harbour management; not to mention the advantage to the whole district from the acceleration of the work. Already the construction has taken nearly a quarter of a century instead of three years as stipulated, and one must reluctantly fear that the deepening of the harbour, from some unforeseen hindrances or other, will be extended over another three instead of two years. Besides this, another important circumstance is, that the proposed depth of the harbour is 16 feet, while sea going ships draw 18 to 20 feet and more of water. In the present year 6 million poods (pood = 36 lbs) of maize besides kerosine, manganese and other products of the Province have been exported.

The same paper in an article published on the 27th ultimo, discusses the state of English politics. We read: —

Political life in England, is as it were, positively numbed by the approach of the Christmas holidays. Telegrams bring no news of interest from London, and is silent as to General Wolseley's expedition, which probably is moving on Khartoum from Dongola. On the eve of important events in the domain of internal home, and external foreign politics, the English are, as it were gathering their strength; and desisting from wasting it on the ordinary political routine. For Gladstone's ministry such a rest is certainly indispensable, for with the advent of the New Year, the Premier will find his hands full, and that with no pleasant work.

First of all, he must secure the passing, by the House of Commons, of the Redistribution Bill. We have already once remarked that among the Radicals of the Government majority there are many opponents of the Bill. These malcontents are endeavouring to excite an agitation for amendments in the Bill, which Gladstone, bound by promises already given, cannot assent to, for he shewed sometime ago that he would make the acceptation of the Bill in its original form a Cabinet question. It will be necessary to convince the Radicals of the unreasonableness of their opposition, which will hinder, for a long time, the practical acceptance of the electoral reforms. If these efforts of Gladstone are crowned with success, there will further remain to him misgivings regarding the Khartoum expedition, still far from its destination. Latterly, a belief in the uncertainty of this military undertaking has shaken the minds of the English public. The possibility of non-success or even of tragic disaster to the English detachment becomes a subject of lively interest, although only as yet based on rumour. The persistency with which certain pessimists aver that Gordon perished long ago, and that Khartoum is in the hands of the Mahdi's partisans, produces its own effect. The fear that the leader of the Soudan insurgents will lure the force to its fall, and cut off its retreat, is almost openly hinted in some political circles. If, by the opening of the administrative session, that is, by the 14th February, news of the full success of General Wolseley's force is not to hand, the Opposition will certainly take advantage of the disturbing situation to begin a new campaign against the Egyptian policy of the Government, and Gladstone will require all his efforts to render harmless the attacks of his opponents.

III.4: "Scrap"

THE ST. PETERBOURGH *Novoe Vremya*, IN A leading article on the 18th January writes: — "from telegrams and from correspondence, we already know that Sir P. Lumsden, the head of the English portion of the Boundary Commission, at the beginning of November, entered the Herat Valley. From the present letters of the *Times*' correspondent, we learn that the troops of the escort behaved very well, and displayed praiseworthy endurance during one hilly and difficult march. The detachment of the 20th Punjab Infantry refused to ride on camels, and marched 57 versts (about 38 miles) in 15 hours. The Beloochees behaved well to the English; but beginning from Lash Jowain to the vicinity of Herat, where the Afghans live, the travellers were received sullenly and inimically. The population of the Herat Valley, which consists of a mixture of Persians with the Turcoman tribe — the Persians having remained there since the time of Jhengis Khan and Timour — behaved in a *very* friendly way to the English. According to the latest news, the party under Sir P. Lumsden, in expectation of the arrival of the Russian section, is occupying itself with a reconnaissance of the locality from Bala Murghab to the Oxus. Vambery, in his capacity of a retired traveller and acknowledged judge of Asian affairs, from time to time writes to the English papers, articles regarding the frontier line of

Russia and Afghanistan; endeavouring to prove our conduct, in the present circumstance, as unsatisfactory and audacious, and to excite the self-love of the English. In his last letter to the *Times*, he points to the non-departure of the Russian section of the Commission, and says that the reason for the delay as put forth by us—*viz.*, the necessity of preliminary negociations [*sic*]—is invalid. The weaker, according to Vambery, can only agree to await the pleasure of the stronger. We, on our side, suppose that the matter will be carried on on a fair basis; and that Russian detachment will set out for the frontier in good time, when the preparatory negociations are concluded. In the present case, Russia will readily shew a tolerance and deference, in clear contrast to England, by having agreed to the Commission. Sir P. Lumsden in traversing our frontier, and making the population acquainted with English money. Lumsden spends on the Expedition 160,000 roubles (£25,600) monthly. This a very substantial sum for a thinly populated tract, such as that in which he now is."

III.5: The Russian Press

We translate below an article from the *Journal de Saint Petersburg* of the 16th February, portions of which have already been quoted by Reuter and the *Times* Correspondent: -

"Our readers know, that for some time past, the greater number of foreign Stock Exchanges do not merely balance their accounts at the end of each month, but twice in the same period. And whenever these dates come round, a rumour of same kind or other, with an influence on the funds, is started by the Bulls or the Bears. There is nothing astonishing then in the fact that the Bourses of Western Europe should have taken alarm at a statement made by the Vienna Correspondent of the *Daily Telegraph*, who informs his paper that Russian troops are about to occupy Herat. He adds that any official negations of this fact, even though they came from Lord Granville himself, need not be credited, as no one knows more about the matter than the correspondent. This is a *canard* of some gravity indeed; and the Bulls have not been slow to take advantage of it. For the past two days the Russian bankers have been continuously asked by their German and English clients whether 'Herat had been really taken.'

"The *Nouveau Temps* assures these perturbed speculators that Herat is not taken, and that the Russians have begun no serious operations against that town. Our contemporary further explains that, near the frontier, are posted a detachment of English troops for the protection of the future Delimitation Commission and with these Russia does not propose to fight. In Herat, further says the *Nouveau Temps,* is a large fortified town occupied by a strong Afghan garrison. Our views with regard to Afghanistan are of the most peaceable nature, and Russia neither desires nor will undertake the least annexation. Our contemporary gives us to understand that the peaceable settlement of the delimitation question between Russia and Afghanistan will depend on the restraint of the Afghans who are not *au courant* with European affairs.

The *Nouveau Temps* adds:-

'It seems to us that the continued presence of an English detachment near our frontier, as well as the British munificence of Sir Peter Lumsden, may have an unfortunate influence on the minds of the too impressionable Afghans; but if, according to the existing agreement, the English have undertaken the expensive and disagreeable task of tutoring the Afghans, they ought, at the same time to restrain them. If England finds herself unable to do this, then naturally, Russia will be obliged to rely on her own resources."

It seems to us that, in the lines which we have just read, the English responsibilities are so well defined that there is nothing left to add. The Vienna Correspondent of the *Daily Telegraph* may profit by them."

III.6: The Russian Press

Specially Translated

The following is an extract from a leading article in the *Novoe Vremya* of 12th February:-

The uncertainty regarding the fate of Gordon is at an end. The daring defender of Khartoum fell by the hand of an assassin on the day of the capture of the city by the Soudanese army. The further problem of operations in the Soudan for the English is thus definitely fixed. It devolves on General Wolseley, who has been invested with full powers, to avenge the loss of Gordon by a complete defeat of the enormous bands of the Mahdi. This obligation the Government have laid on him. This retaliation the whole country unanimously requires from him, through the medium of the most influential journals of the most opposite views. The Radical *Pall Mall Gazette*, the Conservative *Standard* combine on this occasion with the all-powerful organ of the English material interest — the *Times*. In the exasperated cries of the deeply insulted British vanity are heard afar dangers of no fanciful character, namely, the fear that the failure of Wolseley's expedition will not only raise against England all the fanatical Musalmans of the Soudan and Egypt, but will react upon the Mussulmans of India. The question now revolves itself into, not vengeance for Gordon's death, but hits on the prestige of the British name in Asia, and in the Musulman portions of Africa. By the fatal course of circumstances, the leader finds himself in a very dangerous position. The small expeditionary force is split up into three weak bodies, incapable of communication and surrounded by hordes of Soudanese. The base itself has been changed by force of circumstances to Suakim. Between the latter and Wolseley's Head Quarters is interposed the numerous army of Osman Digma of the Soudanese garrison of Berber. It will be first necessary to clear this route. This will take a long time; and meanwhile Wolseley must take up a defensive position, and a policy of inaction, which will give the Mahdi an idea of the weakness of the English. The English army is small, and can with difficulty supply a force of 10,000 to operate from Suakim. Success under the circumstances is possible, and indeed probable against untrained hordes of savages. The complication of the problem, which presents itself to Wolseley, is tremendous, and if he manages it, he will have a right to aspire to the title of one of the most remarkable leaders of our time.

Extract from a London correspondent's letter of 7th February to the same paper.

The St. Petersburg correspondent of the *"Times"* telegraphs that M. Lessar, instead of proceeding to Central Asia, has come to London to aid in settling the preliminary agreement with the English Government regarding the chief points of the Russo-Afghan Frontier. In the telegram the English Government is blamed for dispatching Sir P. Lumsden without coming to an agreement with the Russian authorities regarding certain preliminary questions.

A leading article of the 16th February says:—

A report has been circulated in the city (St. Petersburg) calculated to cause a profound sensation that the Russian Army, quartered in the South Eastern limits of the Trans-Caspian District, have taken Herat. Notwithstanding its evident improbability, this report got abroad and according to private information, some mercantile firms in St. Petersburg received to-day telegrams from Berlin and London with the alarming question. "Is it true that Herat has been taken?"

The reports certainly may be in a way useful, and it must be glittering to our national vanity that they consider abroad we are capable of doing things out of the common, but this time the Bourse Masters can reassure themselves.

Herat is not taken, and no serious operations against it are contemplated from our side. Near the proposed frontier there is, as we have before informed our readers, an English section of the future Delimitation Commission, with which we are not preparing to fight.

Herat is a large fortified town, occupied by a considerable Afghan

Garrison. Our *role* with regard to Afghanistan is most pacific, and Russia does not wish to make captures, and is not going to make any. South western Turcomania joined itself to us peacefully, in consequence of its faith in the might and protection of Russia, and gravitation towards kindred tribes; and only in the interest of our new subjects it behoves Russian diplomatists to display a sensible firmness, and to decide the question of delimitation much more profitably from an ethnographic point of view. Russia sealed her right to Turcomania by the blood spilt under the walls of Geok Tepe. Our wishes are moderate, and it would be hard to withdraw from a once-defined frontier. Since a frontier delimitation is proposed between Russia and Afghanistan, a peaceful solution of the question will very much depend on the prudent behaviour of the Afghans, who are little acquainted with European politics. It seems to us that the continued presence of the English detachment near our frontier, added to the purely British liberality of Sir P. Lumsden, can act injuriously on the impressible minds of the Afghans; and if, according to the existing treaty, the English have taken on themselves the disagreeable and expensive obligation to guard and tutor the Afghans, then they must also restrain them. If indeed England shall appear powerless in this respect, then indeed it will devolve on Russia adopt her own measures.

Two days later the same paper says:-

That the report about Herat called forth a strong sensation in Berlin, the account of the condition of the Stock Exchange at that place shews in the *"Boursen Courier"* received today. They did not at first believe it. Nevertheless shrewd people sent enquirers to the Minister for Foreign Affairs; and when it appeared that nothing was known about the matter, Stocks began to keep firmer. But quiet did not long prevail; categorically confirmed news of the capture of Herat began to arrive in telegrams from London, and simultaneously the fall of Stocks on the London Change was reported. The London telegrams speedily reacted on our paper, and at the end there were so many sellers, that it sensibly fell in value. The *"Boursen Courier"* also explains this fall — that after continued reliance in Russian worth, the news of such an event of the first importance as the taking of Herat, produced a reaction, and mistrust took the place of reliance. The danger arose, that after this cloud which had suddenly risen on the horizon would follow a serious struggle between England and Russia. If in Berlin there was alarm, in London there was almost a panic. In the City great excitement was observed; all believed the report affirming that it was quite reliable because Russia, as it were, had often violated subscribed treaties, taking advantage of any critical position of one or other power. The London correspondent of the Paris *"Gaulois"* says: "Here they are convinced that Russia's glance is obstinately fixed on Herat, but it will be no slight matter to drive England from a district which she unconditionally dominates, whatever they may say. From a military point of view, Herat has for England a tremendously important signification, as this town is disposed at the entrance to a single passage through a long chain of hills. All the roads between Western Asia and India meet there. It is a position of the first degree, and Herat will be a temptation to Russia, until her rivalry with England is at an end. This latter Power twice resorted to armed intervention to save Herat from Persia, who was instigated by Russia, who has succeeded in capturing Merv, and thus arrived at the very door of the city which serves as the object of her ardent desire. Three or four years ago, on the idea alone, that Russia could subdue Merv, such a storm was raised in London, that war was feared on the very first step of Russia in the direction of Herat. Meanwhile Russia has taken Merv, and England even now has not lifted a finger. In truth it is not Lord Beaconsfield that governs England, but Gladstone!"

III.7: The Russian Press

The following is an extract from a leading article, in the St. Petersburg *Novoe Vremya* of the 23rd February:-

The explanations, given yesterday by Lord FitzMaurice, and Mr. Cross, in the House of Commons regarding the newly arisen question of Herat, in reality explain nothing; but they are worthy of remark as regards their tone. Lord FitzMaurice declared that the Russian Government did not consider it necessary to answer the demand for the evacuation of Puli-Khatun before the final decision of the Afghan Frontier Commission had been arrived at; but he abstained from any comment on this fact. Mr. Cross acknowledged the report of the seizure of Herat to be without foundation, in face of Russia's oft-repeated declarations; but he added, as though with intention of uttering a cunning threat, that Herat, at the present time, is held by a large Afghan garrison, and any attempt of the Russians to capture it, would lead to the most serious consequences. In these declarations of Government officers, there is an ardent solicitude to quiet the general suspicion aroused by the reports of the imaginary seizure of Herat; but, at the same time, is seen an anxiety not to irritate the Russian Government by censure of its mode of action in the question of the Afghan frontier. And here, as in many question of its foreign policy, the present St. James's Cabinet is placed apparently between two fires. It well knows, that 'during its present difficulties in the Soudan, good relations with Russia are excessively important. But at the same time it foresees that the

Opposition, who carry popular opinion with them, to a marked degree, can weaken its popularity in the country by hints of those dangers, with which the nearness of Russia to the confines of Afghanistan threaten India. There are strong reasons for conjecturing that, if the Gladstone Ministry did not fear these limits, it would in all probability abstain from any proposals to Russia regarding Pul-i-Khatun, and its orators would not begin to hint in the House about serious consequences by which, as it were, the large Afghan garrison threatens any attempt of the Russians to take persession [sic] of Herat, but would say straight out, that they did not expect any such attempt, calculating on settling by friendly conferences the question of the Afghan frontier. Gladstone has often openly expressed, as regards the Central Asian question generally, opinions which are actually at variance with those second thoughts to which the large military escort with General Lumsden, and the proposals of the British Minister for Foreign Affairs, evoked by the presence of Russians in Pul-i-Khatun, clearly point. At the present moment he is evidently disturbed, and is endeavouring to beat down the paroxysm of Russophobism which has been called forth among a large portion of the London public, and in almost the whole London Press, in consequence of the reports about Herat. All this is clearly understood. But the Russian Government, with all its wish to preserve the friendship of England, cannot sacrifice its own proper interests to alleviate the difficult position of the fresh old English Premier. In London it is well known on what foundations it is ready to decide without any further delay, the question of the Afghan frontier; and the St. Petersburg correspondent, was, as it seems to us, perfectly right in endeavouring to convince his countrymen, that Russia cannot agree to a dismemberment of "Turcomania," leaving a portion of the tribes, who have willingly come under its protection from the power of the Afghan Amir, whose subordinates have succeeded in arousing in themselves an implacable hatred of Turcomans. In place of inciting the Amir to dispatch to Herat a large Afghan garrison, the rulers of India would have done better to compel their Afghan semi-vassal to govern Herat in such a way, that the native population of this district should not feel the necessity of seeking for themselves protection from their powerful neighbour.

III.8: The Russian Press

Specially Translated

The *Novoe Vremya*, of February 23rd, writes as follows:-

At the end of last year, when the English delegate, Sir P. Lumsden, arrived with his escort in north-western Afghanistan, we spoke out our views as regards the signification which the expected Frontier Commission generally bears, and explained those ethnographic conditions to which, in our opinion, Russia must hold in defining the frontier points. Now, in consequence of the diplomatic mission of M. Lessar to London, and of the rumour adroitly published in the Press, of the fictitious seizure of Herat, the question, which bore up to this a political character of secondary consideration, has increased in importance, and provoked a paper war. The last decade of England's Colonial history is remarkable. A series of reverses in Afghanistan obliged the English to evacuate that country; and in place of steel, to have recourse to gold. Hastening over the holes here, somehow or other, they turned to Egypt; but here also the position of affairs, at first sufficiently successful, changed for the worse, and now, until Wolseley receives reinforcements, it may be called critical. We, however, are far from attributing these failures to the weakness of the English. There is not a power which, having been dragged into a colonial war, would not frequently repeat, notwithstanding the lessons of the past, the very same mistakes, which, on the present occasion, were the cause of the English reverses. The mistakes have been rectified; but nevertheless, the English community and Press, have been so seriously roused by the sad occurrences of later times, that, on the annexation by Russia of some 10,000 nomad Turcomans, an attempt to take Herat glimmers in the distance before them, and the formation of a "place d'armes" approaching India. These fears, however, are not new; and are distinguished from former ones, only by their dimensions. Commencing from the taking of Tashkhend to the last minute, the English at our each successive step, have seen a menace to themselves. After the annexation of Ferghana, they expected the appearance of Cossack lances on the snows of the Pamir. They then considered the Alai passes as the keys of India. Understanding well how to reckon on their pockets, the English have never calculated, and never will calculate, all those difficulties, enormous expenses and sacrifices, which a fruitless and needless war with Afghanistan and a problematical march on India, would cost us. The above mentioned fears, though, have a moral foundation. England apparently cannot herself forget that constant inimical policy which she has ever maintained towards us. Paitence [sic] has its limits; and such a puissant power as Russia, probably, will seek interference in her affairs, and a pledge for frank and peaceful relations with England, because even a bad peace is better than a good quarrel.

Only on occasion of extremity will Russia decide on such a ruinous thing as war; but to this extremity England can herself bring us by ill considered pretensions and interference. If Russia raises the sword, then what ever may be the results of the struggle, it will fall, we may say in confidence, no less heavily on the English, than on ourselves. Then will be found also other roads to India, and "all roads are good which lead to Rome." After the annexation of Merv last year, a deputation from the Sarrik Turcomans arrived there, and asked to be our subjects. The Sarriks are located on the Murghab in two oases, Yulatan and Pendjdeh. Their summer camps and pastures are disposed both in the upper parts of the river Murghab, and also generally in the southern half of the district, lying between the rivers Heri-Rud and Murghab. This country has received the name of Western Turcomania. The annexation of the Sarriks to Russia—inconsequence of their kindred Tekkes of Akhal and Merv having already become subject to us, is understood. The occupation of Merv finally quieted the district; and there, where it was only possible to move in armed detachments, unarmed caravans and single horsemen can now move without impediment; pillage has stopped, and the Turcomans can turn to peaceful pursuits. The barren and deserted banks of the Heri-Rud, apparently, will soon be populated with newcomers, seeking land and water; and a number of abandoned canals will again water the fields. A movement of colonists must be expected both from Merv, where there is not sufficient land, and the inhabitants often have to deplore the want of bread; from Khorassan where the persecutions and depredations of local rulers probably call for emigration; and also from the Alai Turcomans, who wander between the Murghab and Amu-Darya, to the north of the Afghan province of Maimena. In this way, on account of the comparative want of water, and of the fact that the greater portion of south-western Turcomania presents deserts, our frontier must pass southward, in such a manner, that from one side, affording the possibility of holding the merchant routes, it should embrace in itself all that region, which has served and will serve, as a place for Turcoman encampments and pasture lands, and should give satisfactory tracts of land for colonization, and consequently for cultivation. In Central Asia, in consequence of the artificial watering of the fields, all habitations are crowded about the rivers and canals. Narrow strips along the hills, watered by few rivers, are distinguished by special fertility. The Tekke Oasis and Atek appear to be thus; and it is necessary to suppose that the northern forelands of the Paropamisus Range—the Borkut chain—in places where there is water, are also suitable for cultivation. As is seen from the English journals, the English Government, having decided to propose to us the dispatch of the Frontier Commission, calculated that we should be satisfied with Merv, and should be quite content if Sir P. Lumsden were to cut off for us a bit of land commencing from old Sarrakhs, and then in a straight line eastward, to the Murghab. This would only remain then to set up in the required direction, a wooden paling, and to ornament it on one side with green and on the other with red paint! We cannot agree to such a frontier. Once the ethnographic principle is considered just, every cession to Afghanistan of Turcoman land would be tantamount to depriving our new subjects of their pasturages. Any artificial dismemberment of that which forms itself one entire whole is pernicious; and never leads, and never would lead, to a desirable end. If south-western Turcomania does not come over to us in entirety, then, besides the fact of the good condition of the people suffering, the Local Government will not be able to answer for the quietness of the district. We do not know the arguments by which our diplomacy is being guided in our conferences with London. Meanwhile these details must play an important part in the settlement of the question. For example, the Caravan route runs from Merv to Herat, is through Yulatan, and Penjdeh, to the Murghab, and then up along the river Kooshk to the hills. Evidently in its trade relation, this route will be held in view, in defining the frontier. Also, as is evident from the reports of M. Lessar, laid last year before the Geographical Society, the salt lakes southwards of the Elbeerst chain, present very rich, and the sole, reserves of salt in the district used by the Turcomans; and by the Persians of Khorassan, for themselves and cattle. It is understood that these must come into our limits. These and many other arguments convince us, that the most complete settlement of the question will be that which leads to the indispensability of marking the southern frontier on the hills of the Paropamisus. Such a frontier will be actually natural; and the English would have done well to agree to this in London, without sending detachments on to our boundaries.

[The translation is followed by a detailed map taken from *Novoe Vremya* of the region between Merv and Herat. The areas occupied by the Saryk Turkomans and the Djemshidis are indicated.]

Appendix IV: Afghan Boundary Commission Reports from Correspondents

(September 18, 1884, to April 29, 1885)

Number	Dateline, date	Author	Publication Date
IV.1	Quetta, Sept. 12	E. Durand	Sept. 18, 1884
IV.2	Quetta, Sept. 18	E. Durand	Sept. 25, 1884
IV.3	Nushki, Sept. 29	E. Durand	Oct. 8, 1884
IV.4		E. Durand	Oct. 13, 1884
IV.5	Sahan, n.d.	E. Durand	Oct. 20, 1884
IV.6	Galichah, Oct. 13	E. Durand	Oct. 27, 1884
IV.7		E. Durand	Oct. 28, 1884
IV.8	Kwajah Ali, n.d.	E. Durand	Nov. 10, 1884
IV.9	(Ibrahimabad ?)	E. Durand	Nov. 11, 1884
IV.10	(Kin ?)	E. Durand	Nov. 18, 1884
IV.11	(Sir Mandal ?)	E. Durand	Nov. 25, 1884
IV.12	(Chah Gazek ?)	E. Durand	Nov. 28, 1884
IV.13	Kuhsan, Nov. 18	E. Durand	Dec. 5, 1884
IV.14	Kuhsan, Nov. 19	E. Durand	Dec. 9, 1884
IV.15	Kuhsan, Nov.19–22	C. Owen	Dec. 9, 1884
IV.16	Kuhsan, Nov. 23–26	C. Owen	Dec. 10, 1884
IV.17	Panjdeh, Dec. 4	E. Durand	Dec. 25, 1884
IV.18	November26-Dec. 6	C. Owen	Dec. 30, 1884
IV.19	Bala Murghab, Dec. 20	E. Durand	Jan. 8, 1885
IV.20	Bala Murghab, Dec. 24	C. Owen	Jan. 17, 1885
IV.21	Bala Murghab, Dec. 26	E. Durand	Jan. 23, 1885
IV.22	Bala Murghab, Dec. 28	C. Owen	Jan. 29, 1885

IV.23	Bala Murghab, Jan. 5	C. Owen	Feb. 2, 1885
IV.24	Bala Murghab, Jan. 5	F. Drummond	Feb. 3, 1885
IV.25	Bala Murghab, Jan. 12	F. Drummond	Feb. 9, 1885
IV.26	Bala Murghab, Jan. 19	C. Owen	Feb. 17, 1885
IV.27	Bala Murghab, Jan. 25	C. Owen	Feb. 20, 1885
IV.28	Bala Murghab, Feb. 1	C. Owen	Feb. 25, 1885
IV.29	Bala Murghab, Feb. 8	C. Owen	Mar. 3, 1885
IV.30	Bala Murghab, Feb. 12	C. Owen	Mar. 10, 1885
IV.31	Aklochi, Feb. 25	C. Owen	Mar. 23, 1885
IV.32	Panjdeh, Mar. 12	C. Owen	Apr. 6, 1885
IV.33	Panjdeh, Mar. 21	C. Owen	Apr. 27, 1885
IV.34	Tirpul, Apr. 8	E. Durand	Apr. 29, 1885

Appendix V: Members of the Afghan Boundary Commission

Commissioner
    Major-General Sir Peter Stark Lumsden (1829–1916)
        Portrait: ILN September 13, 1884 and ILN December 6, 1884

        Publications: "Countries & Tribes bordering on the Koh-I-Baba range," *Proceedings of the Royal Geographical Society*, new monthly series, VII (1885), 561–583.

    Aide-de-camp
        The Hon. George Campbell Napier (1845–1914)
            First named as A.D.C. but later replaced by Barrow
            Twin brother of 2nd Baron Napier of Magdala

        Captain Arthur Frederick Barrow (1850–1903)
            Private secretary and aide-de-camp who kept the record "Precis respecting Afghan Frontier from January 1884 to April 9, 1885, written at Tirpul in 1885,"

    Interpreter, Political Adviser
        Nawab Mirza Hassan Ali Khan

Assistant Commissioner
    Alexander Condie Stephen (1850–1908)
        Portrait: ILN May 16, 1885, p. 510

        Ref.: *Dict. Of Nat. Biogr. 1901–1911*, p. 398: groom-in-waiting to King Edward VII after 1901

    Secretary
        Arthur James Herbert (1855–1921)

Assistant Commissioner
 Col. Charles E. Stewart (1836–1904)
 former Member of 11th Bengal Lancers. He joined Lumsden February 21, 1885 in Islim (between Bala Murghab & Gulran).

 Publications: *Through Persia in Disguise* (London, 1911)

Military Escort

Commander
 Lieutenant-Colonel Sir Joseph West Ridgeway (1844–1930)
 Political officer, who led the Indian section of the ABC and succeeded Lumsden as Chief Commissioner in November of 1885.

 Ref. *Dict. of Nat. Biogr. 1922–1930*, p. 718

Assistant
 William Rudolph Henry Merk (1852–1925)
 Linguist, Political Officer

 Publ.: *Diary of the mark of the Afghan Boundary Commission*, 49 pages (British Library).

Assistant
 Hugh Shakespear Barnes (1853–1940)
 Political Agent of Pishin
 Assisted Ridgeway planning march from Quetta
 Durand made a w/c of his tent, 30. September 1884.

Commissariat Transport, Treasury Officer
 Major Rind

 Assistants: Conductor Lyttle and Mr. Wilson

Cavalry Escort
 11th Bengal Lancers (200 sabres)
 Officers
 Major W. J. Bax (First Officer)
 Donated rugs to the Victoria and Albert Museum in 1909 & 1911

 Dr. Richard Havelock Charles (1858–1934)
 Medical officer

Lieutenant Francis Henry Rutherford Drummond (1857–1910)

Captain Edward L. Durand (1845–1920)
    Political officer

   Burke's Peerage 1893; P.M. Sykes, *The Right Honourable Sir Mortimer Durand* (London, 1926).
   Records and drawings with India House, London

Captain Harry Steptinstall Rose Heath (1850–1922)

Colonel Prinsep

Lieutenant Hedly Wright (1859–1903)

Lieutenant Arthur C. Yate (1853–1929)
    Brother of Charles E. Yate

   Publ.: *Face to Face in Asia: Travels with the Afghan Boundary Commission* (Edinburgh, 1887)

Jemandar Amir Muhammad

Duffadar Mir Baz

20th Panjab Infantry (200 rifles)
    Major William Hope Meikeljohn (1845–1909)
        First Intelligence Officer

    Captain Cotton

    Lieutenant Rawlin

    Subadar-Major Mowla Dad

Political Branch

Officers
    Ridgeway (cf. above)

    Durand (cf. above)

    Captain Charles Edward Yate (1849–1940)
        Portrait: ILN May 16/85, p. 510: "Only British officer who witnessed the affray on March 30 at Pul-I-Khisti"

        Later chief commissioner in Baluchistan 1900–1904
        Clock tower in his honour at Quetta

Publ.: *Northern Afghanistan or Letters from the Afghan Boundary Commission* (Edinburgh/London, 1888)
Ref. *Dict. of Nat. Biogr. 1931–1940*, p. 928.

Merk (cf. above)

Captain De Laessoe (cf. below)

Native Attaches
> Sirdar Mahomed (Muhammad) Aslam Khan
> Brother of British agent at Cabul, Afghan
> Cf. C.E. Yate, p. 48, 82: Kazi Muhammad Aslam Khan

> Ressaldar-Major Baha-u-din Khan
> Central India Horse, Served in every Indian campaign for 30 years, Afghan

> Ressaldar Major Mahomed Hassain (Muhammad Hasain) Khan
> 7th Bengal Cavalry, Employed for several years on Afghan missions

> Sardar Sher Ahmed Khan
> Son of Afghan Governor of Kandahar, Ridgeway's assistant

Survey Branch

Officers
> Major Thomas Hungerford Holdich (1843–1929)
> R.E., Head of Survey Dept., water-colourist
> Replaced Major Hill in Quetta
>
> Ref. *Dict. of Nat. Biography, 1922–1930*, p. 425
> Publ. *Indian Borderlands 1880–1900* (London, 1901)

> Captain St. George Corbet Gore (1849–1913)
> R.E., Surveyor,
>
> Later Surveyor-General of India, 1889–1904

> Lieutenant the Hon. Milo George Talbot (1854–1931)
> R.E., Surveyor
>
> cf. Burke's Peerage, 6th Baron Talbot de Malahide leaving issue Milo John Reginald and Rose Maud b. 1915.
> *Memoir*, written by Sir Reginald Wright
> Papers at Oxford.

Assistants
    Sub-Surveyor Heera Singh (a Gurkha)

    Imam Sharif

    Sub-Surveyor Ata Mahomad (a Yusufzui)

    Mirza Muhammed Taki Khan

    Khan Baba Khan

Intelligence Branch

Officers
    Captain Pelham James Maitland (1847–1935)
        First Intelligence Officer, Bombay Staff Corps

        Publ. Preface to *Land of Uz* by G.W. Bury (London, 1911)

    Captain William Peacock (1848–1931)
        R.E., Second Intelligence Officer

    Sergeant Galindo
        14th Hussars, R.E.
        Sent sketches of battle of Pul-I-Khisti to *The Graphic* 1885 and map in *Travels* by A. Yate, p. V.

Scientific Experts

Durand (cf above)

Captain De Laessoe
    Official interpreter, collected archaeological material (= Capt. Albert Frederic De Laessoe, political agent at Bhowapur), Danish

    Publ. about caves near Penjdeh in *Proceedings of the Royal Geographical Society*, new month series, VII, 561–583.

Dr. James Edward Tierney Aitchison (1835–1898)
    Naturalist, Second Medical Officer, C.I.E.

    Records at Pharmaceutical Society, London and Royal Botanic Garden, Edinburgh

Capt. Charles (Carl Ludolf) Griesbach (1847–1907)
    Geologist

Dir. of India Geological Survey after 1894.
many publications in *Memoirs of the Geological Survey of India* and *Records of the Geological Survey of India*.

Lieut.-Col. Charles William Owen (1853–1922)
Medical Officer, collected ethnographic material, C.I.E.

Assistant
   Pati Ram, medical assistant

Artist from Jaipur School of Art (B. Bux ?)

Correspondents

William Simpson (1823–1899)
   Correspondent of *Illustrated London News*

   Publ. *The Autobiography of William Simpson* by George Eyre-Todd (London, 1903)
   Ref.: *Dict. of Nat. Biogr.*, vol. xxii, suppl.

Dr. Thomas Stephenson Weir
   Correspondent of *Times of India*

   Publ.: *From India to the Caspian, or Journeys with and after the Afghan Mission* (Bombay, 1893)

Others

Captain Korban (Kurban) Ali Berg Mervi
   Head of 50 Turkoman Horse escort,
   Native of Ferozkoh mountain country in Khorassan
   Born in Meshed

   Portrait, ILN, December, 27, 1884, and sketch on horse in *Illustrated Naval & Military Magazine* II (1886), p. 38

General Ghous-ud-Din (died 1885)
   Commander of Afghan troops at Ak Tapa

   Portrait: ILN Mar 7, 1885, 251 and ILN May 16, 1885, 499.

Notes

Chapter 1

1. For a general survey cf. Edward Allworth (ed.), *Central Asia: A Century of Russian Rule* (New York, 1967); Mary Holdsworth, *Turkestan in the Nineteenth Century* (London, 1959); Richard A. Pierce, *Russian Central Asia 1867–1917* (Berkeley, 1960). A. Vambery's *The Coming Struggle for India* (London, 1885) still deserves reading as an introduction to the historical background. The Russian side has been presented by G.A. Khidoyatov, *Britanskaya Exspansiya v Srednei Azii* (Tashkent, 1981). *The Country of the Turkomans: An Anthology of Exploration from the Royal Geographical Society* (London, 1977) with an introduction by Duncan Cummings reviews the literature of the nineteenth century on Turkestan.
2. P. Hopkirk, *The Great Game* (London, 1992), p. 415.
3. Arthur Barrow, "Precis respecting Afghan Frontier from January 1884 to April 9, 1885," unpublished manuscript, private collection, Toronto.
4. *Illustrated London News*, May 31, 1884, p. 522.
5. Arthur Ankers, *The Pater, John Lockwood Kipling: His Life and Times 1837–1911* (Oxford, 1988), pp. 116, 118, and Harold Orel, *A Kipling Chronology* (London, 1990), p. 12. To believe Kipling, he made up half of the European staff, but the foreman was a Scot and other Europeans were employed for specific tasks such as map drawings.
6. Within a few weeks of his arrival, Rudyard Kipling had his trial by fire, when Wheeler was confined to bed after a carriage accident and the new assistant had to assume all the editorial work. In July 1884 Wheeler went through a severe attack of opthalmia, which nearly blinded him: "Wheeler is pronounced ill with "ulcer of the cornea" and fever — videlicet partial blindness and complete prostration." Cf. Thomas Pinney (ed.), *The Letters of Rudyard Kipling* (London, 1990), vol. 1, p. 71. Kipling found himself working 12-hour days with scarcely a break. In a letter to his aunt Edith Macdonald, he complained that, "of late however I have been wildly busy as the Chief hasn't been up to the mark and has let me do a lot of his work confound him!" Cf. Pinney, *op. cit.*, p. 80.
7. Cf. *Civil and Military Gazette*, August 4, 1884, p. 1: "CAPTAIN BARROW, THE LATELY APPOINTED Aide-De-Camp to General Sir P. Lumsden, is peculiarly fitted for such a duty; as he is a first-class Russian scholar. He speaks the language particularly well, having learnt it in a Russian village where he once spent several months of his leave."
8. William Simpson, *The Seat of War in the East* (London, 1855–56).
9. Simpson died in London in 1899. The autobiography he wrote for his daughter appeared in 1903. Cf. W. Simpson, *The Autobiography of William Simpson, R.I.*, ed. by George Eyre-Todd (London, 1903). In addition to the reports sent back to the *Illustrated London News*, Simpson contributed letters to the *Daily News* and he wrote an article about his experiences with the Afghan Boundary Commission for *Harper's Magazine*. Cf. W. Simpson, "With the Afghan Boundary Commission," *Harper's Magazine* 72, 1886, p. 595–605.
10. The organization of the Indian section has been described by Arthur C. Yate in his book *England and Russia Face to Face in Asia* and in reports by Charles Owen, C.E. Yate and T.H. Holdich. Cf. Arthur C. Yate, *England and Russia Face to Face in Asia: Travels with the Afghan Boundary Commission* (Edinburgh and

London, 1887), Charles E. Yate, *Northern Afghanistan or Letters from the Afghan Boundary Commission* (Edinburgh and London, 1888) and Thomas H. Holdich, *The Indian Borderland 1880–1900* (London, 1901). Arthur Yate, brother of the captain, regularly reported on the ABC to the *Pioneer* as that newspaper's special correspondent. In 1921 he presented the Central Asian Society with a bound volume containing almost all the letters he had sent to the *Pioneer* between August 31, 1884, and June 18, 1885. These formed the basis for his book *England and Russian Face to Face*.

11. A.C. Yate, *England and Russia Face to Face in Asia*, pp. 78, 108, 121. According to Thomas Holdich the Indian section consisted of 1600 men and 1600 baggage animals. Cf. T.H. Holdich, *The Indian Borderland 1880–1900* (London, 1901), p. 99.

12. *Illustrated London News*, September 13, 1884, p. 246

13. *Civil and Military Gazette*, September 16, 1884, p. 1.

14. *Rudyard Kipling: Something of Myself and Other Autobiographical Writings*, edited by Thomas Pinney (Cambridge, 1990), p. 30.

15. These generally appeared under the heading "specially translated." In some cases Kipling's authorship can be confirmed by entries in his diary.

16. *Rudyard Kipling: Something of Myself and Other Autobiographical Writings*, edited by Thomas Pinney (Cambridge, 1990), p. 19. Kipling and his wife destroyed almost all of his correspondence from his apprenticeship years. The 1885 diary survived, because he left it behind in the offices of the *Civil and Military Gazette* when he moved to Allahabad in 1887. In 1942 the diary was acquired by Harvard University.

17. *Rudyard Kipling: Something of Myself and Other Autobiographical Writings*, pp. 206–7.

18. Charles Marvin, *The Russians at the Gates of Herat* (London, 1885), p. 68.

19. Cf. *Who Was Who 1918–1928*, vol. 2, p. 622: *Catalogue of Jeypore Exhibits at Calcutta International Exhibition 1883*.

20. National Army Museum, acc. No. 1998-01-121. I wish to thank Alastair Massie of NAM for making photocopies of this material available. Thirty-nine of Owen's letters from the Afghan campaign are in the possession of Fred Sharf, who kindly sent me photocopies of some. The entire contents have been recorded in a 631 page single-spaced transcription. This may have been prepared for the second wife of Owen, Mabel Howard Hopley, who died in 1959 at the age of 86. Massie wrote me: "the person who sold us the letters bought them himself at auction and has no connection with the Owen family."

21. National Army Museum, acc. no. 1998-01-121, transcript, p. 23.

22. The same statement appears as well in Arthur Yate, *England and Russia Face to Face*, p. 18.

23. *Pioneer*, August 29, 1884, p. 84f. Cf. also the same in the *Civil and Military Gazette*, January 20, 1885.

24. Arthur Yate, *England and Russia Face to Face*, pp. 18, 278.

25. Letter of Charles Owen to his wife, dated April 24, 1885. Original in the possession of Fred Sharf, to whom I am indebted for sending me a transcript of the text.

26. The Russians originally set October 13, 1884, as the date of the meeting, but this was later changed to November 7. Cf. T.H. Holdich, *The Indian Borderland 1880–1890* (London, 1901), p. 95.

27. T.H. Holdich, *The Indian Borderland 1880–1900* (London, 1901), p. 96. Cf. A.C. Yate, *England and Russia Face to Face in Asia*, pp. 122 and 155 for details.

28. *Illustrated London News*, June 14, 1884, p. 574. The *Times* carried a similar notice titled "The Northern and North-Western Frontiers of Afghanistan" on June 9, 1884, p. 5.

Chapter 2

1. Omar Khan, *From Kashmir to Kabul. The Photographs of John Burke and William Baker 1860–1900* (Munich, 2002), pp. 122–123 (photo no. 76).

2. *Civil and Military Gazette*, Aug. 30, 1884, p. 3.

3. *Civil and Military Gazette*, September 8, 1884, p. 3.

4. A.C. Yate, *England and Russia Face to Face in Asia: Travels with the Afghan Boundary Commission* (Edinburgh & London, 1987), p. 13.

5. A.C. Yate, *England and Russia Face to Face*, p. 27.

6. *Civil and Military Gazette*, September 18, 1884, p. 3.

7. Owen's papers are housed in the National Army Museum, London, under the number 1998-01-121. The collection was apparently acquired at auction and then sold to the NAM. A previous owner prepared a typewritten transcript of all the letters and diary entries arranged in chronological order.

8. Holdich, *Indian Borderland*, p. 99.
9. A.C. Yate, *England and Russia Face to Face*, p. 12.
10. Holdich, *Indian Borderland*, p. 100.
11. William Simpson, "The Progress of the Afghan Frontier Commission," *The Illustrated Naval and Military Magazine* I (1884), p. 396–399.
12. Durand's letters appeared in reports in the newspaper on October 8, 20, 27, and 28, and November 10, 11, 18, 25, and 28. The arrival in Camp Kuhsan is announced in letters published on December 5.
13. *Kipling Journal* no. 16 (December, 1930), p. 112–113.
14. National Army Museum, 1998-01-121, Owen transcript.
15. NAM, Owen transcript, p. 101.
16. *Pioneer*, November 28, 1884.
17. A. Yate, *England and Russia Face to Face*, p. 105.
18. *Civil and Military Gazette*, October 13, 1884, p. 5.
19. Thomas Pinney, *Rudyard Kipling: Something of Myself and Other Autobiographical Writings* (Cambridge, 1990), p. 30.
20. *Illustrated London News*, November 1, 1884, p. 415.
21. *Illustrated London News*, April 25, 1885, pp. 446–7.
22. *Illustrated London News*, April 25, 1885, p. 448.
23. W. Simpson, "With the Afghan Boundary Commission," in *Harper's Magazine* 72, 1886, pp. 595–6. Alamans were by no means one-sided affairs. The Persian historian Abdur-Rezzak reported that one campaign against the Tekke in 1813 reaped 50,000 camels, cattle, sheep and horses. In another campaign of 1816, all the men of a Tekke settlement were slain and the women, children and possessions captured. The khans of Khiva also launched periodic alamans against the Turkomans. See W. Koenig, *Die Achal-Teke* (Berlin, 1962).

Chapter 3

1. According to the agreement with the Russians the British were to arrive on November 7 (cf. The *Times*, May 18, 1885, p. 6). In his "Precis" Barrow mentions that the Russians then proposed January 27 for the date of a meeting at Puli-Khatun.
2. A calculation of the daily marches from Sarakhs to Kuhsan is found in A.C. Yate, *England and Russia Face to Face*, p. 161.
3. Cf. T.H. Holdich, *The Indian Borderland*, p. 110. The trek is described as well in the diary and letters of Dr. Charles Owen (National Army Museum Department of Archives no. 1998-01-121).
4. National Army Museum, acc. no. 1998-01-121, transcript, p. 110.
5. *Illustrated London News*, March 14, 1885, p. 280.
6. *Civil and Military Gazette*, December 16, 1884, p. 3.
7. *Illustrated London News*, March 14, 1885, p. 280.
8. *Illustrated London News*, March 14, 1885, p. 280. Cf. also the report in *The Times* of March 12, p. 12, and Arthur Yate, *England and Russia Face to Face*, p. 189.
9. In May of 1886 the *Pioneer* published a report stemming from the visit to Penjdeh, which probably came from Charles E. Yate. Cf. *Pioneer*, May 11, 1886. The author described Penjdeh as not a village but "a long narrow valley, some 25 miles in length, and averaging two miles in breadth, containing a series of hamlets of Turkoman kibitka." Simpson's observations concerning Penjdeh can be corroborated by the reports of two of his fellow travellers who later presented papers before the Royal Geographical Society in London. The ABC surveyor T.H. Holdich described the geography of the region in the Proceedings of the Society in May of 1885. Sir Peter Lumsden's lecture before the society in June of the same year appeared in the volume for September 1885. Cf. T.H. Holdich, "The Afghan Boundary Commission; Geographical Notes III," *Proceedings of the Royal Geographical Society*, new monthly series, vol. 7, 1885, pp. 273–292 and Peter Lumsden, "Countries and Tribes bordering on the Koh-i-Baba Range," *Proceedings of the Royal Geographical Society*, new monthly series, vol. 7, 1885, pp. 561–583.
10. The author thanks Lady Durand for sending photocopies of the letters of Sir Edward Durand and for information on Turkoman artifacts she had in her possession. The originals of the letters can be consulted in the National Library of Scotland, Edinburgh (Acc. 10838/3).
11. In the 1980s Lady Durand still had the silver cap mentioned in the letter in her possession and kindly forwarded the author a photograph of it. It is completely covered with small plaques. The ornament at the top, called *gupba* in the Turkoman language, lacks the decoration and gilding of Tekke pieces and has four bells attached around the perimeter. It is

complete with a tuft of red wool at the pinnacle.

A few of the weavings were acquired by Captain Durand were passed on to family members. Marion Campbell of Kilberry, the granddaughter of Sir Edward, wrote me that she had two very fine Turkoman chuvals, which had been mounted on a sofa by her grandparents. Miss Campbell had the pieces removed from the sofa, and creases along the folds were repaired.

A "Royal Bokhara" brought back by Durand apparently survived the bombing of the Durand possessions in Taylers depository in Pimlico during the Blitz. It had already been reduced in size to fit in front of a fireplace. Rugs and silver ornaments from the Durand estate were distributed among the family, but I have been given to understand, that inquiries about their present whereabouts would not be welcomed.

12. T. Holdich, *Indian Borderland*, pp. 119–120.

13. *Daily News*, February 7, 1885, p. 3.

14. The assistant editor augmented his December column count with a description of Chaharshambar by Col. Grodekoff on December 16 and extracts on the ABC from *Saturday Review* and *Daily News* on December 22 and 24.

15. NAM, Owen Transcript. no. 1998-01-121, p. 115.

16. NAM, Owen Transcript no. 1998-01-121, p. 117.

17. *Civil and Military Gazette*, January 27, 1885.

18. *Civil and Military Gazette*, January 20, 1885.

19. NAM, Owen Transcript no. 1998-01-121, p. 128.

20. A. Yate, *England and Russia Face to Face*, p. 210f.

21. The *Times*, April 16, 1885, p. 8.

22. *Daily News*, March 10, 1885, p. 6.

23. "Turcoman Ornaments," *Journal of Indian Art* 1/7 (July, 1886), pp. 53–56.

24. *Illustrated London News*, March 14, 1885, p. 289.

25. Arthur Yate, *England and Russia Face to Face*, p. 269. A search for these Turkoman yurts at various museums in the United Kingdom did not turn up any examples. In his book *The Pater: John Lockwood Kipling, His Life and Times 1837—1911* (Oxford, 1988), Arthur Ankers mentions on page 82 a "Kirghiz tent, composed of felt and a skillfully arrangement of willow-rods" at the Lahore Museum.

26. *Illustrated London News*, March 28, 1885, p. 321.

27. NAM, Owen transcript, p. 137.

28. NAM, Owen transcript, pp. 253–5 (letter of July 22, 1885).

29. *Illustrated London News*, March 28, 1885, p. 321.

Chapter 4

1. The *Times*, January 23, 1885, p. 8.

2. *Illustrated London News*, February 21, 1885, p. 212.

3. The *Times*, March 23, 1885, p. 7. The quotation is from a letter to Lord Clarendon from July 31, 1851.

4. *Pall Mall Gazette*, September 6, 1884, p. 1.

5. Arminius Vambery, *The Coming Struggle for India* (London, 1885), p. 88.

6. *Civil and Military Gazette*, October 8, 1884, p. 5.

7. *Illustrated London News*, March 7, 1885, p. 248.

8. *Illustrated London News*, March 7, 1885, p. 248.

9. National Army Museum, ms. 1998-01-121, Owen transcript, p. 160.

10. NAM, ms. 1998-01-121, Owen transcript, p. 171C.

11. NAM, ms. 1998-01-121, Owen transcript, p. 178.

12. Owen mentions Rudyard Kipling again in a letter to his wife dated March 23, 1886: "You will see a good skit in the C&M on the camp exercise which will amuse you. Kipling must have written it for it reminds me of his style." Cf. National Army Museum, Owen transcript, p. 421.

13. Cf. T. Pinney, *Rudyard Kipling, Something of Myself*, p. 208.

14. Thomas Pinney, ed., *Kipling's India: Uncollected Sketches 1884–88* (London, 1986), p. 78.

15. *Civil and Military Gazette*, April 1, 1885, dated Peshawar, March 28. Cf. also Thomas Pinney, ed., *Rudyard Kipling: Something of Myself and other Autobiographical Writings* (Cambridge, 1990), p. 207 for Kipling's diary entries in March 1885. For text cf. Thomas Pinney, ed., *Kipling's India: Uncollected Sketches 1884–88* (London, 1986).

16. *Civil and Military Gazette*, April 1, 1885, dated Jamrud, March 29.

17. *Civil and Military Gazette*, April 2, 1885.

18. Arthur Yate, *England and Russia Face to Face*, p. 453.

19. Cf. NAM, Owen transcript, p. 232.
20. The same telegram is translated in the *Times*, April 3, 1885, p. 5.
21. Percy M. Sykes, *The Right Honourable Sir Mortimer Durand* (London, 1926), p. 144.
22. Percy M. Sykes, *The Right Honourable Sir Mortimer Durand* (London, 1926). A map of the battlefield also appear in the *England and Russia Face to Face* by A.C. Yate after page 312.
23. NAM, Owen transcript, p. 181.

Chapter 5

1. The *Times*, June 2, 1885, p. 11.
2. *Illustrated London News*, April 18, 1885, pp. 404–408.
3. *Illustrated London News*, April 18, 1885, p. 408.
4. P. Hopkirk, *The Great Game*, p. 431.
5. Thomas Pinney, ed., *Rudyard Kipling: Something of Myself*, p. 208.
6. *Civil and Military Gazette*, April 7, 1885, dated Rawul Pindi, April 5.
7. *Civil and Military Gazette*, April 8, 1885, p. 3.
8. Thomas Pinney (ed.), *Rudyard Kipling: Something of Myself*, p. 208.
9. Rudyard Kipling, *Life's Handicap: Being Stories of My Own People* (London, 1891).
10. Thomas Pinney (ed.), *The Letters of Rudyard Kipling* (London, 1990), vol. 1, p. 82.
11. Thomas Pinney (ed.), *Rudyard Kipling: Something of Myself*, p. 196.
12. Owen mentions the change of editor in a notice in his diary for August 6, 1886: "Heard from Wheeler C&M that he goes home for 4 months from [illegible] and Kay Robinson officiates for him."
13. W. Simpson, *Harper's Magazine* 72, 1886, p. 605.
14. The *Times*, May 25, 1885, p. 5.
15. A. Yate, *England and Russia Face to Face*, p. 342.
16. *The Graphic*, June 6, 1885, p. 560.
17. A. Yate, *England and Russia Face to Face*, pp. 342–346.
18. T. Holdich, *Indian Borderland*, pp. 133–134.
19. Original in the Owen collection of Fred Sharf, dated April 17.
20. NAM, Owen transcript, p. 237 and p. 238.
21. NAM, Owen transcript, p. 205.
22. Letter of Charles Owen to his wife, dated April 14, 1885. Original owned by Fred Sharf.
23. Letter of April 17, 1885, in collection of Fred Sharf.
24. Letter of April 24, 1885, in possession of Fred Sharf.
25. NAM, Owen transcript, p. 196.
26. Owen's letter dated April 17, 1885, in the possession of Fred Sharf.
27. Owen's letter to his wife dated April 24, 1885, in the possession of Fred Sharf.
28. T. Holdich, *Indian Borderland*, pp. 132–136.
29. *Pall Mall Gazette*, April 16, 1885, p. 8.
30. A. Yate, *England and Russia Face to Face*, p. 385. Charles Stewart, second assistant commissioner, was at Herat, when he received the dispatch recalling him to London. Traveling via Russia through Vladikafkaz and Vilna, he reached London on June 9, 1885, three days after Sir Peter Lumsden. Cf. C. Stewart, *Through Persia in Disguise* (London, 1911), pp. 372–374.
31. The *Times*, June 5, 1885, p. 5.
32. *Illustrated London News*, June 13, 1885, p. 601.
33. *Illustrated London News*, May 16, 1885, p. 510.
34. W. Simpson, *Autobiography*, pp. 311–312.
35. *Illustrated London News*, June 27, 1885, p. 656.
36. *Illustrated London News*, July 4, 1885, pp. 5–6.

Chapter 6

1. Arthur Yate, *England and Russia Face to Face*, p. 440–401. The *Illustrated London News* for January 9, 1886, contained a sketch by Edward Durand depicting the fixing of the site of the first boundary post at the Zulfikar pass on November 12, 1885.
2. National Army Museum, Owen ms., p. 339.
3. *Illustrated London News* January 9, 1886. Cf. also Arthur Yate, *Travels*, p. 440.
4. Cf. Holdich's *Indian Borderland*, p. 150ff.
5. NAM, Owen transcript, pp. 323, 362.
6. Arthur Yate, *Travels*, p. 264. Concerning the Ersari, Yate writes: "On both banks are settled the Ersari Turkomans, who live, some in kibitkas, some in mud houses, and cultivate the fertile strip above mentioned." Yate mentions as well the Kara Turkomans, "a section of the Ersari and Alieli."
7. NAM, Owen transcript, p. 349.
8. For names of the motifs cf. Valentina G. Moshkova, *Kovry narodov Srednei Azii kontsa 19-nachala 20 vv.* (Tashkent, 1970).
9. NAM, Owen transcript, p. 276.

10. NAM, Owen transcript, p. 546.
11. NAM, Owen transcript, pp. 156, 436.
12. NAM, Owen transcript, p. 209.
13. NAM, Owen transcript, p. 331.
14. NAM, Owen transcript, p. 309.
15. NAM, Owen transcript, p. 332.
16. His daughter, the Honourable Rose Talbot, informed me that her father's papers are at Oxford.
17. NAM, Owen transcript, p. 421
18. NAM, Owen transcript, p. 557.
19. NAM, Owen transcript, p. 565.
20. NAM, Owen transcript, p. 570.
21. NAM, Owen transcript, p. 572.

Chapter 7

1. Thomas Pinney (ed.), *The Letters of Rudyard Kipling* (London, 1990), vol. 1, p. 125.
2. Thomas Pinney (ed.), *The Letters of Rudyard Kipling*, p. 140.
3. NAM, Owen transcript, p. 579.
4. NAM, Owen transcript, p. 171.
5. Thomas Pinney, *Letters of Rudyard Kipling*, p. 127: Letter to K. Robinson dated April 30, 1886. This material was deemed too extensive to be included in this present study
6. Joy Eldridge at the University of Sussex library could not locate an inventory of the carpets and textiles, but she did find one direct reference to a Turkoman weaving in a guide of Wimpole Hall, Cambridgeshire, the residence of Kipling's daughter, Mrs. Elsie Bambridge. A description of the dressing room mentions a "Saryk Turkoman or Ersari ensi or door rug, early twentieth century."
7. The museum did later acquire one impressive Central Asian artifact which John Lockwood mentions in an article, namely a Kirghiz tent. Cf. Arthur Ankers, *The Pater*, p. 82.
8. NAM, Owen transcript, p. 219.
9. NAM, Owen transcript, p. 425.
10. NAM, Owen transcript, p. 292.
11. Reproduced in Omar Khan, *From Kashmir to Kabul*, p. 172.
12. Omar Khan, *From Kashmir to Kabul*, p. 172–173.
13. Thomas Pinney (ed.), *Something*, p. 27.
14. Thomas Pinney (ed.), *The Letters of Rudyard Kipling*, p. 141: Letter to Edith Macdonald, December 4–5, 1886.
15. Dr. Charles Owen (1853–1922) moved to East Sussex in 1902. This was also the year in which Kipling settled in East Sussex. Owen was Church Warden of St. Mary's Church, Westham for 22 years. His wife, Mary Elizabeth died in 1920 and was buried in St. St. Mary's Church, Weston. Dr. Owen then married Mabel Howard Hopley, daughter of Howard Hopley, Vicar of St. Mary's Church, Weston. Dr. Owen died in 1922, his second wife in 1959. Both were buried in St. Mary's, Weston, Nr. Pevensey, East Sussex.

Appendix I

1. The theme of Russian agents encouraging unrest among the Indians is a major motif in Kipling's *Kim*. The author speaks of the "Amir of Cabul," the spelling used in Kipling's diary, e.g., "to meet the Amir." Kipling's reports from the Rawul Pindi conference were published as "To meet the Ameer," which seems to be the spelling preferred by Stephen Wheeler when proofreading Kipling's reports. The ruler of Afghanistan is generally addressed as "Abdul" in the *Civil and Military Gazette*. By the time of the Rawul Pindi conference he became "Abdur."
2. Kipling mentions working on these pieces several times in his diary for 1885. On January 24 he wrote: ..."worked at long translation from the *Journal de Saint Petersburg* which took home to finish." On the 25th he wrote: "Three hours hard work in the morning finished translation, proofs, papers and all the rest — Did nothing else all day." On January 26 he wrote: "Translation (as I had expected not wanted)." Then on January 27 he wrote: "...Russian translation went in today."
3. This "scrap" appears between two items mentioned in Kipling's diary notes for Monday 2 February: "Scrap on article in Novoi Vremya on relations between Germany and Russia, and two scraps on the Journal of Indian Art." The phrase "we read in the Russian papers" definitely points to Kipling's authorship.
4. Cf. Kipling diary for March 21: "Pindi. Wrote 1st Special on Pindi camp" (T. Pinney, *Rudyard Kipling" Something*, p. 207). Kipling's newsletters from the Rawul Pindi conference are distinguished by the caption "from our own correspondent." After March 31, however, this is changed to "from our Special Correspondent." In this first newsletter Kipling speaks of "Abdur," rather than "Abdul Rahman," which was the spelling in most of the previous reports.
5. Cf. Kipling's 1885 Diary, March 22:

"Peshawur. Where wrote second special of To Meet the Amir." Wheeler corrected Kipling's spelling of "Peshawur" and "Amir" in the title, but the location appears as both Peshawur and Peshawar in the text.

6. Cf. Kipling 1885 Diary for March 25: "Second special 'to meet the Amir.' Knocking about all over the place and cursing Abdur Rahman." Thomas Pinney notes that this is actually the third special (*Rudyard Kipling: Something*, p. 279).

7. Cf. Pinney, *Kipling's India*, p. 77–80 for text and attribution. This is the fourth in the series of 17 newsletters on the visit of the Amir to Rawul Pindi. In his diary from March 27 Kipling mentions his "Third special to meet the Amir" but Pinney points out that this is actually the fourth of the series.

8. This is the first of the series to carry the designation "Special Correspondent."

9. In his diary for March 28, Kipling mentions that he : "Wrote the City of Evil Countenances and saw that it was good." Cf. Pinney, *Kipling's India*, p. 81–85 for text and attribution.

10. Cf. Pinney, *Kipling's India*, p. 85–90 for text and attributions. Kipling's diary for March 29 reads: "Jumrood at Dawn. To Meet the Amir three columns." The author is acknowledged as "our Special Correspondent." The piece is followed in the newspaper by two further reports, one "*From a Correspondent*" and a second "*From our own Correspondent.*" Wheeler again made his mark by changing "Jumrood" to "Jumrud."

11. Cf. Pinney, *Kipling's India*, p. 91–94 for text and attribution. Kipling began this two-part newsletter in Peshawur on March 30 and completed it on the 9:20 night train to Rawul Pindi. Kipling mentions "Messrs. Walker, White-King and Anderson" as participants in the welcoming party. This probably means that James Walker was making the arrangements for travel and accommodation in Jumrood and Peshawur and it was he who suggested to Wheeler that Kipling be promoted to the status of "our Special Correspondent" in the March 31 issue of the *Civil and Military Gazette*.

12. This newsletter appears as an extension of the previous two-part newsletter written on March 30, which were published in the April 2 issue of the *Civil and Military Gazette*. In his diary for March 31, the author wrote: "To Meet the Amir. Still Heavy rain. Reached Pindi. Awfully tired." Kipling had taken the over-night train to get to Rawul Pindi before the arrival of Abdur Rahman.

13. In his diary for April 2 Kipling wrote: "Wild excitement for nothing. Knocking about all over the place and wrote another special." Kipling may have had an inkling of the defeat of the Ameer's troops at Penjdeh, although nothing is mentioned of course in his newsletter. Note the reference to the "great game" in the fifth paragraph. This article is a continuation of the previous one (Appendix I.14) in the April sixth issue of the *Civil and Military Gazette*.

14. In his diary for April 3 Kipling mentions this newsletter and notes that he hadn't been able to sleep for a week. This newsletter follows Appendix I.14 and I.15 in the April sixth issue of the *Civil and Military Gazette*.

15. Cf, Pinney's *Kipling's India*, p. 94–96 for text and attribution. Kipling had a free day and some sleep on April 4: "Got a little sleep at mid-day. Feeling *oh* so tired." On the fifth he wrote this special then "rode about all over the place." The possibilities of a war with Russia were by now openly discussed.

16. Cf. Pinney, *Kipling's India*, p. 97–100 for text and attribution. Parts of this article served as the basis of the piece "Servants of the Queen" in *The Jungle Book*.

17. Kipling's diary entry for April 8 is the last from the conference: "Two and a half columns about the big Durbar. Luckily got a good sleep last night and am fit for anything. Pindi Club crammed. Nothing but cannon all day and half the night." There are no diary entries between April 9 to April 29.

18. In the April 13th issue of the *Civil and Military Gazette* this scrap about the women attending the conference appeared on the front page. It most likely came from Kipling's pen, because he mentions the same women in the report published on April 10 (App. I.21). He wrote: "To allow them at all is a mistake for many reasons, and though it may seem a brutal and ungallant remark, they seriously impair the effect of a ceremony in oriental eyes ... But this is another digression."

19. This newsletter follows the previous one (Appendix I.22) in the April 14 issue of the *Civil and Military Gazette*.

20. Kipling rushed back to Lahore from Rawul Pindi, so he could report on the visit of the Viceroy to his home town. A second "The Viceroy in Lahore" article, dated April 17, followed in the April 20 issue. Of interest is the visit of Lord and Lady Dufferin to his father's museum:

An hour later, Lord Dufferin (to prevent confusion, beit known that any further reference to our ruler, unless otherwise notified, includes Lady Dufferin, Sir Charles Aitchison, Mr. Mackenzie Wallace, all the Aides-de-Camp, and the remainder of the Staff) was on his way in a four-horse barouche to visit the Lahore Museum. Here he was received by the Curator, and spent a long time examining, with much interest, the Buddhist sculptures, which are one of the main features of this institution. At the School of Art, next door, he examined the drawings and the work in progress, with the minutest care; asking the native students questions as to their own and their fathers' trade. Both at the Museum, which give a representation of the present state of arts and industries of the Province, and the School of Art, where Oriental design is studied, there is naturally much to interest any one who is concerned with the artistic and technical progress of the country. Into such details as there was time to consider at any length, the Viceroy entered with critical, but at the same time, cordial appreciation.

21. Thomas Pinney (ed.), *The Letters of Rudyard Kipling* (London, 1990), p. 179. Prof. Pinney kindly forwarded this "scrap," after neither the British Library nor the Dalhousie Kipling Library could furnish it.

Selected Bibliography

Andrews, Peter A., "The Turkmen Tent," *Turkmen Tribal Carpets and Traditions*, ed. by Louise Mackie and Jon Thompson (Washington, 1980), 39–59.

Ankers, Arthur R., *The Pater: John Lockwood Kipling, His Life and Times 1837–1911* (Oxford, 1988).

Archer, Mildred, *British Drawings in the India Office London* (London, 1969).

Azadi, Siawosch, *Turkoman Carpets and the Ethnographical Significance of Their Ornaments*, trans. by Robert Pinner (Fishguard, Wales, 1975).

Barrow, Arthur F., "Precis respecting Afghan Frontier from January 1884 to April 9th, 1885, written at Tirpul in 1885," handwritten manuscript in possession of Mr. Peter Digby Lumsden, Toronto, Ontario, Canada.

Blacknon, James W., "Tent and Town, Rugs and Embroideries from Central Asia. The H. McCoy Jones Collection," *Hali* V/3 (1983), 346–348.

Bogolyubov, Andrei A., *Carpets of Central Asia*, ed by J. M. A. Thompson (Ramsdell, Hampshire, 1973).

Bregel, Yuri, *Historical Maps of Central Asia, 9th–19th Centuries* (Bloomington, 2000).

Bregel, Yuri, "Nomadic and Sedentary Elements Among the Turkmens," *Central Asiatic Journal* 25 (1981), 11f.

Bucherer-Dietschi, Paul (ed.), *Schmuck und Silberschmiedearbeiten in Afghanistan und Zentralasien: Schmuck in Sammlungen* (Liestal, 1981).

Burne, OwenTudor, *Note on some points connected with the North-western Frontier of Afghanistan, with special reference to Badghis and Panjdeh*, ms dated 13 March 1885 at India House.

Dzhikiev, Ata, *Etnograficheskii orcherk naseleniia iugo-vostochnogo Turkmenistana* (Ashkhabad, 1972).

Firouz, Iran Ala, *Silver Ornaments of the Turkoman* (Tehran, 1978).

Holdich, Thomas H., *The Indian Borderland 1880–1900* (London, 1901).

Hopkirk, Peter, *The Great Game: On Secret Service in High Asia* (London, 1990).

Hopkirk, Peter, *Quest for Kim: In Search of Kipling's Great Game* (Oxford, 1996).

Kalter, Johannes, *The Arts and Crafts of Turkestan* (London, 1984).

König, Wolfgang, *Die Achal-Teke: Zur Wirtschaft und Gesellschaft einer Turkmenen-Gruppe im XIX. Jahrhundert*, Veröffentlichungen des Museums für Völkerkunde zu Leipzig, Heft 12 (Berlin, 1962).

Lessar, Pierre M., "Yugo-zapadnaya Turkmeniya. Zemli sarikov i salorov," *Izvestiya imp. russkogo geograficheskogo odshchestva*, XXI (St. Petersburg, 1885).

Loges, Werner, *Turkoman Tribal Rugs*, trans. by Raoul Tschebull (London, 1980).

Lumsden, Peter, "Countries and Tribes bordering on the Koh-i-Baba range," *Pro-*

ceedings of the Royal Geographical Society, new monthly series, VII (1885), 561–583.
Mackie, Louise and Jon Thompson, *Turkmen Tribal Carpets and Traditions* (Washington, 1980).
Marvin, Charles, *The Queen of the World and the Scourge of the Man-Stealing Turcomans* (London, 1881).
McCoy Jones, H. and Jeff W. Boucher, *Tribal Rugs from Turkmenistan* (Washington, 1973).
Menzel, Erich, "Zeichnungen der Saryk-Teppiche," *Hali* II/4 (1980), 282–286.
Moran, Neil K., "Dr. Charles Owen and the Kiplings," 78 *Kipling Journal* (2004), 7–24.
Moran, Neil K., "Turkoman Door Rugs," *Hali* VI/2 (1984), 182–183.
Moshkova, Valentina G., *Kovri narodov Srednej Azii, kontsa XIX — nachala XX vv.* (Tashkent, 1970).
O'Bannon, George W., *The Turkoman Carpet* (London, 1974).
O'Bannon, George W., et al., *Vanishing Jewels: Central Asian Tribal Weavings, A Catalog of an Exhibition by the Rochester Museum and Science Center* (Rochester, 1990).
Ovezberdyev, K., "Materialy po etnografii turkmensarykov Pendinskogo oazisa," *Trudy Instituta istorii, arkheologii i etnografii, Akademii nauk Turkmenskoi SSR*, vol. VI (Ashkhabad, 1962), p. 113–114.
[Owen, Charles,] "Turkoman Ornaments," *Journal of Indian Art* I/7 (1886), 53–56.
Pinner, Robert and Murray Eiland, Jr., *Between the Black Desert and the Red: Carpets from the Wiedersperg Collection* (San Francisco, 1999).
Pinner, Robert, Michael Franses and Donald King, "Turkoman Rugs in the Victoria and Albert Museum," *Hali* II/4 (1980), 301–315.
Pinner, Robert and Michael Franses (ed.), *Turkoman Studies I: Aspects of Weaving and Decorative Arts of Central Asia* (London, 1980).
Pinney, Thomas (ed.), *Kipling's India: Uncollected Sketches 1884–88* (London, 1986).
Pinney, Thomas (ed.), *The Letters of Rudyard Kipling*, vol. 1 (1872–89), (London, 1990).
Pinney, Thomas (ed.), *Rudyard Kipling: Something of Myself and Other Autobiographical Writings* (Cambridge, 1990).
Pittenger, Robert, "Border Patrol: 'Timuri' and 'Baluch' Blue-Ground Prayer Rugs," *Hali* 102 (1999), 78f.
Prokot, Inge and Joachim, *Schmuck aus Zentralasien* (Munich, 1981).
Rudolph, Hermann, *Der Turkmenenschmuck: Sammlung Kurt Gall* (Stuttgart, 1984).
Schletzer, Dieter and Reinhold, *Alter Silberschmuck der Turkmenen* (Berlin, 1983).
Simpson, William, *The Autobiography of William Simpson, R.I.*, ed. by George Eyre-Todd (London, 1903).
Simpson, William, "With the Afghan Boundary Commission," *Harper's Magazine* LXX (1886), 595–605.
Stewart, Charles, *Through Persia in Disguise with Reminiscences of the Indian Mutiny* (London, 1911).
Jon Thompson, *Oriental Carpets: From the Tents, Cottages and Workshops of Asia* (New York, 1983).
Tzareva, Elena, *Rugs and Carpets from Central Asia* (Vienna, 1984).
Tzareva, Elena, "Saryk Tent Bags in the State Museum of Ethnography of the Peoples of the USSR," *Hali* I/3 (1978), 277–280.

Tzareva, Elena, "Salor Carpets," *Hali* VI/2 (1984), 126–135.
Vambery, Armin, *The Coming Struggle for India* (London, 1885).
Vambery, Armin, *Travels in Central Asia* (New York, 1865).
Weir, Thomas, *From India to the Caspian or Journey with and after the Afghan Mission* (Bombay, 1893).
Yate, Arthur C., *England and Russia Face to Face in Asia: Travels with the Afghan Boundary Commission* (Edinburgh and London, 1887).
Yate, Charles E., *Khurasan and Sistan* (Edinburgh & London, 1900).
Yate, Charles E., *Northern Afghanistan or Letters from the Afghan Boundary Commission* (Edinburgh and London, 1888).

Index

Abdur Rahman, Amir (Ameer) 2–3, 7, 10, 16, 31, 35–36, 48, 52, 55, 57–61, 71–77, 82, 84–85, 87, 93–95, 97–98, 100, 104, 109–110, 120, 124–135, 138, 140–157, 159–160, 162–168, 170–176, 180–189, 192, 218–219
Abistada 22
Abonguine 116
Abyssinian War (1867–68) 7, 170
Adam Yolan 121
Afghan Boundary Commission: in Bala Murghab 38–47; demarcating the border 86–93; establishment of 4–6, 8, 14–19; in Kabul 93–95; in Lahore 96–105; retreat to Tirpul 79–81; traveling through Baluchistan 18–24; traveling to Bala Murghab 30–38
Afghan Khan 133
Afghan War: First 3, 11; Second (1878–1880) 3, 7, 111, 170
Afreedde (Afridi) 58–59, 103–104, 136, 139
Afridi *see* Afreedde
Aftaba 160
Aga 133
Aga Hyder-Shah 133
Ahmed Jan Khan 134
Airakhta 122
Aitchison, Lt. Gov. Charles 75, 99, 172, 175, 185–186, 220
Aitchison, James E. T. 8, 18, 20, 40, 210
Ak Mahommed (Saryk) 67
Ak Tapa 30–32, 52–54, 65, 67, 211
Akhal Tekke region 114
Aklochi 205
Alai pass 201
Albert Victor, Prince 85
Alexander, Capt. 177–179
Alexander the Great 21, 38
Alexander III, Czar 16, 71
Alexandoff 115
Alexandra, Princess of Wales 85
Ali Musjid 59, 132–133, 138

Alikhanoff, Major 9, 24, 35, 52, 65–68, 78, 108, 187
Allahabad 12, 16, 77, 214
Allen, George 96
Allgemeine Zeitung 6
Allworth, Edward 213
Amir Mohd, General 93
Amu Darya 122, 202
Anderson, Mr. 127, 143, 146, 219
Andhui (Andkhoi) 40, 89
Ankers, Arthur 213, 216, 218
Aral Sea 116–117, 122
Armageddon 104
Army: Bengal Cavalry: (3rd) 123, 164; (7th) 209; (12th) 129, 138, 140, 143; (15th) 148–149, 155, 164; (18th) 155; Bengal Lancers: (9th) 123–124, 164; (11th) 8, 17–18, 31, 81, 101, 207; (14th) 123, 148–149, 164, 186; (19th) 123, 164; Bengal Sappers and Miners 130, 142; Campellpore Elephant Battery 123–124, 165; Carabiniers 123, 164; Cheshire Regiment 123, 164; Dorsetshire Regiment: (2nd) 129, 142; (99th) 129; Field and Horse Battery 165; Goorkhas: (1st) 123, 163; (4th) 123, 163; (5th) 157, 163; Guides 7, 164; Highland Light Infantry 123, 164; Infantry Division: (2nd) 123; King's Dragoon Guard 148–149, 164, 182; King's Rifles: (4th) 129; Manchester Regiment 123; Mountain Battery 129, 143; Native Infantry: (8th) 129, 142; (9th) 129; (13th) 129, 142; (30th) 129; Punjab (Panjab) Native Infantry: (1st) 164; (3rd) 60; (9th) 142; (19th) 123, 164; (20th) 8, 17, 30, 86, 93, 101, 208; (21st) 163; (24th) 164; (25th) 123, 164; (30th) 129, 142; (31st) 163; Punjab Volunteers 148, 156; Regiment: (33rd) 162–163; Rifle Brigade: (4th) 123, 163; (60th) 134, 142, 144; Royal Artillery 129, 138, 165; Royal Horse Artillery: (K Battery) 182; (L-A) 123–124; (L.2) 123;

225

(L.3) 123; Royal Irish Fusiliers 148, 182; Royal Irish Regiment 123, 163; Scotch Regiment: (78th) 164; Seaforth Highlanders 123–124, 171; Sikhs: (3rd) 164; (14th) 163; Wiltshire Regiment: (2nd) 129, 142
Askabad 93, 116
Astrabad 78, 83
Astrakhan 122
Atak (Atek) range 70, 202
Atkins, Thomas 124, 139, 143, 171, 183–184
Atta 126
Attar 158, 172
Attock 129
Ayub Khan 11
Azad kan, sirdar 20

Baboo *see* babu
Baboo Abdur Rahman 126
Babu 126, 155
Badghiz (Badghis/Badgheis) 10, 47, 53, 120
Badshah 133
Baha-u-din Khan, Ressaldar-Major 209
Bahawulpur (Bahawulpore), Nawab of 101, 103, 124
Baku 13, 52–53, 78, 119, 193
Bala Murghab 30, 33, 36–40, 43, 48, 50, 53, 111, 194, 204–205
Balkh (Balk) 6, 111–112, 114, 120, 207
Balla Ischem 116
Balmoral 84
Baluchistan 13, 18, 22, 208
Bambridge, Elsie 218
Bamian 43, 89, 93
Barnes, Hugh Shakespear 207
Barrow, Arthur Frederick 4, 7, 29, 31, 50, 83, 206, 213, 215
Batoum (Batumi) 78, 83
Bax, W. J. 86, 92, 95, 105, 207
Beatty 180
Beddy, Mr. 178–179
Bek 117
Bekovitch, Prince Alexander 115
Bekovitch-Tcherkaskey expedition 115
Beliavsky (Beliavski), General C. 115–116, 122
Belmont, Mr. 180
Benmore 21
Benton, Mr. 143
Beresford, Lord William 178–179, 182
Berlin 56, 78, 197–198
Bhisti 126, 157
Bhopal 154
Bhusa (bhoosa) 132, 136
Bhutan 170
Bibuiani 18
Biddulph, Michael 148, 163, 169

Bikaneer, Rajah of 154
Black Sea 13, 78, 83, 193
Blackburn 177–178
Blue Beard 139
Bokhara 3, 10, 27, 36–37, 125, 190–192, 216
Bombay 4, 8, 19, 33, 106
Bond, Lieutenant 143
Borkut chain 202
Bosphorus 51
Boursen Courier 198
British Library 73–74, 76
British Museum 37
Broughton, Mr. 179
Bruce, Mr. 177, 179
Bunder Gez 78
Bundobust 130
Bungalow 126, 134–135, 142, 145, 149
Burke, John 15, 73–74, 104–105, 214
Burney, R. T. 105
Burrows, Brigadier George 3
Bux, Meeran 54
Bylawalla 165

Cabuli 61, 145–148, 161
Calcutta 4–5, 12, 132, 145, 214
Calcutta Review 134
Calico 167
Campbell of Kilberry, Marion 216
Carandini, Capt. 178
Carlyle, Thomas 184
Caspian Sea 13, 52–53, 70, 78, 103
Cavagnari, Louis 3, 11
Chah Gazek 204
Chaharshambar 216
Chaman-i-Bed (Chaman-i-Baid) 31, 79
Chamba 171
Chapgal Pass 31
Chaprasi *see* Chaprassi
Chaprassi 132, 145, 152
Char Aimak tribe 40
Charpoy 57, 133, 152, 161
Charles, Richard Havelock 31, 207
Chasma Sabz Pass 79, 81
Chemsford, Lord 84
Cheroot 143, 160
Chick 155
Chirag 136
Chisholme, Major Scott 177–179
Chit 123
Chitral 111–112, 114, 120
Chobdar 172, 186
Civil and Military Gazette 4–6, 9, 11–12, 14–15, 17–19, 24, 26, 30–32 35, 38–40, 43–44, 49–51, 53–54, 58, 62, 68, 77, 81–82, 92–93, 96–99, 101–205, 213–219
Clarendon, Lord 216
Close, Lieutenant 143

Index

Coates, Dr. 143
Codlin and Short 133
Colonial and Indian Exhibition (1886) 44
Colvin, Auckland 14
Connaught, Duchess of 181
Connaught, Duke of 2, 55, 71, 74, 76, 97–99, 101–102, 104, 106, 149–140, 153, 172–173
Constantinople 51, 83
Cook, Major 177–178
Coolie 138, 148, 175, 186
Cophes 22
Cossack 59, 66–67, 87, 103, 141, 201
Cotton, Capt. 86, 93, 208
Crimea 170
Crimean War 7, 170
Crore 159
Cross, Richard Assheton 119–120, 199
Cummings, Duncan 213
Czarwitch Bay 115

Dagestan 24
Daily News 34, 40, 213, 216
Daily Telegraph 91, 195–196
Dâk 126, 128, 135
Dalli 145
Dandridge, General 143
Dardja 116
Dash-Kepri 66
Daukala 121
Dbobie 148
Deccan 164
DeGex, Mr. 177, 179
De Laessoe, Albert F. 8, 31, 65, 86, 91–92, 209–210
Delhi 18, 169–170
Derby, Lord 21
Devon 5
Dhakka (Dakka) 125, 132, 134
Dhar 154
Dholepore, Rajah of 143
Dilawer Khan 133
Dogan 18
Dogarou 121
Dongola 193
Drummond, Francis H. R. 41, 54, 86, 205, 208
Dublin 89, 164
Duffadar Mir Baz 208
Dufferin, Lady 153, 156, 185–186, 220
Dufferin, Lord 2, 55, 71–77, 84, 94, 97, 99, 101–105, 110, 113, 123–125, 128, 132, 149–150, 152–159, 161–163, 166, 168–175, 178, 182–185, 219–220
Duftar 131
Dunnage, Major 143
Durand, Edward L. 8, 11, 17–22, 25, 30–33, 38–41, 43, 54, 63, 86–87, 92–93, 99, 105, 207–208, 215–217
Durand, Henry 11
Durand, Henry Mortimer 11, 54, 66, 71
Durand, Marion 33
Durand, Stella 215
Durani 141–142
Durbar 30, 52, 55, 60, 72, 74–77, 93–95, 97–98, 104, 110, 130–132, 145, 149–150, 152–159, 161, 166–167, 170–175, 178, 182, 219
Durzie 126
Duserah gorah lao 147

Edward, Prince of Wales 7, 78, 85, 99
Egypt 12, 21, 51, 53, 121, 170, 194, 196, 201
Ekka 135
Elbeerst chain 203
Eldridge, Joy 218
Elisabeth Feodorovna, Grand Duchess 119
Elisabeth Mavrikievna, Grand Duchess 119
Elphinstone, Gen. William 14
Ewart, Colonel 113
Eyre-Todd, George 211, 213

Faizulla Khan 134
Faridkote (Faridkhot), Rajah of 99, 124, 171
Ferghana 201
FitzMaurice, Lord 199
Friday 161
Furrah 112

Galichah 204
Galindo, Sergeant 210
Gardi Sharkhani 133
Gaulois 198
Gazette de Moscow 117
Gazette de St. Petersburgh 115
Gelzai (Ghilzai) 127, 188
Geok Tepe 3, 10, 70, 198
George, Prince 85
German French War of 1870 7
Ghat 186
Ghee 126, 136
Gholam Hyder Khan, General 61–62, 134, 142, 146, 181
Ghous-ud-Din Khan 32, 52, 66, 68, 211
Ghuzni 112; *see also* Guzni
Gladstone, William 4, 6, 10, 15, 51–52, 54, 71–72, 84, 100, 159, 193–194, 199–200
Globe 97
Godown 130, 135
Godwyn, Major 143
Goolar 29
Goorbund 127
Gordon, General Charles George 51, 194, 196
Gordon, Brigadier Gen. T. E. 74, 128–129, 132, 140–141, 144, 172, 194

228　Index

Gore, St. George Corbet 8, 17, 86–87, 92–93, 209
Gortschakoff, Prince 116
Grant, Field-Marshall Sir Peter 84
Granville, Lord 6, 9–10, 53, 63, 84, 121, 195
Graphic 81, 210, 217
Griesbach, Charles 8, 40, 86, 210
Grodekoff, Col. N. L. 216
Gulran (Gurlin) 46–47, 50, 53, 63, 68–69, 78–79, 82, 207
Gurgan River 70
Guzni 127; *see also* Ghuzni

Hamilton, Mr. 180
Hardinge, General 175
Harper's Magazine 26, 30, 78, 92, 213, 215, 217
Harvard University 77, 108, 214
Hastings, Mr. 143
Hazara 127
Heath, Captain Harry S. R. (Mark) 31, 53, 68, 208
Helmund River 13, 20,
Henderson, Colonel 148, 182
Herat 6, 13, 17, 22, 24–25, 29–30, 32, 36–37, 49–53, 55–56, 63, 82–83, 85–86, 104, 110–114, 119–122, 187–189, 194–195, 197–201, 203, 214, 217
Herbert, Arthur J. 206
Heri-Rud (Hari-Rud) River 13, 29, 31, 78, 82, 85, 115, 202
Hill, Edmonia 187
Hill, Major 8, 209
Himalayas 37
Hindu Kush 36, 93, 107, 112
Hindustanee 160
Holdich, Thomas Hungerford 8, 19, 31, 34, 81–83, 86–87, 91–92, 209, 214–217
Holdsworth, Mary 213
Holkar 154
Homer 21, 38
Hookah 130, 135, 147, 173
Hopkirk, Peter 213, 217
Hopley, Mabel Howard 214, 218
Hotuk 127
Howdah 148
Hussein Abdul 63
Hyderabad 154–155

Ibrahimabad 204
Ilbert, Courtenay 12, 107, 175
Ilbert, Mrs. Jessie 92
Illustrated London News 4, 6–8, 11, 13, 23, 25–28, 30–33, 35, 37, 43–46, 52–56, 60, 62, 65, 69, 84–85, 87–88, 213–217
Indian Mutiny 7, 170
Indus River 18

Indus-Valley-State Railroad 18
Islim 79, 207
Istanbul 94

Jacobabad 18
Jaipur (Jeypore) 12–13, 18, 91, 211, 214
James, Fitz 21
Jamma Khan 133
Jamrud (Jamrood/Jumrood) 58, 63, 76, 95, 97, 128, 132–133, 138, 140, 143–143, 216, 219
Jamshedis (Jamshidis/Djemshidis) 37, 39, 44, 187–188, 203
Jan Mahomed Khan 133–134
Jellalabad 95, 133
Jemandar Amir Muhammad 208
Jeypore, Rajah of 154
Jheel 152
Jhelum 123–125, 162–164
Jhengis Khan 194
Jhind, Rajah of 100, 150, 154–155, 165, 172
Jhool 131, 148
Jodhpore, Rajah of 154
Johnson, F. G. 177–178
Journal de St. Petersbourg 6, 51, 111, 192, 218
Journal of Indian Art 42–43, 98, 216, 218
Jowaki 170
Jowral 154

Kabul (Cabul) 3, 8, 11, 14–16, 36, 54–55, 93–94, 97–98, 112–113, 118, 127, 144–148, 159, 161, 168, 209, 214, 218–219
Kafir 136–137, 173
Kandahar 3, 7–8, 11, 14, 16, 55, 83, 111–112, 120, 209
Kandahar and Sind Railroad 18
Kannat 151
Kapurthalla, Rajah of 99, 165
Kara-Kum desert 26, 70
Kara Tapa 31, 188
Kareschout-Khan-Kila 114
Kashmir (Cashmere) 112, 150, 214, 218
Kazi 117, 133
Kazi Abdul Kadir 127
Kazi Kootb-ud-din 133
Kazi Saud-ud-din, Governor 188
Kazi Shahb-ud-din 133
Kendall 178
Keosque 150
Khadim 179
khakee *see* Khaki
Khaki 151, 163, 170
Kham-i-Ab 93
Khan 128, 135, 145–146, 191
Khanna plain 60, 74, 123–124, 151–152, 155–157, 159, 166–167, 171, 177, 181–182
Kharsan 20
Khartoum 51, 119–120, 193–194, 196

Index

Khattak hills 58, 138
Khawaja Ali 25
Kheradj 115
Khidoyatov, G. A. 213
Khiva 3, 27, 44, 70, 191, 215
Khodga Salekh (Khoja Saleh) 10, 111
Khorassan 4, 13, 36, 70, 113, 202–203, 211
Khurarezm lake 116
Khwaja Salar 87
Khyber Pass 3, 58–59, 128, 134, 138, 140
Kibitka 28, 32–35, 39, 43–45, 54, 68, 93, 115, 121, 215, 217
Kila-i-Maur 68, 78–79, 89
Kimberley, Lord 84
Kin 204
Kinkab *see* Kinhob
Kinkob 130–132, 167, 173, 185
Kinsman, Major 181
Kipling, Alice 1, 5, 12, 77–78
Kipling, Alice (Trix) 77–78
Kipling, John Lockwood 1–2, 5, 12, 37, 39, 43, 57, 76–77, 98, 105, 218–220
Kipling, Rudyard: *Amir's Homily* 77; assistant editor in Lahore 1–2, 5–6, 9–10, 17, 19, 21, 38, 43, 49–50, 52–56, 75, 77, 93, 100, 107–203, 213, 216; correspondent at Rawal Pindi conference 57–63, 71–76, 95, 123–183; correspondent in Simla 77; *Departmental Ditties* 97; diary of 1885 10, 57, 62, 71, 76–77, 108, 218–219; East Sussex 106, 218; *Jungle Book* 77, 219; *Kim* 18, 218; *Life's Handicap* 217; *Quartette* 77; *Something of Myself* 9, 105, 214–215, 218
Kipling Journal 5, 215
Kirghiz 34, 118, 216, 218
Kirta 18
Kizil Arvat 53, 119
Kizilbash 127, 133
Koenig, Wolfgang 215
Kohistan 58, 127, 136
Kokchail 37
Komaroff, General Alexander 35, 52, 65–67, 83
Kouldja 118
Koun 117
Kouschine, M. 116
Krasnovodsk 3, 53, 119
Kubberdar 147
Kuhlberg, Colonel 86–88, 93
Kuhsan 22, 25, 29–32, 37–38, 204, 215
Kungrad 115
Kurban Ali Berg Mervi 211
Kurban Ali Khan 133
Kushk (Kooshk) 30–32, 37, 52, 65–68, 79, 85, 188, 203
Kutcha 123, 131, 151, 167
Kwajah Ali 204

Lahore: ABC in 95–105, 219; government house 186; Jehangeer's tomb (Shahdera) 186; museum 216, 218–220; New Mayo School of Art 5, 39, 98, 220; office of *Civil and Military Gazette* 1–2, 4–6, 55, 57, 97; train station 18, 99, 184–185
Lakh 137
Lancashire 164
Landi (Lundi)-Khana 128
Lasgird 25–26
Lash Juwain (Lash Jowain) 25, 194
Latabund 95
Lauson 180
Leigh, Lieutenant 134
Leiningen, Princess of 85
Lessar, Pierre 48, 56, 84, 86–87, 100, 114–115, 121, 197, 201, 203
Little, Mr. 177–178, 180
Log 152
Loga (Logar) 58, 127, 136
London 4, 7, 9–10, 13, 19, 25, 38–39, 47–51, 53–54, 56, 65, 69, 78–79, 82–87, 99–100, 118–119, 193, 197–201, 203, 208
Lorne, Marchioness of 85
Lumsden, Harry Burnett 7, 83
Lumsden, Peter Stark 4, 6–7, 9, 13, 15, 17, 24–25, 29–32, 34–35, 37–39, 44, 49–50, 52–53, 56, 63, 79–80, 82–85, 100–101, 120–121, 194–198, 200, 202, 206–207, 213, 215
Lundi Kotal 125, 132, 134
Lyall, Sir Alfred 172, 175
Lyttle 207

Macdonald, Edith 77, 97, 213, 218
Mach 18
Maclean, General 187
Macpherson, Mr. 179
Madras 172
Mahdi 150, 154, 194, 196–197
Mahomed Akbar Khan 133
Mahomed Alum Khan 134
Mahomed Azim 134
Mahomed Jan 133
Mahomed Khan, chessplayer 133
Mahomed Nahin 133
Mahomed Omar Khan 133
Mahomed Sirwa Khan 134
Maidan 140, 151
Maimana 37, 40
Maitland, Pelham James 8, 86, 210
Maiwand 3
Malahide Castle 89, 211
Malcolm, John 14
Malli 126
Manners-Smith 180
Martini-Henry (Henri) rifles 141, 144, 147, 184

230　　　　　　　　　　Index

Marvin, Charles 4, 11, 13, 119, 214
Massie, Alastair 214
Maund 126, 130, 132
McCausland, Captain 143
McGregor, Charles 14–15
Mehmandar 129
Mehter 158
Meikeljohn, William Hope 17, 208
Meredith 180
Merk, William R. H. 40, 47, 86, 207, 209
Mertvy-Koultuk (Mertvi-Kultuck/Kultuk) 115, 122
Meruchak (Maruchak) 37, 114
Merv (Merve) 3–4, 6, 9–10, 16, 24, 32, 34–35, 50, 56, 70–71, 89, 93, 107–108, 111, 114–116, 119–120, 122, 192, 199, 202, 211
Meshed 13, 25, 63, 78, 85, 187, 211
Metcalfe, Lord 14
Miandasht 25
Mihrab 130
Miller, T. 145
Milton, Mr. 177, 179–180
Minar 186
Mir Mahomed Husein 133
Mirza Abdul Rashid 134
Mirza Assidulla Khan 119
Mirza Mohommed Nubbia Khan 134, 156
Mohamed Aslam Khan, Sirdar 31, 95, 209
Mohurri 130, 135
Montaigne, Seigneur de 22
Mooltan 18, 97
Moscow 108
Moscow News 122
Moshkova, Valentina Georgievna 90, 217
Mowla Dad, Subadar-Major 208
Mufti 117
Multah Khan (Saryk) 67
Mungal 127
Murghab River 19, 30, 32, 37, 46, 52, 66, 68, 85, 115, 120–121, 202–203
Musnud 130–131

Nabha (Naba), Rajah of 101, 124, 150, 154–155, 165
Nahun, Maharajah of 101
Naib Salar 67
Naini Tal 106
Napier, George Campbell 206
Napier of Magdala, Lord 84, 206
National Army Museum (London) 1, 12, 214–217
National Library of Scotland 215
National Review 49
Natore, Raja of 102
Nawab 146, 155
Nawab Mirza Hassan Ali Khan 7, 31, 80, 86, 206

Nazar Safed Mahomed 133
Neeld, Captain 178
Nejrob 127
Nekrassova, Natalia 90
Nepal 164
New York 24
Nishapore 25
Nixon, Captain 143
Nobel Brothers 52, 119
Nouveau Temps 114, 190, 195–196
Novoie (Novoe) Vremya 6, 9, 51, 56, 121, 192, 194, 196, 199–200, 203, 218
Nowshera 129
Nubbee Buksh 183
Nushki 20, 22, 25, 204

Odessa 78
Official Messenger (St. Petersburg) 66–67, 116
Oliver, Mr. 177
Oodeypore, Rajah of 154
Ooreha 154
Orel, Harold 213
Orenburg (Orengburg) 116, 122
Osman Digma 197
Ourga 118
Oust-oust plateau 115–116
Ouzboi 116
Owen, Charles William 8, 11–13, 17–19, 22–25, 30–47, 53–56, 63, 65, 67, 72, 79–82, 86–87, 89, 91–99, 101, 105–106, 210, 214–215, 218
Owen, George 63
Owen, Mary Elizabeth 12–13, 30–31, 53–54, 63, 81, 86–87, 91, 93, 217–218
Oxus River 10, 13, 19, 36, 40, 89, 104, 111, 115–117, 192, 194

Page, David 5
Paisley 164
Pal 132, 139
Palin, Lieutenant 143
Pall Mall Gazette 49, 51, 196, 216–217
Palmerston, Lord 48–49
Pamirs (Panier) district 10, 34, 191
Pan 158
Panjsheer 127
Pardahneshin 160
Paris 38, 198
Paropamisus range 202–203
Parsee 155
Pathan 57, 136
Pattiala, Maharaja of 75, 124, 150, 155, 171–172
Peacock, Captain William 40, 86, 210
Penjdeh (Panjdeh) 1, 7, 10, 29–37, 39–40, 43–44, 47–48, 52–55, 63, 65, 67–68, 71,

Index

78–79, 82–85, 89, 100, 111, 114, 120–121, 176, 203–205, 210, 215, 219
Pepys, Samuel 149
Perkins, Mr. 148, 182
Perwana Khan 98
Peshawar (Peshawaur/Peshawur) 57–59, 61–63, 76, 125–134, 137, 140, 142–143, 145–148, 176, 181–182, 216, 219
Peshin 159, 176
Peter the Great, Czar 115
Pierce, Richard A. 213
Pinney, Thomas 108, 213–220
Pioneer 12, 16, 24, 91–92, 121, 214–215
Plowden, Edith 57, 76
Ponsonby, Sir Henry 84
Poshteen 136
Poti 192–193
Prinsep, Colonel 17, 208
Pucca *see* Pukka
Pugdundie 151
Puggri 162
Pukka 131, 167
Pul-i-Khatun 13, 29, 48–49, 112, 119–121, 200
Pul-i-Khisti 31, 65, 67–68, 91, 208, 210
Punjab (Panjab) 8, 17–18, 60, 73, 75, 86, 93, 99–105, 113–114, 123, 142, 147–148, 150, 154–158, 161–165, 171–172, 175, 177, 183, 185–186, 194, 208
Punjab Northern State Railroad 123–125, 129, 145–148, 154, 162, 182–183, 186, 219
Punna 154
Pushtu 146–147

Quetta 13, 17–20, 24–25, 36, 54, 106

Raj 113
Rajah 155
Rajputana 154
Ram, Pati 211
Rao, Sir Dinkur 102
Rattigen, William 4, 12
Rawal Pindi (Rawul Pindi/Rawalpindi) 55–57, 59, 61–62, 71–77, 82, 94–95, 108–110, 123, 128–129, 132, 145, 147–149, 152, 155, 157, 161–162, 166, 168, 170, 175, 180–182, 185, 217–219
Rawlin, Lieutenant 208
Resht 13
Reuter 187, 195
Rewah 154
Reza, Imam 25
Rezai 130
Ridgeway, Joseph West 7–8, 14–18, 20, 24–25, 29–31, 37–38, 40, 47, 53, 63, 82, 86–89, 91–92, 94–95, 97–98, 100–102, 104–105, 207–209

Rind, Major 207
Rindli 18
Ripon, Lord 4, 15
Roberts, Gen. Frederick 3, 7–8, 11, 14–16, 55, 75, 77, 91, 106, 175, 177
Roberts, Lady 92
Robinson, E. Kay 78, 93, 96–97, 99, 105–106, 217–218
Robinson, Jun. 177
Robinson Crusoe 161
Rohri Bunder 18
Rozabagh 95, 98
Rudbar 22
Rus 51
Rustam 21
Rutlam 154

Sabzewar 25
Sahan 204
Sahara 140
Sahib 139, 152, 160
St. Petersburg 4, 9–10, 49–51, 54–56, 65–67, 84, 93, 108, 115, 119, 122, 190, 197–200
Salar Jung 155
Salisbury, Robert Gascoyne-Cecil, 3rd Marquess of 94
Salisbury, Robert Gascoyne-Cecil, 7th Marquess of 6, 8, 27, 33, 45
Samarkand 3, 98
Sarakhs (Sarrakhs) 4, 13–14, 25, 29, 48–50, 53, 111–112, 201
Sardar Sher Ahmed Khan 209
Sari Yazi (Sari Yari) 52, 68, 119–121, 215
Saro Tar 22
Saryskamysch (Sarakamysch) 116–117
Saturday Review 216
Schariat 117
Scindia (Schindiah) 150, 154
Seistan 21
Semiramis, Queen 21–22, 38
Shahrud (Shukrood) 25, 29, 78
Shamiana 141, 150, 153, 167, 171
Sharf, Fred 214, 217
Shere Ali Khan, Amir 15, 127
Shignan 36
Shore, Lieutenant 60
Shuldari 151
Siakh-Puschem 114
Simla: foreign office 17, 19, 54, 91, 188; Kevin Grove 5; military headquarters of India 3, 5, 7, 9, 11, 15, 36, 52, 54, 76, 91
Simpson, William 5, 7, 19, 25–28, 30–31, 33–34, 39, 43–47, 69–70, 78–79, 83–85, 211, 213, 215, 217
Sind, Punjab and Delhi Railroad 18
Singh, Maharaja Kishore 177–178
Sinja 86

Sir Mandal 204
Sirdar 126–128, 130–133, 145, 152, 155
Sirdar Nur Mahomed Khan 133
Siriab 19
Sister Anne 139
Skobeleff, Gen. Michel 70
Slater, John 5
Smith 180
Soboleff, General L. N. 51
Soorkee 135
Soree-Kul lake 10, 191
Soudan (Sudan) 51, 53, 70, 111, 118, 121, 154, 194, 196–197, 199
Sowar 139, 149–150, 153, 155
Standard 51, 187, 196
Stanhope, Edward 48
Stephen, Alexander Condie 7, 31, 53, 63, 82, 84, 99, 209
Stewart, Charles E. 7, 17, 82, 99, 207, 217
Strathnairn, Lord 84
Suakim 197
Sue, Eugene 135
Sukkar 18
Sutton and Co. 37
Swat hills 58, 138
Syce 138, 147
Syed Ahmed Khan 133
Sykes, Percy 66, 208, 217

Talbot, Captain 174–175
Talbot de Malahide, Milo George 8, 18, 86–87, 89–90, 93, 209
Talbot de Malahide, Milo John Reginald 209
Talbot de Malahide, Rose Maud 209, 218
Tamasha 152–153, 174
Tartar 118, 147
Taschkend (Tashkend/Tashkhend) 115, 201
Taylor 197
Tchernaieff, Colonel 115, 122
Teapoy 134
Teheran 7, 13, 25, 39, 50, 118
Tejend 111
Terai 85
Thornton, Sir E. 55
Thuillier, Mr. 177, 179
Thugs 27
Ticca gharri 125, 138, 162
Tidy, Major 143
Tiffin 153
Tiflis 13, 193
Times (London) 24, 30, 35, 48, 78–79, 81–85, 194–197, 214–217
Times of India 8, 31, 211
Timour 197
Tingey 177–178, 180
Tirpul 79–81, 83, 86

Tomaun-Agha 29
Tonga 158
Toorkhee 127
Toronto 90, 213
Tourbaieff 115
Trans-Caspian Railway 3, 112–113, 119, 193
Tucker, Mr. 143
Turkestan (Turkistan) 3, 16, 18–19, 23–24, 28–29, 36, 39, 50–51, 55, 70, 98, 112, 114, 117, 213
Turkomans: Alieli (Alai) Turkomans 38, 202, 217; carpets 32–35, 37, 39–41, 53–54, 87, 89–90, 216, 218; customs 41, 98; Ersari Turkomans 89, 217–218; Goklan Turkomans 70; jewelry 38–40, 42, 54, 89, 215–216; Kara Turkomans 217; raids 26–28, 37, 44, 70; Salor Turkomans 10, 52; Saryk Turkomans 7, 10, 31–36, 38, 40–44, 50, 52, 54, 56, 63–65, 67–68, 78, 89–91, 107, 114, 188, 203, 218; Tekke Turkomans 3, 10, 43, 52, 66–67, 70, 79, 89–91, 188, 215; Yomut Turkomans 70
Tut-i-Kurkht 29

Ulwar, Rajah of 154
Umballa 173
Umbeyla 170
University of Sussex 2, 218
Usbegs 36, 51, 59, 61, 72–73, 114, 141, 144, 147, 154, 160–161

Vaman 122
Vambery, Arminius 49, 69, 194–195, 213, 216
Vanuschine 115
Verandah 131, 148, 155
Victoria, Queen 2, 39, 78, 84–85, 95, 102–103
Victoria and Albert Museum 207
Vienna 13, 83

Wakkan 36
Walker, James 4–5, 10–12, 15–16, 55, 57, 59, 62, 77, 91–92, 98, 107, 143, 219
Wallace, Donald Mackenzie 76, 182, 220
Waller, Mr. 180
Warduk 127
Waterfield, Colonel 95, 132, 140–141, 181
Weir, Thomas Stephenson 8, 31, 33, 54, 211
Westward Ho! 5
Wheeler, Stephen 1, 5–6, 15–16, 19, 24, 35, 40–41, 55–57, 62, 77–78, 81–82, 93, 96–97, 106–109, 189, 213, 217–219
White-King, Mr. 127, 143, 219
Willet, Mr. 179
Willoughby, Major 177–178
Wilson, Corp. 22

Index

Wilson, Mr. 207
Wolseley, General Garnet 51, 193–197, 201
Wright, Lieutenant 17, 80, 208
Wright, Reginald 209

Yaboo 138–139, 146–148
Yakoob Khan, Amir 11
Yalatan 50
Yalintoosh (Yaluntush) Khan 32, 67, 120
Yarim Tapa 66
Yate, Arthur C. 18–19, 24, 39, 44, 63–64, 67, 80–81, 89, 91–92, 208, 213–217

Yate, Charles Edward 8, 17, 40, 47, 53, 63–66, 68, 80, 86, 91–92, 208, 213–215

Zamindawiri 188
Zelenoy, General 9, 13, 29,
Ziafat 129, 132, 145, 149
Ziafut *see* Ziafat
Zimam Islam (Saryk) 67
Zulfagar (Zulfikar) Pass 29, 86–88, 121, 217
Zurabad 121
Zurmat 127

www.ingramcontent.com/pod-product-compliance
Lightning Source LLC
Chambersburg PA
CBHW061346300426
44116CB00011B/2016